P9-AFK-461

Books by John E. Mack

NIGHTMARES AND HUMAN CONFLICT

BORDERLINE STATES IN PSYCHIATRY
(Edited by Dr. Mack)

A PRINCE OF OUR DISORDER:
The Life of T. E. Lawrence

A PRINCE OF OUR DISORDER

The Life of T. E. Lawrence

Sketch of Lawrence made in 1919 by Augustus John. Gift of Lawrence
to J. W. Wright, manciple of All Souls College, Oxford, and presented
to the college by Wright's brother. Courtesy of the Warden and
Fellows of All Souls College, Oxford

John E. Mack

A PRINCE OF
OUR DISORDER

The Life of T. E. Lawrence

WITH MAPS AND ILLUSTRATIONS

LITTLE, BROWN AND COMPANY
BOSTON – TORONTO

D

Acknowledgments of permission to reprint excerpted material appear
on page 538.

LIBRARY OF CONGRESS CATALOGING IN PUBLICATION DATA

Mack, John E   1929–
   A prince of our disorder.

   Bibliography: p.
   Includes index.
   1. Lawrence, Thomas Edward, 1888–1935. I. Title.
D568.4.L45M28   941.083′092′4 [B]   75-22481
ISBN 0-316-54232-6

BP

Designed by Janis Capone

Published simultaneously in Canada
by Little, Brown & Company (Canada) Limited

PRINTED IN THE UNITED STATES OF AMERICA

To my father, Edward Mack

The reasonable man adapts himself to the world: the unreasonable one persists in trying to adapt the world to himself. Therefore all progress depends on the unreasonable man.

— George Bernard Shaw

If I have restored to the East some self-respect, a goal, ideals: if I have made the standard of rule of white over red more exigent, I have fitted those peoples in a degree for the new commonwealth in which the dominant races will forget their brute achievements, and white and red and yellow and brown and black will stand up together without side-glances in the service of the world.

— T. E. Lawrence

Acknowledgments

The writing of this book has been a very personal undertaking. I have talked with many people who knew Lawrence and they have become an important part of the book. This is true not only because of information they provided, but also because they helped to re-create for me the times and places in which Lawrence lived. Through them I learned to appreciate the impact his personality could have on other people.

It is not possible to thank all those who have helped me through interviews and letters. Some I have omitted mentioning because I believe they would prefer to remain anonymous. Because of the timing of the writing, many of my informants died after the project began in 1964 and could not see this book. I am sorry they could not have had the latest word about their friend.

I wish to give special thanks to Mrs. Christine Longford and Mrs. Seton Pringle of Dublin, to Miss Lily Montgomery, and to Miss Fitzsimon and other villagers in Delvin, County Westmeath in Ireland. I am also grateful to the villagers of Tremadoc in Wales and the townspeople of Kirkcudbright in Scotland, to members of the Laurie family — Andrew, Molly and Janet — and to Lady Pansy Lamb. I wish also to express my thanks to A. H. G. Kerry, C. F. C. Beeson, Theo and Hilda Chaundy, Elsie Newcombe, Stewart Newcombe, Jr., Sir Basil Blackwell, William Hogarth, E. F. Hall, R. W. Bodey, James Fowle, W. O. Ault, Richard Brinkley, William Sargent, Robert Graves, Basil Liddell Hart, Fareedah El Akle, William Yale, Phillip Knightley, Colin Simpson, Lincoln Kirstein, L. H. Gilman, shaykhs and members of the Howeitat tribe of Jordan, my Bedouin guides R'faifan and Sabah, Lord Rennell of Rodd, Dermot Morrah, E. F. Jacob, Thomas Beaumont, Lowell Thomas, Philip Townshend-Somerville, Henry Williamson and Bertram Rota. I wish to thank especially

Professor Arnold Lawrence and his wife Barbara for their sustained help, understanding and tolerance.

In the application of psychoanalytic concepts to biography Erick Erikson has been the pioneer and provided me with valuable help. I was particularly fortunate in having excellent consultation and help in the course of the research from Manfred Halpern, P. J. Vatikiotis, Irene Gendzier, Robert Wolff, Gregory Rochlin, Ray Hodgkins, Basil Kohler, Helena Deutsch, and Robert Coles. Jack Ewalt, former chairman of the Department of Psychiatry at the Harvard Medical School, kept after me until the job was done. Help in Arabic translation has come from Basim Musallam, Wasmaa Chorbaji, Antoine Hallac and Andrawes Barghout. David Pollack was of great assistance in the transliteration of Arabic names. George Vaillant, Bennett Simon, Charles Hofling, and my mother, Ruth Mack, provided valuable critical readings of portions of the manuscript. I feel a particular debt of gratitude to Walter Langsam and L. Carl Brown for page-by-page reading of the manuscript, for their helpful suggestions, and for protecting me from such glaring errors as they were able to spot.

Others not only helped me with their ideas and knowledge, but also offered special friendship and companionship. I would include in this group, among others, Arabella and Charles Rivington, Jeremy Wilson, A. E. ("Jock") Chambers, Edward Nevins, Gladys Page, and many colleagues in the psychiatric and psychoanalytic communities. I am thankful to the staff of the Department of Psychiatry at the Cambridge Hospital and the Cambridge-Somerville Mental Health and Retardation Center, especially to Lee Macht and Robert Reid, for their support and for permitting me leave to complete the book. In a more personal vein I am grateful to my father, Edward Mack, for his ideas about Lawrence as a critic and to my wife, Sally, for her steady encouragement and support at times when the project was foundering.

I have been fortunate in having a great deal of help from directors and staff members of archive collections and libraries. I wish especially to thank Dennis Porter and his staff at the Bodleian Library, Oxford; Sarah Graham-Brown at St. Antony's College, Oxford; Rodney Dennis and Carolyn Jakeman and other members of the staff of Houghton Library, Harvard; June Wilcox at the Huntington Library in Pasadena; and E. F. Jacob at All Souls College, Oxford. Jane Page offered valuable research assistance; Rosanne Kumins and Judith Risch were of great help in preparing the manuscript. I owe special thanks to my assistant, Patricia Carr, for her work on the manuscript and for seeing me through the throes of its preparation, and to Lilith Friedman who selflessly over a period of several years devoted her own time to the realization of this work. Finally, I wish to thank my editors, Llewellyn Howland and Jean Whitnack, for their unusual patience and care in the preparation of the book.

                                                              J.E.M.

Contents

Illustrations

Maps

Introduction

We have a natural fascination with individuals of extraordinary talent, achievement or power. We are drawn by their glamour and curious about the special abilities that make it permissible, indeed essential, for them to enact upon the public stage the hopes and dreams we all possess but fear or do not choose — or simply have no opportunity — to carry out ourselves.[1]

We follow with great interest the fortunes and decisions of persons in positions of leadership: Our self-regard rises and falls with their successes, vicissitudes or failures, and we second-guess the choices they make. For many of us the identification will continue — for some, more readily than before — if the leader's purpose deteriorates to the expression of personal, often destructive, impulses that are no longer associated with the constructive solution of human problems.

The destructive leader, and the eagerness of a large segment of the population to identify with him, comprise one of the central threats — if not the greatest threat — that faces human society. The power, or potential power, of such leaders in the contemporary world is awesome, and the public is acutely aware of this fact. There is perhaps an increasing unwillingness to entrust our well-being and our lives to individuals whose motives and characters we do not understand and whose ultimate purposes we are ignorant of. There is available in modern depth psychology, if used appropriately in conjunction with other disciplines of the social sciences and the humanities, an approach to the understanding of public figures that may help us to choose more rationally those we would wish to allow to govern us or at least to designate those to whom we would deny this privilege.

This book is the historical and psychological study of a public figure whose decisions and actions have affected, and continue to affect, the lives of millions of people.

It is historical in the sense that I have chosen to examine T. E. Lawrence's actions in the context of the history and politics of the West and the Middle East. As history, the study is limited by the restrictions of biography, which does not attempt, in its focus upon a single person, to provide a balanced or complete view of the events in which the subject played a part, however significant it may have been. Since the analysis must concentrate upon him, it cannot deal fully with all the forces — social, political, economic — that operate simultaneously in the production of historical change.

The study is psychological in the sense that I have chosen to seek an understanding of Lawrence as an individual, to show how one deeply and intensely motivated person affects events of historical importance and how they, in turn, affect him. Yet, though I draw on my training as a psychiatrist in discussing Lawrence, I do not claim a primacy for the psychological determinants of history. Accordingly, I find the term "psycho-historical" unsatisfactory in its implication that the psychological lies outside the historical and acts upon it. On the contrary, individual psychology operates within established, though shifting, historical contexts and becomes one of the many agents of historical change. And historical change depends for its realization upon the joining, through circumstance and chance, of private individual purpose with public or historical opportunity.

I must confess that in the beginning I sought to do a psychological study of Lawrence of the sort more familiar to those engaged in clinical work. I have long been affected by Lawrence's suffering and have found that I could readily identify with the personal elements from which it grew. His conflicts were familiar to me from psychiatry — since they derive from the usual human needs that confront the healthy and the troubled alike — and I attempted to understand them through the skills and methods I had been taught.

But as time went on, I found myself diverted by two dilemmas. First, no matter how fully I was able to "understand Lawrence" through the explication of his personal conflicts, the understanding added little to my appreciation of Lawrence's accomplishments as a man. From the psychological standpoint, although his struggles were interesting and compelling, they differed little from those of many other persons of his or our age and could therefore contribute little to the understanding of human psychology. Second, I found myself becoming steadily more interested in Lawrence's achievements than in his problems; or, stated more precisely, I became fascinated with how he was able to adapt his personal psychology to the historical realities that he came upon, or was able to surmount his personal conflicts in the accomplishment of valuable public services.

When I presented "psychological material" about Lawrence at conferences or meetings, my audience would inevitably offer interpretations about his psychopathology which, however accurate they may have been, left me always feeling that they had not seen Lawrence as I knew him to have been. In reading other psychological studies of historical figures I found myself becoming impatient with the failure of their authors to come to grips with the salient fact of unusual accomplishment, and kept registering the same objection that Lawrence himself had made when he commented upon a biographical essay about a famous British general: that the article "left out of him his greatness — an extraordinary fellow he was."[2]

I do not wish to imply that I do not think that individual purpose and psychology produce historical change. For I believe strongly that history is often the result of individual choice and motive, and of human responsibility, both individual and collective. I agree fully with Sir Isaiah Berlin's warning that "the invocation to historians to suppress even that minimal degree of moral or psychological evaluation which is necessarily involved in viewing human beings as creatures with purposes and motives (not merely as causal factors in the procession of events), seems . . . to rest upon a confusion of the aims and methods of the humane studies with those of natural science. It is one of the greatest and most destructive fallacies of the last 100 years."[3] And I believe with Sir Isaiah that individual human motive and responsibility are among the dominant forces of history and that the evaluation of these determinants is an essential part of the historian's task.

What I *am* stressing is that the personal psychology of a historical figure cannot be studied apart from the familial, social and cultural context in which he developed and functioned. At the same time, his actions and their public impact need to be looked at in terms of a dynamic interplay between his inner drives and purposes and a number of concurrent political, social and historical opportunities and realities. What is happening around him and to him of course plays upon his psychology and affects his actions, a process he may not be completely aware of.

I believe that Lawrence's historical reputation has been damaged by the use (or misuse) of psychology to devalue his accomplishments, and by misguided efforts to explain complex decisions and behavior through simplistic explanations or psychological reductionism. Although Richard Aldington's biography, *Lawrence of Arabia: A Biographical Enquiry,* is the most flagrant example of the use of psychology for such denigrating purposes (psychology is not the only instrument of Aldington's devaluation), Lawrence has been the object of an enormous amount of psychologizing, much of it demeaning. Lawrence's candor about his deeper motivations and about the nature and impact of his psychosexual conflicts and traumata, which he offered for the purpose of achieving a fuller understanding of himself and thereby of helping others, has, paradoxically, further served to tarnish his reputation. His historical reputation has been hurt since his death by the vestiges of the same Victorian intolerance from which he suffered throughout his life.

Perhaps every biographer feels to a certain extent that his subject has been incompletely or poorly understood. Otherwise why should there be a need for another biography? I have certainly felt that this was true of Lawrence. Although I have attempted to give as thorough and objective an exposition of the historical evidence as possible in order to achieve a balanced view of the man, and to examine any personal reactions of my own which might lead to distortions of the data, I do not claim to be neutral to my subject. I unabashedly regard him as a great man and an important historical figure, and intend in the pages that follow to show how the evidence led to my opinion. But I have sought to suppress nothing that would lead to a contrary view.

Custom does not require that biographers justify or explain their choice of subject. Ordinarily, the freedom of the biographer to indulge whatever affinity or aversion exists between himself and his subject is taken for granted, and his biases or special intentions may or may not become evident as his book is read. But because this work on Lawrence is not, after all, the kind a psychiatrist usually undertakes, and is one that explores the psychology of a person no longer living, I feel constrained to add a word explaining why I chose to write of Lawrence. The reasons are more ordered in retrospect than they were as they evolved over the years I devoted to the research and writing.

I have long been fascinated by the relationship between the inner life — between dreams, hopes and visions — and action or activity in the "real" world. Perhaps because Freud and the other early psychoanalysts concentrated upon exploring new territories of the mind and the inner mental life of their patients, psychoanalytic research has not formulated a systematic theory of action. Yet the study of action or activity from the standpoint of behavior alone can hardly be adequate: all activity derives from inner drives or impulses, or at least from an interplay between outside influences and internal forces. Direct observations of children; the experience with adults who come to professional attention in the community through their actions; and the influences of the social and community psychiatry movements, which stress the need to obtain knowledge about the environments or "real worlds" in which patients live — all have furnished data about the relation between the inner mental life and action in the outside world. The biographical study of an individual "public" figure who characteristically lives out elements of his inner life in the public arena can, if data about his interior life are obtainable, provide yet another valuable source of information about the psychology of action.

Lawrence has proved to be an extraordinarily rich subject for such a study. Deeply introspective — a trait unusual in men who act forcefully in the outside world — he was driven by painful events he experienced in World War I and in the postwar period to probe his motives and to examine the relation between them and his public actions. Lawrence was highly gifted as a depth psychologist, and although he holds back even as he reveals, he has left in writings and in conversations others have remembered, a record of an intricate pattern of connections among the influences of his personal development, his feelings, his motives, and his actions. His individual psychology and mental life directly relate to the psychology of his followers and his age. The need to know and make known was highly developed in Lawrence and he applied this need to himself as he did to any matter that commanded his attention.

In addition, a particular currency attaches to Lawrence's life and work. Not long before these pages were written, a major war — the fourth in a quarter of a century — led to great loss of life among Arabs and Israelis. Political and economic strife among the peoples of the Middle East continue to threaten the world's peace and stability.

It was out of the defeat of the Ottoman Empire in World War I and the partitioning of it afterward that the present shape of Western Asia took form. Lawrence strongly influenced both the military outcome and the political aftermath. He powerfully and effectively encouraged Arab nationalistic hopes and dreams, and strove to diminish the political dominance of the Western powers in the Middle East before such a change was contemplated in the West. He hoped, too, that the Jewish people would provide leadership in the Middle East by sharing their greater economic and technological sophistication with the Arab people to the advantage of the whole region. It is a hope which, having seemed forlorn for more than twenty-five years, appears less odd or remote at the present time.

But, ultimately, my choice of Lawrence must be seen as a subjective one, deriving from my own predilections and psychological makeup. Lawrence's struggles have been consistently important and moving to me. I have found it easy, though at times disturbing, to identify with his hopes, his actions and his pain. He has enabled me, as he did so many others, to see possibilities that were not dreamed of before.

Several other important associations between individual psychology and public action ("psycho-historical" relationships) are examined in this book. They are less directly related to the *choice* of Lawrence as the subject than those I have already mentioned, but they are sharply illuminated by the example of his life and work. In brief, I am using the example of Lawrence as a paradigm in the discussion of these larger issues. The particular psycho-historical relationships embodied in his life and legend serve as an *approach* to problems which, by their very nature,

are interdisciplinary or multidisciplinary. Part of the value of this work
will be its applicability to the study of other public figures or historical
materials.

There is the general question of the psychology of the individual
(applicable to all of us in some degree) who lives out or tries to find
solutions for his inner conflicts on the public stage. In addition to the
study of the person himself (his family influences, early development and
personal motivation), the relationship between his own drive or purpose
and historical opportunity becomes of central importance. I have in mind
the process whereby a person like Lawrence, with a particular set of
personal needs, talents and abilities, finds an appropriate external medium
or stage for their fulfillment.

There is an equally tantalizing reciprocal question to be raised: how do
governments, peoples, or individuals functioning historically at a particular time find and use a person like Lawrence for their own purposes? The
role of chance looms large in human history. Lawrence recognized this
fact well in his own case. Near the end of his life he wrote to the poet
C. Day Lewis, "As an historian by training I shouldn't like to think that
accidental participation in this one war of the infinite series past and to
come had made me put it bigly in the foreground of any but its victims."[4]

If one adds the dimension of time or "history," the social system gains
further elements. In addition to his immediate relationships with contemporary employers or followers, a public figure may develop over time
a lasting significance for another heterogeneous group, one that may be
called the "audience of posterity." The life and work of a figure like
Lawrence will take on new meaning for future "audiences" depending on
what facts about his life, or interpretations of historical materials, are
known to the societies or nations for which he has importance and which
are themselves undergoing processes of economic, political and ideo-
logical change.

Finally, there is the relationship of the subject to his biographers and
they to him (and I include in this group the radio and television broad-
casters and filmmakers who present public figures, often deliberately distorted, to their audiences). One might call them the representors. The
representors discover, rediscover, and even on occasion reinterpret the life
and work of a historical figure when he takes on new meaning for them
and when they in turn find responsive currents in a public for which the
figure has assumed new or renewed meaning.

In the world of mass communication, where trends and fads emerge
and disappear in weeks, the importance and meaning of historical figures
for their appropriate audiences often shift with great rapidity. One might
hypothesize two levels in the reciprocal relationship between a historical
figure and his public: a superficial, commercially influenced view or interpretation which is subject to quite fickle contemporary trends; and a

more lasting, stable view based on accumulated and accurate scholarship, which will, in the end, come to dominate. I believe, though, that this division will not prove to be entirely valid. It is quite possible that a commercially motivated view of a public figure, distorted but convincing — for example, the popular film *Lawrence of Arabia* — could be the lasting one in the public's mind, however inaccurate it may be from the factual standpoint. A hero may be seen as a scoundrel, and a rogue may be lionized for decades, if not for centuries, and there is no guarantee that, from the public standpoint, "the truth will out."

Beyond these broad considerations of the relation between the public figure and his public, Lawrence's life and example have provided an unusual opportunity to consider the specific psychology of the political leader or military commander and to examine a number of psychosocial issues related to the commander's activity. Lawrence's own epic narrative, *Seven Pillars of Wisdom*, was partly written "to show," as he phrased it, "how unlovely the back of a commander's mind must be."[5] As he assumed what seems to be such exaggerated responsibility for the lives of others, Lawrence invites us to reconsider the very nature of the leader's responsibility to society and to the individuals his actions affect. Because he was so troubled by the moral complexities of his part in the desert campaigns, and in the political settlements that followed the war, and was, to begin with, a man unusually concerned with ethical matters, Lawrence felt compelled to raise a number of questions about the morality of his own actions as a military commander.

They were and still are embarrassing questions, as they concern ultimately the right of one man to endanger other men's lives in a political or military cause. It is of the very nature of warfare that men are encouraged or forced by their leaders to follow political purposes they may not understand, or to take part in wars for whose ends they would not voluntarily have chosen to fight. Such psychosocial questions as the morality and responsibility of leadership are, of course, culturally and historically time-related. A particular leader who examines such questions from a different point of view or who assumes a unique kind of responsibility, may contribute through his personal example to shifting expectations and standards of leadership viewed not only from the political and strategic standpoint, but from the ethical and moral vantage as well.

Related to the issue of leadership or command is the question of heroism. The problem of heroism is in its fullest sense a uniquely psychohistorical matter. It depends upon a series of relationships involving the psychology of an individual (the hero); other individuals or followers who identify with him; the society (or societies) that defines its criteria for the heroic and its expectations for the hero; and, finally, the biographers, historians, journalists, dramatists or other mythmakers who create the narratives and legends from which examples of heroism are drawn. For a biographer who is interested not only in heroism as a psycho-historical problem, but in historical accuracy as well, there is the additional problem in treating a historical figure like Lawrence, around whom legends have developed, of distinguishing actuality from myth and legend. This is not to say that a figure who becomes a hero, even an epic one, cannot in fact have performed great deeds. Rather, the problem is that stories, myths and legends — often of the hero's own telling — surround and embellish the actual deeds, creating a particularly thorny problem for the biographer or historian who tries to tease them apart.

The criteria of heroism, like the expectations of leadership and command, evolve historically, although certain heroic values, such as individual courage and initiative, seem to be the most nearly absolute or the least time-bound. Lawrence is in many ways a transitional hero, standing as he does between the neo-medieval romantic heroes of the nineteenth century and the moral realists of the twentieth. Although there have been few studies of the family history or childhood development of persons who later become heroic figures, Lawrence's family background and early history seems to conform remarkably to what has been hypothesized about the childhood of the hero from the study of myths or the psychoanalysis of the hero fantasies of children who did not become heroes in reality.

And lastly, Lawrence possessed to a unique degree a quality I have called "the capacity of enabling." He enabled others to make use of abilities they had always possessed but, until their acquaintance with him, had failed to realize. The enabling ranged from helping an airman enjoy a day's work to encouraging a people and its leader to achieve a revolution they could not accomplish unaided. Enabling depends upon a unique kind of relationship between the enabler and the enabled. In some ways it resembles the relation between teacher and student, especially that between master and apprentice, which depends heavily on identification. But teaching is, in purpose, didactic: the teacher is often an active giver and the student a more or less passive recipient. Enabling is a more balanced or mutual activity, one in which individuals are helped to realize themselves. Enabling is closer to psychotherapy, but unlike psychotherapy it is not marked by the necessary element of psychopathology or psychological difficulty in the one enabled — only an initial lack of fulfillment or self-realization.

Surely one of the first responsibilities in biography is self-knowledge on the part of the writer. This does not mean that the work can be completely free of bias or distortion. But it does imply that the biographer will find it useful to examine and try to understand the motives that determined his selection of subject, the choice of materials he intends to use and any subjective purposes within himself that might influence the presentation or interpretation of the material. To be sure, some biographical studies are openly denigrating or idolatory; some are written primarily to make money; and others are written principally to advance a political point of view, or even an individual candidacy. But a biographer who sets out to write a historically factual and objective study has the responsibility of trying to identify hidden purposes in himself that might distort the work. I would not offer this caution only to biographers who, like myself, lay great emphasis upon the use of psychological materials. Anyone who explores deeper psychological issues and emphasizes the use of psychological data is brought into a particularly close relationship with his subject. He develops strong feelings toward the subject and in the course of his study personal needs of his own may be aroused that continually tax his powers of analysis.

With regard to sources in this biography, I have made use of the usual written documents upon which biographers and historians must rely: letters, diaries, autobiographical notes, public records, other biographies and essays. In addition I have made extensive use of interviews with persons who knew Lawrence during the various periods of his life. In using the documents, I have, of course, had to consider the relationship between the writer and the recipient, the time and context in which the document was written, and the readers whom the writer might have imagined his words would reach in the future. This is true not only of documents with important psychological significance, although elements of defensive distortion are naturally more likely with such material. The truth of even ostensibly neutral documents, such as military dispatches, is not, as Lawrence well understood, absolute. They often serve for the self-justification or personal aggrandizement of military and political leaders. All accounts of war in particular, he noted, would be unfair in their assignment of credit until "the un-named rank and file" could write the dispatches themselves.[6] Historians, Lawrence wrote in 1927, tend to accept too uncritically the truth of documents. "The documents are liars," he wrote to one historian friend. "No man ever yet tried to write down the entire truth of any action in which he has been engaged."[7]

With interviews the biographer must, as Erik Erikson wrote in *Gandhi's Truth,* assess the information obtained in the light of an understanding of the informant's relationship to the subject — for example, whether the informant is personally attached to him, or seeks (sometimes unconsciously) to seem important to the interviewer or to himself through claiming a special relationship with the great man. Less frequently in my experience — usually when the person being interviewed knew the subject very little — distorted information is provided that discredits the subject. I have found it very valuable in interviewing to make the informant a kind of partner in the work by explaining in detail the nature of

my study and sharing our areas of common interest or empathy in relation
to the subject.

The diagnosis of conventional psychopathological entities is of so little
value or contemporary relevance in the study of public figures that it is
somewhat surprising that it has remained such a popular pursuit. Even
in studying destructive leaders like Stalin and Hitler it does little to
establish that they were paranoid personalities (or whatever), for this will
not distinguish them from other persons who are paranoid. Furthermore,
the judgment of pathological behavior is not absolute. It depends upon
the social context of the behavior and on what is expected of the subject
by those judging him within that context. This is especially true of one
who is a leader of some sort. Judging the appropriateness of his behavior
is difficult without full knowledge of the forces and stresses constraining
him, and it is subject to bias that derives from political preferences. The
person who seeks in his expectations of himself to reach beyond what
ordinary men are willing or able to undertake draws upon extraordinary
means of adaptation and also exposes himself to great failure and disappointment. He is especially vulnerable to the development of pathological symptoms and unusual behavioral responses.

With Lawrence, the more acquainted I became with the social context
in which his public actions took place, and the public demands with
which he had to contend, the more understandable I found his troubled
personal responses to be. This by no means implies that an understanding
of the emotional elements in Lawrence or in any leader is irrelevant to a
study such as this. Rather, these internal elements, deriving from the
leader's own psychology, must be seen as operating within a constant field
of forces making up the elements of the social and political world. Conventional psychiatric diagnosis, with its emphasis on a given moment in
time and upon behavioral outcomes looked upon in their own right, fails
often to consider this fuller context.

More important than the leader's pathology is how he was able to reach
positions of power and through his actions affect the course of history. An
understanding of his personal psychopathology will be of value in this
connection only if it sheds light on how he was able to achieve positions
of leadership, maintain power, or draw other men into destructive courses
through living out his madness in the public domain.

The development of psychoanalysis at the turn of the twentieth century
provided a new method for the understanding and treatment of the
psychoneuroses. Its students became interested in the armchair analysis
of the works of writers and artists like Shakespeare and Leonardo. In
fragments of their writing examples were sought of repressed sexuality
and other childhood conflicts that had been found to play a part in the
etiology of the neuroses and in the formation of dreams. Similar uses —

not by the psychoanalysts themselves usually — were made of the concepts of psychoanalysis in biographical studies of public figures ("pathographies"). Such studies were common in the early decades of the twentieth century and often were used for debunking purposes.[8]

In studying the life of a person of great accomplishment, we are interested in how the influences of parental figures, other family members, nannies, teachers, colleagues and friends fostered through love, or promoted through a variety of relationships and examples for identification, the development of the special qualities that enabled him to achieve what he set out to do or become. We are particularly interested in how areas of conflict worked together with special abilities and shaped the direction of later accomplishments or intensified the motive for achievement. Even if the events or traumata of adult life play upon the vulnerabilities incurred in the earlier years and lead to emotional difficulties (like those Lawrence suffered from in the war), or even produce grossly psychopathological reactions, our interest nevertheless remains focused upon the person's creative efforts to surmount the disorder, rather than upon the psychopathology as such.

A biographical study of a figure no longer living, which seeks to examine and interpret psychological data, suffers from the absence of the kind of psychological information that direct interviews with the subject himself can give. But it may have certain advantages. For one, it may be more balanced. From written documentation and interviews knowledge can be gained of every phase of the subject's life and a fuller, richer picture of his character emerges, one less weighted in the direction of psychopathology, a picture more equable in its view of strength and weakness, love and hate, bitterness and humor. This is fortunate for the biographer's purposes. He is interested in his subject, not as a figure alone with his suffering, or allied with a therapist in order to resolve his personal dilemmas, but rather as one who lives and acts in the context of a series of relationships with others, whose lives he influences and whose needs and demands move his own life in directions not always of his choosing.

This book is divided into six parts. The first deals with Lawrence's family background, childhood and adolescence up to the time of his admission to Oxford in the fall of 1907, with the exception of two summer trips to France that seem related more to the years that followed and thus are included subsequently. Part Two deals with the period of Lawrence's youth from the age of nineteen, when he went up to Oxford, to the beginning of World War I when he was twenty-five. It includes his undergraduate years; his trips to France in 1906, 1907, and 1908; his first trip to the Middle East; and the three years spent at Carchemish working as an archeologist. Part Three describes the critical years of

World War I, out of which Lawrence's principal fame as a historical figure derives. Part Four is concerned with the four years of Lawrence's participation in the political struggles over the postwar fate of the Middle East. These are also the years in which Lawrence wrote *Seven Pillars of Wisdom*. Part Five deals with Lawrence as an enlisted man in the ranks of the RAF and Tank Corps from 1922 to his death at forty-six, two months after his retirement in 1935. Finally, Part Six contains discussions of aspects of Lawrence's intimate life and personality that spanned his thirteen years in the ranks.

Because the emphasis of this book is upon the relations between Lawrence's inner life — the psychological forces that shaped and moved him — and the actions and events that grew out of them or through which they were played out, more space has been devoted to the social and political-historical aspects of his life than to his importance as a literary figure. His writings are used as source materials, to bring out aspects of his psychology or to help in the understanding of the development of his historical reputation and legend. Likewise, I have not concerned myself with Lawrence as a literary critic, although his letters are full of literary criticism. I have taken great pains to develop as complete a picture of Lawrence the human being as I could, even including seemingly small details that illuminate particular aspects of his personality. For I believe that his fundamental importance for human history, and his lasting ability to influence the lives of others, derives as much from the example of what he was as from what he did.

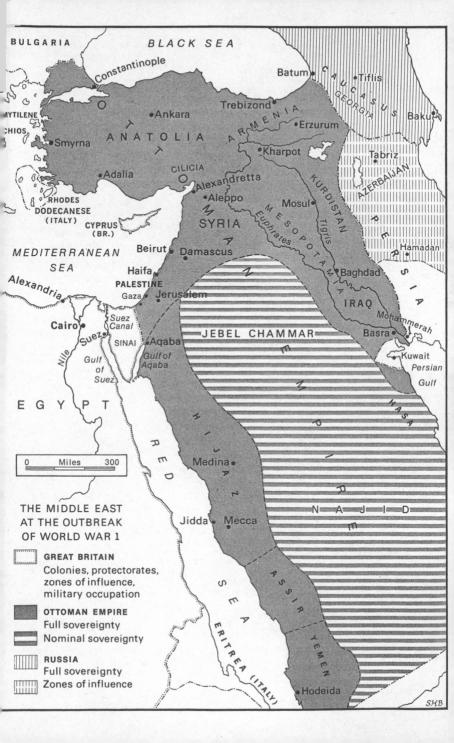

THE MIDDLE EAST
AT THE OUTBREAK
OF WORLD WAR 1

GREAT BRITAIN
Colonies, protectorates,
zones of influence,
military occupation

OTTOMAN EMPIRE
Full sovereignty
Nominal sovereignty

RUSSIA
Full sovereignty
Zones of influence

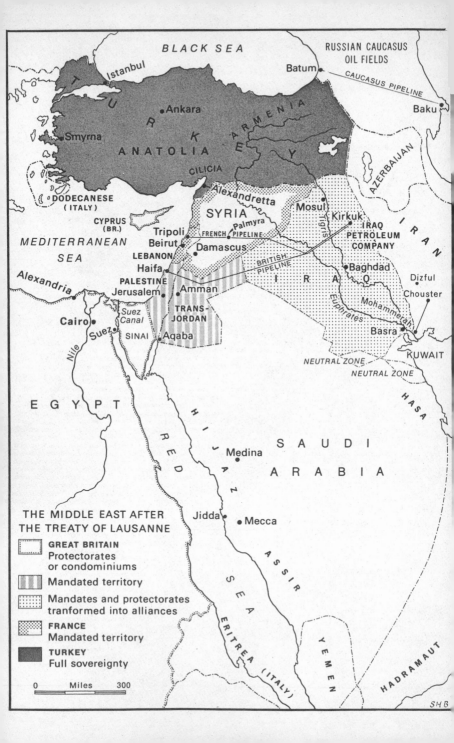

THE MIDDLE EAST AFTER
THE TREATY OF LAUSANNE

GREAT BRITAIN
Protectorates
or condominiums

Mandated territory

Mandates and protectorates
tranformed into alliances

FRANCE
Mandated territory

TURKEY
Full sovereignty

0   Miles   300

ONE

FAMILY BACKGROUND
AND
CHILDHOOD

1

Chapmans and Lawrences

Many, but by no means all, the significant facts regarding T. E. Lawrence's ancestry are now known, especially since the publication in 1955 of Richard Aldington's *Lawrence of Arabia: A Biographical Enquiry*. Yet despite a good deal of speculative psychologizing, we still lack a full understanding of Lawrence's family background and the meaning of his childhood experiences for his personal development, later life experiences and historical place.

In giving information about his forebears, Lawrence provided a characteristically provocative and puzzling assortment of bits and pieces from his own incomplete knowledge. He both revealed and concealed in what he told his biographers, in part to protect family members still living, but also because such hide-and-seek behavior was an element in his personality. When he wrote to Basil Liddell Hart, for instance, he prefaced the information he gave (which was, in fact, quite extensive) by saying: "There are (as I hinted at Hindhead) things not quite desirable in this. Without wanting to censor I suggest alternatives — written with the allusiveness that hints at knowledge refusing to betray itself between the lines."[1]

Lawrence's psychological uncertainties regarding his own identity correspond nicely with the ambiguities of his ancestral background, which, naturally, constituted one of the underlying causes of his later psychological confusion. In the 1927 manuscript of Robert Graves's biography (corrected by Lawrence, who had already supplied the basic data), appeared exotically: "He was born in 1888 in North Wales, of mixed blood, none of it Welsh; it is Irish, Spanish, ~~Isle of Skye~~ [*Hebridean*], Dutch and ~~Swedish~~ [*Norse*]."[2] He tried to put off further inquiry from Graves by declaring that sources of information regarding his family background and childhood were "nil."[3] Later, Lawrence answered Liddell Hart's questions about his origins with: "Father Anglo-Irish, with ¼ Dutch. Mother Anglo-Scotch with a dash of Scandinavian."[4]

Lawrence's fullest account of his paternal family background is contained in a letter to John Buchan: " 'Lawrence', like 'Shaw' [he had by that time changed his name to Shaw], was an assumption. My father's people were merchants in the Middle Ages: then squires in Leicestershire. In Tudor times they had promoted themselves to soldiering, and had married with a Devon family: by favour of one of these cousins (Sir Walter Raleigh) they got a huge grant of County Meath in Ireland, from Queen Elizabeth: and they lived till the Irish Land Acts did away with most of the estate. My father had other troubles too, which made him change his name, and live abroad, in Wales and England, the latter half of his life. So there weren't any Lawrence ancestors or relations: but it's not my line to say so, since the fiction is less trouble than the truth."[5]

Lawrence's father, Thomas Robert Tighe Chapman, was born in 1846 and inherited his father's estate in 1870, when his older brother died. In 1914, after the death of his cousin Benjamin James, he became the seventh and last Chapman baronet, but he lived only five years after succeeding to the title. Little is known of his life or personality when he was in Ireland. He married a cousin, Edith Sarah Hamilton, in 1873 and by her had four daughters between 1874 and 1882. Edith Chapman was described by my informants as having been a most severe, sour and religiously strict person who was known locally as "the Vinegar Queen."[6]

The Chapman family settled on an estate at Killua in County Westmeath northwest of Dublin, and in 1782 a Chapman baronetage was established.[7] The Chapman manor house, Killua Castle, now in ruins, was formerly a preceptory of the medieval religious order of the Knights Hospitalers. The branch of the family from which Lawrence was descended acquired in due course a large manor house called South Hill, near the village of Delvin. Like the other members of the displaced Protestant gentry of English origins, the Chapmans looked to England for help, married into their own group, mingled little if at all with the surrounding Irish Catholic peasantry (who regarded them with suspicion and resentment), and satisfied their sense of social responsibility by doing good works of the Lady Bountiful variety in the local community. As one Irish schoolteacher of Delvin told me, the "planters" were "not Irish," did not look after their tenants who worked the farms, "grabbed" land from the people, and gave little in return.[8]

Lawrence was quite conscious of the family connection with Sir Walter Raleigh, which served the fantasy of his derivation from a heroic past. He would like, he wrote in 1927 to Charlotte Shaw, George Bernard Shaw's wife, to buy some acres of land in the Irish county from which his father had come, in order "to keep some of Walter Raleigh's gift in the family of which I have the honour of being not the least active member!"[9] To another friend he pointed out his father's resemblance to Sir Walter, but disclaimed a direct lineage: "Raleigh isn't an ancestor, only the son of one. My father, middle-aged, was his walking image. I'm not like that side of the family though."[10] Lawrence related his later actions to his ancestry, but not specifically to the heroic aspects. "My matter of fact ancestry compels me to carry my impulses into action," he wrote to Charlotte Shaw in 1926.[11]

According to a family companion with whom I spoke, Thomas Chapman was described by his daughters as having been a somewhat morose and not very effective man in Ireland, one rather uninterested in the usual country pursuits of hunting, shooting and fishing.[12] He drank a good deal then, and one daughter recalled that he had to hide liquor from his intolerant wife. Lady Chapman also disapproved of the things he did well and tried to deprive him of any enjoyment in them. An old gardener remembered that the Chapmans held frequent prayer meetings.[13]

Sometime between 1878 and 1880 — the exact date is unknown — the father brought from Scotland to South Hill a young girl to be a companion and governess for his children. Sarah, as she called herself, was attractive, strong-willed and highly capable. The daughters grew very fond of her, and the father likewise. One of them recalled that whenever their father came into the room and the governess was present his ordinarily dour manner changed: his face brightened noticeably and he became "all gay."[14] Efficient and energetic, Sarah was soon managing the house in a businesslike way.

Eventually, at an undetermined date, she left the family's employ, and soon thereafter Chapman took lodgings in or near Dublin, where the two lived together as Mr. and Mrs. Chapman when he was in the city. In this period, according to one story of doubtful authenticity, he joined the Salvation Army and went about Dublin wearing a blue Army jersey with the name across the front.[15] Their first child, Montague Robert, was born in Dublin on December 27, 1885. On his birth certificate, they gave their address as 33 York Street. According to a Chapman cousin, they were ultimately found out by the Chapman butler, who overheard Sarah in a grocery store giving her name to the grocer as "Mrs. Chapman" and followed her home. Shortly after the inevitable row at South Hill, Thomas and Sarah with their child left Ireland for North Wales.[16] They settled in the village of Tremadoc, where in due course their second child, Thomas Edward, was born — on August 16, 1888.

The embittered Lady Chapman's refusal to permit a divorce prevented Thomas and Sarah from ever marrying. Soon after Robert's birth, they assumed the name of Lawrence ("privately, not by deed poll or other instrument," T.E. told a friend many years later).[17] On the birth certificate of their third son, William George, they stated that they had been married in St. Peter's Church, Dublin,[18] but no record of the ceremony exists in the church's registers.

The Lawrences stayed in Tremadoc for a little more than a year, then moved to Kirkcudbright, Scotland, where it was less damp. They rented a large comfortable house on the edge of town, one that had formerly belonged to the provost (mayor). Here William George was born on December 10, 1889. From Scotland the family moved to the resort of Dinard on the Brittany coast, and then to the Isle of Wight and the New Forest in Hampshire. The fourth son, Frank Helier, was born in St. Helier, Jersey, in 1893. The family settled finally in Oxford in 1896. Mrs. Lawrence told a woman friend in Oxford that between 1893 and 1900 she gave birth to three other sons; two of them were born dead, and the other lived for only a few hours.[19] In 1900 the last son, Arnold Walter, was born.

Before settling in Oxford, the family chose to live in places on the seacoast, where they could make friends with English people not of their class (and thus less likely to identify them or be suspicious of the relationship). The seacoast also facilitated communication with Ireland and enabled the family to enjoy sailing.

Because Thomas Lawrence was less dominant and overwhelming than Sarah, his effect on T.E.'s development and character has been slighted by biographers. And because he died forty years earlier than Sarah (in 1919, at seventy-two), we have fewer firsthand recollections of him and fewer documents concerning his life. The picture of Thomas Robert Tighe Chapman that emerges has, as with T.E. himself, elements that are difficult to reconcile. Many of them found later expression in T.E.'s personality.

There is to my knowledge nothing written about Thomas Chapman by anyone who knew him before he left South Hill in the mid-1880's, when he was in his late thirties. The Debrett and Burke baronetages of the period states that he was a justice of the peace for County Westmeath. His dourness, which Sarah's presence dissipated, was due, one assumes, to his unhappy marriage.

Little is known of his early life or family relationships. According to T.E., his father had no interest in the land, but was a fine snipe and pheasant shooter and a yachtsman.[20] T.E. pictures him rather romantically as "on the large scale, tolerant, experienced, grand, rash, humoursome, skilled to speak, and naturally lord-like. He had been 35 years in the large life, and a spend-thrift, a sportsman, and a hard rider and drinker."[21] This swashbuckling image of Chapman in Ireland is superseded in T.E.'s accounts by that of the domesticated Thomas Robert Tighe Chapman Lawrence in England, "remodeled" by Sarah. He never attained a stature in his son's eyes comparable to that of the revered military and political chiefs under whom T.E. was to serve. Lawrence once wrote to his friend Hugh Trenchard, marshal of the RAF and the third and last of the leaders he idolized: "If my father had been as big as you, the world would not have had spare ears for my freakish doings."[22] A kind of uncomplaining riches-to-rags image adds to the picture of Mr. Lawrence. T.E. wrote later, "It was my father who was wonderful in throwing up all his comforts to go away with her: and I never remember his being sorry at having so little, as we grew bigger."[23]

The picture of the grand lord of the manor, carried off and transformed by a powerful woman, is, though accurate in certain respects, probably exaggerated at both its Irish and English poles. It is difficult, for example, to explain altogether satisfactorily how such a strong, heroic and religious man could be induced in his prime to give up his name, estates and entire status in life for love, living thereafter a quiet life as a displaced country gentleman, no matter how comely or compelling the woman. Except for the notation in the baronetages that Thomas Chapman heard cases as a J.P. in County Westmeath, we have no concrete evidence to support our suspicions that Thomas Robert Chapman was less grand a figure in Ireland than T.E. liked to believe. But there is evidence that he was somewhat more of a personage in England than the accepted biographical accounts might suggest.

The earliest description of Thomas Lawrence I have been able to obtain came from members of the Laurie family, who were neighbors and friends of the Lawrences in the New Forest (1894–1896) and maintained ties with them at Oxford. They pictured him as a slender man whose clothes fitted loosely, "like a scarecrow," gentle and kind, but diffident, shy and unsure of himself, seeming to feel terribly out of place in the genteel English surroundings of Oxford.[24] He had become a teetotaler, and the sometimes sad countenance, which had been observed in Ireland, was in evidence once more. A photograph of him taken about 1900 shows a man with a long face, a large Roman nose and narrow shoulders. He was not, according to his oldest son, physically strong.[25] Another member of the Laurie family, a boy named Andrew, who lived for brief periods in the Lawrence home (because he suffered from asthma attacks in his own house but not in theirs), described the father as thoroughly domesticated and extremely kind. Andrew recalled the father's judicious intercession in a playful scrap with six-year-old T.E., who was generally "lively and mischievous": "I was in bed and Ned [T.E.] came in and took hold of the bedclothes and yanked them off. I ran after him and slapped his head. His father said, 'Andrew, Andrew, he's a smaller boy than you.' "[26]

Mr. Lawrence enjoyed spending time with the boys, playing word-guessing games or going through boys' magazines with them. In England he was an enthusiastic sportsman, with a license to shoot in the New Forest, one who retained the manners of a gentleman. Although T.E. and his older brother, Bob, did not hunt with him — "Our sympathies were with the game," Bob said — Mr. Lawrence would frequently come home at the end of the day with a "couple of snipe."[27] Mr. Lawrence's other interests, which he shared with his sons, included photography, the architecture of medieval castles and cathedrals, and bicycling, of which he was one of the earliest enthusiasts. He had considerable skill as a carpenter (T.E. himself was extremely skillful in building and making repairs around the house or at a campsite) and once, at Mrs. Lawrence's request, built a meat safe in which recently killed game was stored.[28]

In his later years at Oxford, Mr. Lawrence is remembered by family friends as a gentle soul, tall, sensitive and quiet, dominated absolutely by Mrs. Lawrence, "the drum major."[29] A neighbor offered this description of him: "[The] Father was a tall, slender man, very distinguished looking, looking rather like Bernard Shaw, I should say.[30] He had a red beard and whiskers, and he always went about in a Norfolk jacket and breeches, and was always waving when we passed him — very friendly looking." He was "stately, courtly and friendly, an obvious aristocrat in hiding."[31] Others recall him at home as anxious, smoking a great deal, retiring to the smoking room to calm himself; or as "a country G.B.S." in tweed knickers.[32] T.E.'s teacher at the City of Oxford High School and at Oxford University, L. Cecil Jane, wrote in a letter to Robert Graves that Thomas Lawrence was "one of the most charming men I have known — very shy, very kind."[33]

According to his youngest son, Arnold, Thomas Lawrence was a rather unworldly, impractical man. He could, however, on occasion be sound in business matters. At one time he had holdings in an Irish railroad that was in financial difficulty. He was effective through his personal intervention in making it solvent again. He was dissuaded by Mrs. Lawrence from investing in the first pneumatic tire company on the grounds that he would be throwing his money away. The company made such a fortune that the family could have been millionaires. (Arnold Lawrence, reflecting upon this fact, remarked that he was glad for his own offspring that his father had not made this investment: "children who are born rich are nervous about it.")[34]

When Thomas Chapman broke away from Ireland and became Thomas Lawrence, he had to leave his estates and most of his money to his wife. It then became necessary for him to receive support from the family estate in Ireland. He would make trips there, perhaps twice a year, in connection with the management of his affairs and to see old friends and hunting cronies, and would be gone as much as a fortnight. Although Chapman-Lawrence was able to find a group of hunting companions in Oxford, his move naturally brought about a considerable fall in social standing.

Sarah Lawrence was a remarkable woman, possessing unusual energy, great charm and prodigious will and determination. She was short of stature, like T.E., and had similar piercing china-blue eyes, a fair complexion and a firm chin. In her strong character she maintained as many contradictions as her famous son did in his. The story of her life is fragmentary and has, aside from a few published sources, been pieced together from the accounts of those who knew her personally and in whom she confided.[35]

Her stoicism was legendary. In her nineties, when she broke her leg and was confined to a wheelchair, she insisted on getting in and out of the chair by herself, without help. "It's good for me!" she asserted.[36] A fine firsthand account of Mrs. Lawrence at ninety is provided by Victoria O'Campo in her book *338171 T. E.: Lawrence of Arabia*.

Lawrence told his biographer Liddell Hart that his mother was, like himself, illegitimate.[37] She was born "Sarah Junner" on August 31, 1861, near Sunderland in County Durham in the north of England. Her father was John Junner, a "shipwright journeyman," and her mother, Elizabeth Junner, whose maiden name is also given as Junner, may have been a relative of his.[38] In the Chapman household, however, she used the surname Lawrence, and on Robert's birth certificate in Dublin she is registered as Sarah Chapman, "formerly Laurence" (sic). On T.E.'s birth certificate she gave her maiden name as Maden, but on Will's certificate, she appears with the surname of Jenner.

In her earliest years, Sarah was taken to Scotland, where she spent the remainder of her childhood, although it is not known at what age she moved there from County Durham. She told T.E. that her mother died of alcoholism, and according to Arnold Lawrence, T.E. believed she never knew who her father was.[39] Convinced that there was a predilection for alcohol on both sides of the boys' family — she believed, perhaps even more than other Victorian parents did, that alcoholism was hereditary — she warned the children sharply against its evils, and apparently tried with the power of her own will to overcome the influence of heredity on her husband.[40]

In Scotland, according to her friend Elsie Newcombe, Sarah spent some years of her early childhood on a farm owned by one of her grandfathers in Perthshire. She told an Oxford friend that she had had to walk six miles back and forth each day to school in Blairgourie near Perth. By this time her grandmother had died, and she was looked after by an aunt who was married to the rector of an Evangelical (low-church) parish. She recalled her aunt and uncle as strict but "just" and described a rather forlorn childhood. Sometime during her adolescence she moved to the Isle of Skye where, when she was about eighteen, it was arranged by a Mr. Andrew Balfour, agent for the Chapman estate, that she be sent to Ireland as a nursery-governess for the Chapman daughters.[41]

In the New Forest, when she was in her early thirties, she was described as "hardheaded" but kind, speaking with a soft Scottish burr and occasionally mispronouncing words.[42] A photograph of her from about this period shows a handsome, attractive woman with a full, strong face, good complexion and a pert, straight, rather sharp nose.

At Oxford, Mrs. Lawrence was remembered as very straitlaced by the boys' friends. She did not approve of dancing or the theatre (Shakespeare was the exception). Once during Lawrence's undergraduate years he, Will and Frank wanted to go with a young girl to a light musical comedy they knew Mrs. Lawrence would disapprove of. They told her they were going to see Shakespeare so as to forestall her objections. Another time Ned or Will mentioned Oscar Wilde, and Mrs. Lawrence told the boy not to say that name, especially in front of a girl.[43]

Despite her puritanical severity Mrs. Lawrence was described with deep affection, and at times with awe, by her Oxford friends and acquaintances. Mrs. Thomas Hardy once called her "a heroine, and a very sweet one."[44] She was on the one hand hospitable and generous, and devoted to her friends ("her friends were her friends for life once she liked someone"), while on the other extremely definite in her opinions — "clear as a brook," according to Elsie Newcombe.[45] Mrs. Newcombe, whose son was about to leave to join the armed services in World War I, remembers her also as an emotional person who sat knitting a Balaklava helmet for him while tears streamed down her face.[46] She was "fearfully keen on walking," even in her eighties and nineties, and martyrlike, forced herself to hobble about soon after she had broken her leg.[47] Despite her strict religiosity she confessed shortly before her death that she doubted the existence of an afterlife.

Those who knew her agreed that she seemed at times to suck or draw the vitality out of people. David Garnett called her "a terror," a person who devoured people "like a lion." He felt that it was necessary to handle her as one would a lion: "If you know what to say it won't eat you up. Better to step out of the way."[48] Others — especially people who did not know her well — found Mrs. Lawrence overpowering and terrifying. Although not intellectual, she possessed an extraordinary memory, read a good deal, especially botanical books, and in her nineties could remember the names of a great variety of plants.[49]

Arnold Lawrence felt that his mother tried to redeem herself vicariously through all her sons, to whom she transmitted her sense of sin. She wanted each of them to become a missionary and to devote his life to God and Christianity. In this ambition she succeeded only with Robert. It also seemed to Arnold that his mother tried to swallow, absorb, or smother her sons.[50]

In 1955, with the publication of his biography of Lawrence, Richard Aldington disclosed publicly that the Lawrences had never married. The fact was well known by then in Oxford and had been indicated earlier in less widely circulated books, but had not been acknowledged in Mrs. Lawrence's presence by her friends. They wished to spare her the knowledge that the fact had been made public, and so one day when it was learned that there would be a discussion of the Aldington book on the BBC, they tried to keep Mrs. Lawrence, now ninety-five, from the radio. But Robert, who had denied the facts even to himself, led her straight to the room where the program was on the air.[51] Mrs. Lawrence sat through it stoically, without moving or speaking out. At the end she got up and walked stiffly out of the room without comment.[52] At the end of her life she admitted — the confession gave her visible relief — that she had had a responsible part in T.E.'s "nervousness." During a febrile illness late in her life, she was heard murmuring, "God hates the sin but loves the sinner," and "God loves the sinner but he hates the sin."[53]

Mrs. Lawrence survived her husband by forty years. As an old woman she was well accepted and had many good friends. For her ninety-fourth birthday one of them had a party in her honor to which many of the leading scholars and citizens of Oxford were invited.[54] She died in 1959 at ninety-eight.

One of the most difficult tasks in my research concerning the Lawrence family has been attempting to understand the motivations of the parents and the manner in which they were able to reconcile the discrepancies between their avowed principles and the reality of the situation in which they were living. I must stress that we are not dealing with the world of the 1970's (in which it is still difficult socially and psychologically for a middle-class couple to live and rear children out of wedlock) but with late Victorian England. As Arnold Lawrence stated the matter: "In that day someone who did that was odd — it just wasn't done."[55]

How was Mrs. Lawrence, reared according to strict fundamentalist codes, and later to become a devoted mother herself, able to take a man from his wife and children forever and live with him thereafter "in sin"? Her friends in Oxford have speculated from their knowledge of her that she believed she was giving up her own soul to save from worse sins the soul of a somewhat morally lackadaisical Irish country gentleman who drank too much, and it is true that except for an occasional glass of claret he stopped drinking. Or perhaps she believed — easy to speculate after what ensued — that she would be serving God if she were to bear sons to a man who had served the Lord less than well in having only daughters. One of Mrs. Lawrence's Oxford friends, knowing her interest in biblical teachings, is of the opinion that Mrs. Lawrence justified her actions, at least in part, through the example in Genesis 16, where Sarah, unable to bear Abraham children, suggested that he have a child by Hagar instead (the Chapman daughters, in Mrs. Lawrence's view, presumably did not count).[56] Always conscious of her unmarried state, and insisting upon a scrupulous literal truthfulness, Mrs. Lawrence referred to Mr. Lawrence as "Tom" or "the boys' father" — never as "my husband."

One may suspect, in view of her own illegitimacy and severe upbringing, that she was living out elements in her personal psychology derived from early childhood and her own birth out of wedlock. But a suspicion is not always a fact. What can be well documented, however, is the impact her conflicts had upon the lives and characters of her sons, conflicts she could not help imposing on them.

Although the change in Mr. Lawrence's social status is well established, there is no material that reveals what it was like for him to live with his decision, or what the radical change in his life, whereby he gave up so much, meant for him personally. Our richest source is T.E. himself, but his view of his parents' relationship is deeply colored by its effect upon his own psychology. From India in 1927 and 1928 he wrote long passages about his mother in letters to Charlotte Shaw, who had become, T.E.'s denials notwithstanding, a kind of mother-confessor for him. "My mother [was] brought up as a child of sin in the Island of Skye by a bible-thinking Presbyterian,"[57] he wrote Mrs. Shaw in 1927 (a year later he phrased it "brought up as a charity child in the Island of Skye"),[58] "then [she became] a nurse maid, then 'guilty' (in her judgment) of taking my father from his wife. . . . To justify herself, she remodeled my father, making him a teetotaler, a domestic man, a careful spender of pence. They had us five children, and never more than £400 a year: and such pride against gain, and such pride in saving, as you cannot imagine. Father had, to keep with mother, to drop all his old life and all his friends. She by dint of will raised herself to be his companion: social things meant much to him: but they never went calling, or on visits, together. They thought always that they were living in sin, and that we would some day find out."[59] Later he wrote: "Mother was always caring (to my mind) too much about such essentials as food and clothes. Life itself doesn't seem to me to matter, in comparison with thought and desire. That was how my father acted. Our pinched life was very hard on him: — or would have been if he had pinched with [sic] only he didn't. He was pinched, instead, and that's a mere trifle."[60]

The social isolation to which Lawrence refers was confirmed by others who knew the family in Oxford. The isolation was partly self-imposed; for the fact that the Lawrences were unmarried was not known in Oxford while Mr. Lawrence was living (in London it was gossiped about from the time the couple left Ireland).[61] To one of his biographers Lawrence wrote: "The mother kept to herself, and kept her children jealously from meeting or knowing their neighbours."[62] The self-consciousness of the parents meant that the family members were thrown upon themselves more than would be usual and may account in part for Robert Lawrence's reflection: "Our parents were always with us."[63] Sir Basil Blackwell, who was at Oxford with Lawrence, stated bluntly that the family was ostracized. Blackwell and the other undergraduates knew "something was odd" in the Lawrence family. "Oxford was very correct in those days," Sir Basil said; yet even by Oxford standards "they were so punctilious, churchgoing and water-drinking."[64]

One direct result of the father's descent in the social scale, and the restriction in his outside contacts, was that he was forced to accommodate himself more to the mother's way of life. For example, the mother, who had limited formal education, was quite comfortable and friendly with the men who did construction around the house, with other working people, and with the local solicitor, but less so with the gentry. However congenial she found these men, they were not persons of the same social level as her husband. Nevertheless, Mr. Lawrence made considerable concessions to Mrs. Lawrence's choices and became friendly with these men to please her.[65]

The union was, according to T.E., "a real love match,"[66] and all my sources, which include several of his childhood playmates, agree that the Lawrence home was a warm and loving one, a household that other children liked to visit.[67] The parents were affectionate with each other and devoted to their children (though not physically demonstrative towards them), and they made other children feel welcome.[68]

Arnold Lawrence feels that his father's role in the family has been distorted by those writers who have depicted Mr. Lawrence as weak in relation to Sarah. Although Mr. Lawrence tended to be gentle, quiet and reserved, and reluctant to show his feelings, he could be very firm when necessary. At times of family crisis he was the one who stepped in and made the basic decisions. Arnold Lawrence also feels that his father was an understanding person who had a considerable capacity to make peace: he could often find the right words to ease family tensions. Also, through his knowledge of people and skill in handling social situations, he was able to make others feel better, an ability T.E. grew up to possess as well. Although most of the time he left the handling of the children and the household to Sarah, on occasion he would raise his voice to intervene when he felt that she was being unduly harsh, and she would subside. His gentleness was such, however, that it was she, as we shall see later, who administered the physical discipline in the family.[69]

Arnold Lawrence was impressed with his father's quiet authority. He recalls an incident from his own childhood when a carter was beating a horse. Mr. Lawrence went up to the young man and spoke to him softly and the beating stopped. On another occasion Arnold was surprised how firmly and effectively his father dealt with a group of Oxford undergraduates who were acting obstreperously.

The family belonged to the Evangelical congregation that worshipped at St. Aldates Church, where the Reverend Alfred M. W. Christopher, a leader of the nineteenth-century Evangelical revival, was rector. Canon Christopher and others of his congregation believed literally in the Bible.

An Evangelical atmosphere filled the Lawrence household, with the mother practicing her religion as a matter of course and expecting her sons to follow suit. For Thomas Lawrence religion was a less concrete or ritualistic matter and more a question of emotional experience.[70] The family attended St. Aldates Church regularly, contributed financially to it,[71] and held Bible readings in their home every Sunday and in the morning before the children went to school. Thomas would lead the readings as the children drew around him. He would also kneel, according to Bob, and lead prayer sessions. I have seen the well-thumbed and extensively annotated and underlined Bibles from which the parents read to their children.[72]

The five Lawrence boys were "a most happy band of brothers," Mrs. Lawrence wrote after T.E.'s death, and to a major extent this seems to have been true.[73] A group of sons may form close ties in a family in any circumstances, but the Lawrences' self-imposed isolation when their children were growing up in Oxford may have fostered a still closer attachment among them. This close comradeship within the family may have contributed to Lawrence's predilection throughout his life for the companionship of a society of men. Lawrence made the connection himself, rather grimly in sentences he wrote for Liddell Hart: "The five brothers . . . were brought up to be self-sufficient, and were sufficient till the war struck away two and left in their sequence gaps in age that were overwide for sympathy to cross. Then their loneliness seemed to rankle, sometimes. To friends who wondered aloud how he could endure the company of the barrack-room and its bareness T.E. might retort, almost fiercely, that he had gone back to his boyhood class and was at home."[74]

Although he was the second son, Lawrence was clearly the leader among the children, and played the role of oldest brother oftener than Bob did. Bob studied medicine under the famous British physician Sir William Osler, and served with great courage as a doctor on the front lines in France during World War I.[75] Later he became a medical missionary in China, where he was joined by Mrs. Lawrence. But aside from these achievements, Bob was so overprotected and stifled by her, and absorbed so literally by the exaggerated climate of religiosity through which she sought to justify herself, that he was unable to deal directly with any of the emotional issues that arose within the family. He remained attached inseparably to his mother until her death. Lawrence wrote to Mrs. Shaw in 1928: "The chickens are beyond her cluck, you see: all except the elder brother and he's queer company. You will not persuade him of anything, if you do see him. He is illuminated from inside, not from out. His face, very often, shines like a lamp. Such an odd family."[76]

In 1964 and 1965, when I visited with Dr. Lawrence, he was living in a vicarage and was vigorous, alert and kind. He had retained fundamentalist religious beliefs and considered beauties of nature, such as a recent ice storm that had turned the small branches of trees in the churchyard into gleaming ropes of ice, to be evidence that the second coming of the Lord was not far off. He died in 1971 at eighty-six.[77]

T.E.'s preeminence among his brothers had several aspects. He was the most inventive and imaginative of the boys and thus their leader in family games and activities. He also had a strong maternal side, derived from his identification with his mother, which manifested itself quite early in a readiness to help her take care of the younger children, and in a lively capacity for empathy — a quality often associated more with women than with men. "Mrs. Lawrence once gave my wife and myself a tin travelling bath for our children," Robert Graves wrote. In a note accompanying the gift she had written: "I used to bathe Ned in it, and Ned later bathed Arnie. He was a very good nursemaid." Later, when T.E. saw this bathtub in Graves's home, he remarked that it gave him a "violent revulsion to recall such physical dependency."[78]

T.E.'s extensive knowledge and early travel experience added to his natural inclination to assume the role of teacher with his younger brothers, and in his letters to them he delighted in sharing experiences he thought they would enjoy or information he believed they might profit from. At times he could sound rather pedantic. When he was eighteen, he replied to a letter from Will, who was a budding archeologist: "Your letter bristles with inconsistencies." He then proceeded to lecture Will on the differences among Roman, Celtic, Saxon, British and Danish structures and artifacts.[79] Finally, when he came to recognize his mother's smothering qualities, he offered to help his younger brothers, especially Arnold, achieve physical and even emotional distance from her.

The most important relationship among his brothers for Lawrence during childhood and youth was with Will, only sixteen months younger than himself. From all descriptions Will was an attractive boy, tall, handsome, finely built, graceful and intelligent. He was thought by some to have been the mother's favorite. One of his friends said of him, "He was really an Adonis to look at, beautiful in body, and I think in many ways he might have been as great a man as Ned."[80]

Will was a fine athlete and won the City of Oxford High School gymnastic cup two years in succession. He won a history exhibition (a type of scholarship), as T.E. had done, to St. John's, and after graduation from Oxford became a teacher of history at a college in Delhi, where he had unusual success in gaining the trust and affection of the Indian students.[81] Will had a deep religious faith that complemented his intellectual abilities, and an affectionate and generous nature. His friend E. F. Hall tells the story that he came upon Will practicing high dives from Brighton pier one day during a vacation. He was surprised to see this — diving was not a skill or interest Will was known to possess — and asked him why he was doing it. Will replied that he was standing in for another young man who was in a diving contest but had broken his leg. "He's got a large family to support and I'll do the high diving for him and give him the money if I win," he explained to Hall. "That kind of thing," Hall added, "came from the mother."[82]

Though T.E. and Will were deeply devoted to one another and close companions throughout childhood, Will's greater success in athletics, his tall stature and striking good looks, and the possibility that Sarah favored him, may all have contributed to T.E.'s avoidance of conventional athletic achievement and competition, and to his intense need to prove himself through overwhelming physical adversities. Although he never spoke or wrote of jealous feelings toward Will, it would have been only natural for him to have had them. Hall said to me, "I've often wondered whether Ned's tiny stature may have in some way or other made him a little bit inhibited in relation to his rather beautiful brother."[83] When the young woman to whom Ned proposed marriage preferred, and then became betrothed, to Will his feelings toward Will became further complicated. After Will was killed in France in World War I, Lawrence found that he could no longer "go on living peacefully in Cairo" and sought out a more active role in the war.

The next brother, Frank, was the least unusual of the group, but an able person in his own way. He was the only one of the boys to go in for team sports, which earned him some disdain from T.E. Like T.E. he went to Jesus College, and one of his contemporaries has offered this picture of him: "He was a born leader, was Captain of Football for two years, 1911–13, and also of cricket. Very quiet in speech and manner, he was the embodiment of school loyalty and keenness in everything. He was an excellent shot and Captain of the School Miniature Rifle Club when it did so well in the Oxford League and later, as an undergraduate, he was Captain of the Oxford Twenty."[84] Like Will, Frank was killed in World War I.

The youngest brother, Arnold, twelve years younger than T.E., was the only one of the five to marry and become a parent. Lawrence's affection for this "child-of-the-old-age of my two extraordinary parents" comes through clearly in his many letters to "Arnie." As an interested big brother T.E. served as an inspiration as well as a buffer against their mother's dominating influence. Although he helped Arnold carve a separate life for himself, told him about their illegitimacy, and advised him to leave home as soon as he could manage it, Lawrence could never quite reconcile himself to his brother's marriage. "Prostitution is marriage à la carte," he told Arnold jokingly in a letter when he learned of his plans. "I always thought we wouldn't go in for it in our family."[85]

Arnold, like T.E., became an archeologist, but unlike his older brother had the opportunity to pursue an academic career in his chosen field. However (also like T.E.), Arnold did not follow the path of conventional scholarship. He went to Ghana to start a new national museum and found that he got along better with the illiterate tribesmen in the bush than with the officials.[86] T.E. wrote of him in 1927: "He gets enthusiastic never, except in denunciation."[87] Elsie Newcombe, a friend of both brothers, told me that she could share jokes and plain fun more openly with Arnold than with T.E.

Fundamentally kind behind his reserve and critical wit, Arnold has borne the burden of having to live two lives. For forty years he has conducted the job of being his famous brother's posthumous keeper with rare skill, fairness and, most of the time, patience, while living simultaneously his own private life.

2

Childhood and Adolescence

T. E. Lawrence was born in a cottage called Gorphwyspha ("place of rest") at the edge of Tremadoc village. As was then the usual practice, he was delivered by a midwife. Although according to his birth record in Portmadoc Lawrence was born on August 15, 1888, his mother said that he was born in the "early hours" of August 16, the date Lawrence used as his birthdate.[1]

The principal available sources of information about the earliest years, before the family moved to Langley in the New Forest, are the published accounts written by his mother and older brother (the latter was still living during much of the time the research for this book was undertaken).[2] T.E.'s own accounts are probably based primarily on information supplied to him by his parents.[3] I have no reason to question his mother's reports on matters of neutral fact, although she might, in her pride over the accomplishments of an extraordinary son, have exaggerated somewhat his precocity. Her assertions of complete harmony within the family may be questioned, and of course her omission of any reference to the family's situation or to Lawrence's conflicts is not unexpected. Robert Lawrence, even more than the mother, expunged from his own mind, not to mention the printed record, any material suggesting that family life was anything but idyllic ("We had a very happy childhood which was never marred by a single quarrel between any of us"),[4] or that T.E.'s childhood was other than completely virtuous. However, I believe that he too in matters of neutral family history has been a reliable reporter.

The family moved when Lawrence was thirteen months old to Kirkcudbright, a port in the southern part of Scotland, where Will was born. For three years, between the time T.E. was three and six, the Lawrences lived in Dinard, a French port and resort on the Brittany coast, a popular watering place, where many English people lived or vacationed. The fourth son, Frank, was born during the Dinard years at St. Helier in Jersey when Lawrence was four and a half. Because any boy born in France was due to serve as a conscript in the French army, the parents arranged to have Frank's birth take place in the Channel Islands in order to assure the child of English citizenry. (A photograph of Ned at the age of five shows a boy with piercing eyes dressed in a dark outfit with richly embroidered lace about the neck, and black velvet stockings.)[5]

At Dinard the boys had lessons from an English governess, and went briefly to the Frères school near where they lived. Lawrence attended private gymnastic classes with other English boys in the larger port city of Saint-Malo, near Dinard. The Lawrences evidently kept in touch with several French families in Dinard, as there were many tidings conveyed by Lawrence to his parents from French people he visited there during his 1906, 1907 and 1908 trips in France, and he stayed for considerable periods of time with one of these families in Dinard, the Chaignons, during his travels.

Although Mrs. Lawrence regularly employed "nannies" to help her in bringing up her children, the first four were breast-fed by their mother for at least a year.[6] Mrs. Lawrence stated that T.E. was big as a child and from infancy was particularly active and energetic, "constantly on the move," exploring and mastering his environment.[7] Once he followed his father up a ladder into a loft, and on another occasion early in his second year he had to be rescued by his mother from a high window ledge, which he had reached by climbing over a sewing machine.[8] Before he was nine, he had become the leader of the brothers in inventing games for them to play. These were usually war games and were marked by both humor and imagination. A favorite was the assault by virtuous and noble, but very aggressive, dolls or animal figures upon a tower, which had to be entered in order to rescue it from enemies ("fourscore of men") within.[9]

The nannies played a significant role in the boys' upbringing as they did in so many English families of the period. One of them, Kate Vickery, lived with the family for several years, until she had to leave abruptly when T.E. was six or seven to be with a sister in Canada. T.E., who called her "Kattie," was distinctly her favorite. After her departure she was never seen again by the boys except for one reunion several years later.[10] Miss Vickery was succeeded by Florence Messham, with whom Lawrence later corresponded.[11]

Lawrence's precocity as a child has been a matter of great interest to some of his biographers. Aldington, especially, has taken considerable pains to challenge T.E.'s claims to exceptional childhood accomplishments, particularly intellectual ones.[12] Aldington quibbled over the accuracy of Lawrence's claim to an early ability to read and write. He

challenges Mrs. Lawrence's statements that T.E. learned the alphabet
before he was three through hearing Robert taught and he also questions
Robert's recollection that T.E. was able to read a newspaper upside down
at about five.[13] Lawrence himself wrote that he was "reading (chiefly
police news) at four"[14] and "could read and write before I was four."[15]

Although it is possible that both he and members of the family exaggerated the facts or distorted them through faulty memory, their statements are quite consistent with the exceptional intellectual abilities
Lawrence demonstrated throughout his life. Such early milestones are
familiar among very gifted children. They are also consistent with the
statements that he had a child's fluency in French by the age of six (or
"as a boy")[16] — not so remarkable considering that by six he had lived in
France for two and a half years — and began learning Latin at five.[17]

In the spring of 1894 before Lawrence was six, the family moved from
Dinard to the Isle of Wight and then to Langley on the edge of the New
Forest, where they remained for two years in a red-brick villa called
Langley Lodge. According to his mother, Ned was already able to read
English books "at a glance" and remember their content. Strong and big
as a young child, he was able to climb trees without falling. Soon after
coming to Langley, he impressed his family by proving that distant rum-
blings were the guns of the fleet, not thunder. He had observed the smoke
from a high perch in a tree.[18] He also learned to swim and ride a pony
at this time. As Langley Lodge was near the Solent and Southampton
Water, and the fleet was at Spithead, there were many opportunities to
see ships of all kinds — oceangoing steamers, naval vessels and yachts.
According to Robert, T.E. demonstrated a precocious ability to identify
fossils on the beach near Langley, anticipating his later skill in identifying
archeological findings. Robert Lawrence showed me several specimens
that Ned had found, which contained imprints of sea urchins and other
fossil remains.[19]

The first observation of Ned by someone outside of the family comes
during this period. The Lawrence boys were friendly with several children of the agent of a nearby estate in the New Forest. One of them,
Janet Laurie, recalled the first time she met Ned. Her parents had
wanted another son and so kept her hair short and dressed her like a boy.
She was in church, and behind her were two or three Lawrence brothers
with their nanny, Florence Messham. She heard one of the boys, who
proved to be Ned, say to Miss Messham, "What a naughty little boy to
keep his hat on in church." She turned around and put out her tongue
and said, "I'm not a boy, I'm a girl." She overheard Miss Messham ("I
took a great dislike to her") say, "Well, she may not be a little boy, but
she's a very rude little girl." Thus the friendship began.[20] On another occasion, Ned refused to come down out of a tree to have tea with her. "I'm
not going to have tea with any girl," he protested. He climbed like a

monkey and seemed to have no fears. The children had a donkey and cart at their disposal, and enjoyed chasing the donkey and riding about in the cart. Even at six, she said, he could be "frightfully bossy; he used to order us about, but in a very nice way." He exerted "a quiet authority."

Like Mrs. Lawrence and Bob, Janet had lively recollections of T.E.'s humor and sense of fun, and spoke of the generally happy atmosphere in the Lawrence home. But she observed that "there was always something he was not satisfied with, even as a small child," something sad, "a secret something of unhappiness," which inspired the feeling that she ought to take care of him or protect him. These qualities seemed to grow stronger as he grew older. He was always outside the ring of children, had odd eating habits (he ate chiefly porridge and bananas), and was not good at group games, such as cricket, which he later came to disdain proudly.[21]

In 1896, when T.E. was eight years old, the family settled in Oxford in order, according to Bob, to obtain a proper education for the children.[22] They lived in a red-brick Victorian house at 2 Polstead Road in a middle-class neighborhood on the outskirts of town. We are fortunate in having detailed, published descriptions of Lawrence's boyhood by those who knew him in Oxford. Allowing for the glow that tends to bathe in a golden light the memory of a great figure, the picture is nevertheless of a child who was remarkable in many ways.

Even as a boy of eight or nine Lawrence demonstrated extraordinary energy, curiosity, powers of observation and invention. What is also remarkable — the significance of this I will discuss later — is that there was no discernible transition from early childhood to adolescence, as we understand adolescence, with its frequent rebellious storms and the development of sexual interests. Lawrence had, in my opinion, no real adolescence at all, his energies remaining in many respects those of a lively and lively-minded schoolboy. "His great abilities and interests," as George Bernard Shaw wrote, "were those of a highly gifted boy."[23]

Lawrence's insatiable curiosity about the past and its evidences in the present dominated his childhood interests. His rummagings and excavations about Oxford, beginning when he was eight or nine, for pieces of old pottery, stone and glass, or his tearing away at the pews of churches in and around Oxford to find brasses of medieval knights to rub (he perfected the technique), are well documented. Indeed, so intense was Lawrence's perseverance in the levering up of pews and furniture to get at old brasses that an article once appeared in a local paper complaining of vandalism.[24] On another occasion, when he was fifteen or sixteen he pulled a whole roof, or a large piece of one, that interested him, off a collapsing old house on a main Oxford street. This interest was no ordinary childhood exploration but, as one of his friends, C. F. C. Beeson, described it, "a passionate absorption beside which my urge was more akin to the curiosity of a magpie in a Baghdad Bazaar."[25]

Lawrence also avidly sought information about other structures and artifacts of earlier times, especially of the Middle Ages — castles, armor, costumes, heraldry, crypts (possessing human bones), illuminated manuscripts, leatherwork, and old coins. The earliest account of Lawrence's archeological explorations occur in an essay he wrote himself — his first "published" writing — entitled "An Antiquarian and a Geologist in Hants [Hampshire]," which appeared in the City of Oxford High School magazine when he was fifteen.[26] The article, signed "L.ii," describes a family cycling tour in Hampshire ("it was unanimously decided, by the votes of the family council . . ."). Included in it are descriptions of a thirteenth-century abbey and depictions of the countryside and wildlife that demonstrate Lawrence's intense powers of observation. Of this quality in Lawrence Sidney Webb would one day remark, "This fellow describes every blade of grass and foot of gravel he walked over."[27] The article concludes with a description mingled with an awkward and childish effort at humor: "We crossed over to Whiteparish, in which all things ought to be white, yet we saw a big black horse, a chimney sweep, some dirty ducks, and a drove of brown cows, with one black one."

Lawrence's adventures as a boy, especially his travels by boat with his friends on the Trill Mill Stream have often been told. What struck me most in talking over these times with his friends from childhood, who remembered them with great delight, is the unselfconscious way in which Lawrence would lead them on escapades they would never have thought to undertake themselves.[28] These were not ordinary childhood pranks or adventures. To carry out the Trill Mill Stream voyages (the Thames divides near Oxford and one of its streams passes under the city and emerges at Folly Bridge) Lawrence had to know when the level of the water was lowest (in summer), how to smash the lock on the iron gates which blocked the exit at Folly Bridge, the right kind of punt to use, and an effective method of illumination.

What also needs to be emphasized is the excitement, humor, and sense of delightful mischief he inspired in his companions, raising their usual existence to a special level. One passenger, the only girl to my knowledge to pass under the city of Oxford in a punt with Lawrence, described how thrilling the adventure was but also her fear that passage would be made stormy by the rush of someone's bathwater emptying into the stream. Other examples of the mischievous, affectionate and adventurous aspects of Lawrence's boyhood nature are provided in the early contributions to *T. E. Lawrence by His Friends.*

Lawrence attended the City of Oxford High School from the time of his arrival in Oxford in 1896 to his graduation and entrance into Jesus College, Oxford, in 1907. The high school was opened in the nineteenth century, when the dons were allowed to marry and thus sought a school to which they could afford to send their children.[29] It was not a public school in the English sense, but more like an American public school, with an independent board of governors drawn from the city and the university.[30]

The Lawrence boys, dressed by Mrs. Lawrence in their blue-and-white striped jerseys, were thought somewhat sissyish at first, but became popular when they were better known.[31] One school friend has described how T.E., with a characteristic "mask" or "grin," would stand silently on the edge of groups playing cricket or football.[32] "At school they used to stick me into football or cricket teams," he wrote Mrs. Shaw, "and always I would trickle away from the field before the match ended."[33] Although he avoided these group and contact sports, preferring to play chess with a pocket set, he enjoyed cross-country paper chases and inventing games of mock warfare with his playmates.[34]

Lawrence's second essay in the school magazine is a satirical piece written in pseudo-technical style about how to put together an improvised game of playground cricket. The short article reveals Lawrence's cynicism toward this "folly" and concludes, "The balls go, some into the side windows of the school, some through those of [a] factory, others again attach themselves to the windows opposite."[35] A third essay, written when he was eighteen, is also a satirical piece directed principally at himself, on how to "annex a vacant emolument" (that is, obtain a scholarship) in history by showing an interest in antiquities and admiring the right books. Lawrence expressed contempt in later years for his early education,[36] but the contempt seems in part to have been the result of later embitterment; it is not discernible in documents or data from the time itself.

As a schoolboy Lawrence read voraciously and widely but not necessarily deeply. At this time he became interested in the Middle Ages and its feudal, romantic and chivalric traditions and myths, and clearly enjoyed his private reading more than the formal lessons. From the age of about sixteen, he told Liddell Hart, he studied war because he was filled with the idea of freeing a people — from what he did not say.[37]

He also told Liddell Hart that "the long school hours and the plague of homework cut into the pursuit of archeology that was already the child's passion,"[38] and to another friend he complained that these school years were "miserable sweated years of unwilling work . . . nor do I think the miseries of grown-up feelings are as bad as those of boys."[39] In a passage in *The Mint*, Lawrence's account of his RAF initiation, he revealed that he suffered during his school years from a constant fear of being punished by his teachers, although there is no evidence that he actually elicited much disciplinary action. "Hazardously suspended penalty," he wrote, "made my life from eight to eighteen miserable, and Oxford, after it, so noble a freedom."[40]

A contemporary record dispels any notion that Lawrence neglected his studies in favor of his other interests. One of his teachers wrote the following report when Lawrence was thirteen years and nine months old: "I have every confidence in stating that Thomas Edward Lawrence is a very persevering boy and works well at his lessons and is exceedingly well-behaved. I have attended the prize givings at the Oxford High School for Boys and can therefore speak with some authority. I also notice he has been successful in gaining prizes on several occasions and is well up in his form."[41] One of his prizes at school was for an essay on Tennyson, whom he had selected for special study.

Lawrence did, however, sometimes find that his studies afforded him an opportunity to make gentle fun of his teachers. When he was in the fifth form, there were two tutors, one named Binney, the other Tubbie. In translating a passage on ancient games from the *Aeneid*, Lawrence reported that some object was brought in tubs. His tutor asked if he couldn't think of another word. "In bins," he suggested.[42]

His efforts to inure himself, as if for some important future hardship, danger or important task, first became evident during his early teens: "Right from a boy he was preparing himself for some big thing that fate had in store."[43] Lawrence delighted in teasing a friend who was born on August fourteenth by pointing out that he was less fortunate than Lawrence, who was born on the fifteenth — like Napoleon. In his home he had a coffin-shaped box almost six feet long, two feet high and two feet wide. His mother complained, "That boy of mine's sleeping there every night now."[44] Overhead were brass rubbings — "the room was hideous with them," another friend recalled[45] — one of which depicted a corpse being eaten by worms. Every night when he went to bed "he'd think of this chap dying, eaten by worms."[46]

Lawrence told Liddell Hart in 1929 that he had enlisted in the artillery "about 1906" and "did eight months before being brought out."[47] When he was going over the passage concerning this episode in the manuscript of Liddell Hart's biography, Lawrence wrote: "This is hush-hush. I should not have told you. I ran away from home . . . and served six months. No trouble with discipline, I have always been easy; but the other fellows fought all Friday and Saturday nights and frightened me with their roughness."[48] There is also a veiled reference to this episode in *The Mint* (written in 1922) in connection with a discussion of the violence and bullying of enlisted men in the barracks: "Twenty years ago — or seventeen years, my limit of direct experience — they [the troops] were indeed brutal. Then every incident ended in dispute and every dispute either in the ordeal of fists (a forgotten art, today) or in a barrack-court-martial whose sentences were too often mass-bullying of anyone unlike the mass."[49] I have been unable, however, to unearth any confirming evidence of these six or eight months of military service between 1904 and 1907 before he went up to Oxford at the age of nineteen in October 1907.[50]

Granted, his mother states that Lawrence was "out of school for a term" when he broke his leg rescuing a smaller boy from a bully, but the time was spent convalescing, not bicycling off to the army. She states that he did not grow much after the accident (she is mistaken in implying that his growth was halted as a result of the injury), which would indicate that it occurred quite late — when he was seventeen or eighteen.[51] I have been unable to obtain school or army records that shed any light on the matter. Several of Lawrence's childhood friends, including C. F. C. Beeson, who attended the City of Oxford High School, recall no period of absence, such as Lawrence described to Liddell Hart, and doubt that the six months could have been "fitted in." Bob Lawrence once told Arnold that it was not possible that T.E. was away from home for six to eight months.[52] The most likely explanation is that the episode was the elaboration of something real but smaller, perhaps a period of a week or two, which Lawrence needed later in his life to embellish into something greater when writing as a military expert to a well-known military historian.

During the adolescent years Lawrence showed no interest in girls, according to C. F. C. Beeson, a close companion at this time.[53] Whereas Beeson would go to St. Giles Fair (a traveling fair still held on the widest street in Oxford each September, at which teen-agers have an excellent opportunity to be together) to meet girls "for roistering and philandering," as he put it, Lawrence had no interest and stayed away. Beeson would also go to dances and parties at Christmastime and found them "exhilarating," while Lawrence avoided them altogether. Similarly, Lawrence would avoid the "Eights Week" festivities, a kind of annual springtime regatta on the Thames, with dances, picnics and entertainment and "every possible chance for flirtations."[54]

3

Lawrence and His Family:
The Burden of
Illegitimacy

Lawrence's illegitimacy, and its meaning for him throughout his life, cannot be separated from his relationships with his parents, from his conscious and unconscious views of them, their personalities, their lives and relationship with one another, and above all, from his identification with them. The evidence regarding the great significance of Lawrence's illegitimacy for him is beyond dispute. However, it is not the mere fact of illegitimacy, with its social consequences, but rather the complex interplay of psychological and psychosexual developmental forces and social realities that gave the illegitimacy its weight in the formation of Lawrence's character and the emergence after the war of his psychological and sexual conflicts. Lawrence's offhand, sometimes humorous dismissals of the matter not only show his attempt to reject its importance, but reflect also a kind of enlightened social viewpoint, above the battle.[1] A more tolerant social climate might have eased somewhat the burden of Lawrence's conflict over his illegitimacy, but it could not have relieved him completely of the deeper psychological problems it occasioned.

It is not possible to establish a precise time when Lawrence "learned" that his father had another family and that his parents were not married. A childhood friend recalls hearing Lawrence say, "My father told me I was a bastard when I was eleven"; yet in his only written statement on the subject (the only one, that is, of which I am aware) Lawrence denies flatly that his parents told him.[2]

In view of the intense and precocious curiosity of his young mind, what probably happened is that he pieced together the reality from his own observations. Arnold Lawrence told me that Lawrence wrote either to his friend Lionel Curtis or his mentor David Hogarth that when he was four and a half he began to discover what the situation was from trying to understand a discussion his father was having with a solicitor about managing the estate in Ireland. In the years after that, Lawrence told his brother, he "worked it out for himself."[3] Although this is psychologically possible, and even likely, I have not found the letter in which the statement occurs. Arnold Lawrence is convinced his brother understood the fact of their illegitimacy by the time he was nine or ten years old.[4] I disagree emphatically with Aldington's statement that Lawrence's claim to have known before he was ten was "very likely a rhetorical expression deriving from Lawrence's vagueness over numbers."[5]

Whether or not a solicitor was discussing the situation within earshot of the four-and-a-half-year-old Ned, it is true that as a child Lawrence had other opportunities to overhear discussions between his parents. No matter how scrupulously discreet they may have been, they could well have underestimated what a lively-minded and intensely curious child like Ned might pick up and piece together from bits of conversation. In addition, the father sometimes made trips to Ireland and visited with former Irish friends in London, and the mother kept up correspondence with relatives in Scotland, all of which provided puzzling, incongruous clues for Lawrence to work out. Land agents were in fact coming from Ireland to meet with the father at least once a year to discuss arrangements with the tenants and other matters.[6]

The fact that T.E.'s parents never told him directly of their situation but left him to figure it out for himself only served to underscore the deception and intensify his resentment of them for it. The paragraph that follows the passage in which Lawrence tells Mrs. Shaw that he discovered his illegitimacy as a child demonstrates clearly his resentment and conflict, together with the self-hatred thus engendered. Written in 1927 at a time when there was considerable strain between Lawrence and his mother, the letter reveals as well how inextricably intertwined were his feelings about his parents (especially his mother) and their relationship, his illegitimacy, and his views of marriage and parenthood as they applied to himself. "They thought always that they were living in sin," he wrote, "and that we would some day find out. Whereas I knew it before I was ten, and they never told me; till after my father's death something I said showed mother that I knew, and didn't care a straw.

"One of the real reasons (there are three or four) why I am in the service is so that I may live by myself. She has given me a terror of families and inquisitions. And yet you'll understand she is my mother, and an extraordinary person. Knowledge of her will prevent my ever making any woman a mother, and the cause of children. I think she suspects this: but she does not know that the inner conflict, which makes me a standing civil war, is the inevitable issue of the discordant natures of herself and my father, and the inflammation of strength and weakness which followed the uprooting of their lives and principles. They should not have borne children."[7]

It is the conflict described in this letter, deriving from the discrepancy between his parents' avowed Christian values and their position as pillars of their church in Oxford society and the actualities of their unmarried state, that was the most disturbing aspect of the illegitimacy for Lawrence and had the greatest influence upon his later development. It would not have been so difficult had his parents not felt forced to maintain the deception with the children. A person's inner sense of worth derives from an identification with valued parents, but Lawrence's parents were on the one hand persons of high ideals and standards while at the same time their actual lives violated fundamentally what they purported to represent. His identification with them includes both elements. He is identified with their ideals, which he accepts, but also with their failure to live up to them. They are, furthermore, deceivers, and he has been made a part of the deception.

To make matters still more difficult his mother required of him that he *redeem* her fallen state by his own special achievements, by being a person of unusual value who accomplishes great deeds, preferably religious and ideally on an heroic scale. Lawrence did his best to fulfill heroic ideals. But he was plagued, especially after the events of the war activated his inner conflicts, by a deep sense of failure. Having been deceived as a child he was later to feel that he himself was a deceiver — that he had deceived the Arabs — although, as we shall see, his conviction about this far outweighed the reality.

I do not mean to imply that the influence of the illegitimacy on Lawrence's development was altogether negative. Part of his creativity and originality lies in his "irregularity," in his capacity to remain outside conventional ways of thinking, a tendency which I believe derives, at least in part, from his illegitimacy. Lawrence's capacity for invention and his ability to see unusual or humorous relationships in familiar situations come also, I believe, from his illegitimacy. He was not limited to established or "legitimate" solutions or ways of doing things, and thus his mind was open to a wider range of possibilities and opportunities.

In addition to its psychological meaning, Lawrence's illegitimacy had important social consequences and placed limitations upon him, which rankled him deeply and preyed on his mind. Certain schools and social opportunities were not available; he was excluded from some social groups and may have been considered a liability for a number of professional posts, especially in governmental circles.[8] At times he felt socially isolated when erstwhile friends shunned him upon learning of his background.[9] Lawrence's delight in making fun of regular officers and other segments of "regular" society (however well deserved the mockery) derived, one suspects, at least in part from his inner view of his own irregular situation. His fickleness about names for himself is directly related, of course, to his view of his parents and to his identification with them. As far as I have been able to discern, Lawrence did not share with his childhood friends or with schoolmates at Jesus College the facts of his illegitimacy, for none of those I interviewed who knew him during that period were aware of it.

According to Elsie Newcombe, the wife of Colonel Stewart F. Newcombe, an officer and good friend with whom Lawrence served during the war, Lawrence told her husband in 1914 that his parents were not married and he "had no right" to the name Lawrence.[10] What induced Lawrence to start telling his friends at this time in his life is not known. Perhaps it was because the matter was becoming known in Oxford anyway, or he had lived away from home so long his views of it had changed. During the decades that followed he told a number of his friends about it and wrote hints and bits to others. (Copies of these letters are among the Lawrence papers in the Bodleian Library.)

Lawrence's bitterness, pain and anxiety lest the matter come out publicly are evident behind the humor and the tone of inconsequence with which he sometimes dismissed it. In giving his address to Lord Winterton in 1923 he wrote casually, "My constant address (as Lawrence — did you know that wasn't my real name?) is at 14 Barton Street, Westminster."[11] To Lionel Curtis in 1926: "Your remark about ancestry, for which you apologized, I've entirely forgotten! So what can it have been? Bars Sinister [the heraldic sign erroneously believed to be the sign of illegitimacy] are rather jolly ornaments. You feel so like a flea in the legitimate prince's bed!"[12] Or to A. E. "Jock" Chambers, whom he wrote in 1924: "This address is my safest one: it may be any name. 'Shaw' I call myself, but some write Ross and others Lawrence. Hippocleides doesn't care!"[13] He signed this last letter: *

$$\left[\begin{array}{l} \text{TES.} \\ \text{ea J. H. R.} \\ \text{ea TEL.} \\ \text{ea E.C.} \end{array} \right]$$

More seriously he wrote to Sir Fred Kenyon, who was cataloguing the *Seven Pillars of Wisdom* in 1927: "My 'Lawrence' label (an invention for his own reasons, of my father's late in life) is worn out."[14] To the American publisher F. N. Doubleday: "So you see the name 'Lawrence' bars itself. It is worth a lot of money, because of Arabia: whereas my father chose it because it meant nothing, to his family."[15] And again to Curtis, who was preparing an entry for *Who's Who* about him: "Of

* From the Bodleian Library, Oxford.

course write anything you please; so long as you don't give away (i.) my
original family (ii.) my present address."[16]

In trying to understand Lawrence's relationship with his parents, one
should not presume that the documents, especially the letters to Mrs.
Shaw, which disclose his deeply ambivalent attitude toward them, depict
the family relationships as they actually existed when he was a child.
(Lawrence's relationship with Charlotte Shaw will be explored in Part
Five.) The letters to Mrs. Shaw, written in the loneliness of India, are
introspective. They follow a decade of experiences that had destroyed the
relative inner harmony that T.E. had achieved in childhood and young
adulthood. They disclose thoughts and feelings Lawrence might never
have become conscious of, or at least ones he might not have dwelled
upon, had his life and character not become so severely dislocated. They
represent an effort on his part to understand himself, a kind of self-
analysis directed toward a mother-figure who evoked his inner attitudes
toward his mother but with less experience of pain. (In her letters to him
Mrs. Shaw spoke of similar conflicts with her own parents.) Lawrence's
letters reveal his inner mental representations of his parents — not
literally the parents themselves.

This is not to say that these ambivalent attitudes toward his parents
did not begin to form in Lawrence's childhood. Rather, the words of his
letters reflect the impact of the complete life experience which followed
childhood, the insights and conflicts established thereafter, and the
strained relations between Lawrence and his mother, which resulted from
his insistence upon remaining beneath his station in the ranks.

Lawrence's father and mother, even by the high standards of the day,
were in many ways very good parents. Their religious and moral strict-
ness did not prevent them from giving their sons wide freedom to learn,
to explore their environment, and to travel, opportunities which Ned and
Will in particular took advantage of. And they provided a secure, loving
home and rich educational opportunities.

Lawrence's father from all accounts was devoted to his sons and their
welfare, and as mentioned previously, he enjoyed many activities with
them.[17] Lawrence's letters contain a number of references to these mutual
interests, especially photography ("he taught me before I was four years
old") and bicycling. They went together on summer bicycle tours in
England from as early as 1903 and in France in 1907. Lawrence acknowledges his father's kindness to him, and Arnold states that the elder
Lawrence was very fond of his second son.[18]

T.E. wrote to Liddell Hart that his father's family seemed unaware
that the five sons existed, "even when after [my father's] death, recognition of their achievement might have done honour to the name."[19] But it
is not clear to whom this statement referred. Lawrence's difficulty with

his father was quite different. It lay in the defeat of his masculinity, and of his view of himself as a strong and effective person — the result of being identified with the elder Lawrence as his son. For in Lawrence's eyes his father was a devalued person, transformed and reduced by his mother. Whereas once Thomas Lawrence had been "on the large scale," "grand," "naturally lord-like," "a hard rider and drinker" and a "spendthrift," in the mother's hands he had been "remodeled" into "a teetotaler" and "a domestic man." We have seen that in reality the father was somewhat less heroic in his former life than Lawrence imagined, and a good deal more of a person in the home in Oxford than the letters to Charlotte Shaw would suggest. But for reasons of his own psychology, Lawrence viewed him in the way that he did.

Much of Lawrence's resentment of his mother, which had a number of causes, was related to her role, in his view, in reducing Thomas Lawrence. Not only did Lawrence accuse his mother of carrying off his father and cutting him down, but in a passage which has something of the tone of a jealous son, he also accuses her of devoting herself too fully to keeping him that way. The following passage also reveals the dominant element in Lawrence's relationship with his mother, the deeply ambivalent love-hate attachment by which he was both drawn to her and yet repelled: "Mother is rather wonderful: but very exciting," he wrote. "She is so set, so assured in mind. I think she 'set' many years ago: perhaps before I was born. I have a terror of her knowing anything about my feelings, or convictions, or way of life. If she knew they would be damaged: violated: no longer mine. You see, she would not hesitate to understand them: and I do not understand them, and do not want to. Nor has she seen any of us growing: because I think she has not grown since we began. She was wholly wrapped up in my father, whom she had carried away jealously from his former life and country, against great odds: and whom she kept as her trophy of power. Also, she was a fanatical housewife,[20] who would rather do her own housework than not, to the total neglect of herself."[21] The letter also reveals Lawrence's intense struggle to grow as a separate person despite his mother's overpowering personality.

The terror of closeness with his mother lest she destroy his inner self (a conflict most sons resolve, at least in part, in childhood and adolescence) is further revealed in another letter to Mrs. Shaw a year later. "I wonder how you will like her," Lawrence wrote (a meeting between Mrs. Shaw and Mrs. Lawrence was anticipated); "she is monumental really! and so unlike you. Probably she is exactly like me; otherwise we wouldn't so hanker after one another, whenever we are wise enough to keep apart. Her letters are things I dread, and she always asks for more of mine (I try and write monthly: but we haven't a subject we dare be intimate upon: so they are spavined things) and hates them when they come, as they do, ever so rarely. I think I'm afraid of letting her get, ever so little inside the circle of my integrity: and she is always hammering and sapping to come in. A very dominant person: only old now, and, so my brother says, very much less than she has been. She has so lived in her children, and in my father, that she cannot relieve herself, upon herself, at all. And it isn't right to cry out to your children for love. They are prevented, by the walls of time and function, from loving their parents."[22]

Again, three months later he wrote: "I've not written any letters of this sort to anyone else, since I was born. No trust ever existed between my mother and myself. Each of us jealously guarded his or her own individuality, whenever we came together. I always felt that she was laying siege to me, and would conquer, if I left a chink unguarded."[23]

Lawrence's relationship with his mother, deeper, more complex and more troubled than that with the father, played a central role in his personal development, the direction of his life, and the formation of his character. He was probably not her favorite in the conventional sense of receiving the most affection, and she seems not to have been especially demonstrative toward him physically (although the nannies were more so).[24] However, all my informants agree that Lawrence was adored by his mother, who was deeply devoted to his welfare, and that he was the child in whom both parents had the most important emotional investment. He was treated differently, as if he were special, and it was expected from childhood that it would be Ned of all the sons who would do something important with his life.[25]

Mrs. Lawrence's original hope that her sons would provide her personal redemption by becoming Christian missionaries was fulfilled only by Robert. Frank and Will were killed in the war, and Arnold resisted intensely ("I just didn't pay any attention to her") and ceased in his own estimation to be a Christian.[26] As for T.E., in Oxford he took part in the family Bible readings, attended faithfully Canon Christopher's sermons at St. Aldates, and even taught Sunday School classes, although according to one of his friends Lawrence lost a Sunday School post for reading the class a beautiful story of Oscar Wilde's (Wilde was then in disgrace).[27] Mrs. Lawrence saw in T.E.'s reverent 1908 letter describing Chartres Cathedral an indication of his love of God and she had copies of it made and distributed to her friends.[28] But a careful reading of the emotion-filled letter indicates that Lawrence's response was largely aesthetic, and that his appreciation was not of God Himself but of the cathedral as "a place truly in which to worship God."[29] A year later, when he went to Syria, his mother believed that he was on a special mission of some kind, one with religious significance.

But the direction of Lawrence's later life, ascetic though it may have become, was secular in the extreme. When Bob went out to China as a medical missionary, accompanied by the mother (perhaps it would be more accurate to say that he accompanied her), T.E. disparaged their missionary activity in a number of letters.[30]

Lawrence's closeness to his mother, his need to please her, his sensitivity, and his intense identification with her and with her conflicts made it almost inevitable that the imposition of her ambitions, emotional needs, guilt and demands upon him would ultimately have a devastating effect upon his personality. His psychological vulnerabilities may be traced in large part to their relationship. "The strongest impression I have," his younger brother Arnold once wrote, "is that his [T.E.'s] life has been injured by his mother."[31] Lawrence struggled to resist her smothering and absorbing influence, to become completely separate and distant from her. Even his puckish rebellion against every form of authority and his conspicuous pursuit of "nonsuccess" may be seen in part as a defiance of her authority.

Lawrence's resemblance to his mother, which extended beyond their physical similarities to include basic personality characteristics, was obvious to his friends. One, a woman, remarked to me: "T.E. got his firm chin and the piercing blue eyes from his mother, his strength of character and ability to martyr himself in the desert. She had those martyr qualities. . . . She forced herself. Nothing would get him down either."[32] And his resemblance to his mother was well recognized by Lawrence himself, although he seemed pleased when Charlotte Shaw wrote to him after meeting Mrs. Lawrence that she did not see the resemblance. Lawrence replied: "It interested me very much that you found no likeness between us. I had taken it for granted (not knowing myself at all) that we're so like that we clashed. You'd suggest it is because we are unlike: or rather, if you are right, it is unlikeness which is a possible cause of our clashing so, when we meet: for we do rub each other up the wrong way."[33]

Lawrence's resistance as a child to his parents' authority often took familiar forms of naughtiness. Discipline, according to Arnold, was administered in the form of severe whippings on the buttocks and was delivered by his mother because his father was "too gentle, too imaginative — couldn't bring himself to."[34] Arnold remembered receiving only one such beating himself. His mother once told him, "I never had to do it to Bob, once to Frank and frequently to T.E." The beatings seem to have been brought on by nothing more than routine childhood misbehavior, such as T.E.'s resistance to learning to play the piano. In any case, what was unique about them, Arnold felt, was that they seemed to be given for the purpose of breaking T.E.'s will.[35] Never losing her faith in such punishments, Mrs. Lawrence once remarked in her later years that the reason Lord Astor's horses never won was because he wouldn't whip them.[36]

In actuality T.E. was a dutiful and devoted son. Robert Lawrence stressed to me T.E.'s sensitivity to their parents' feelings and his affectionate ways in the family. He wrote long, devoted letters home when he was away, especially before the war, describing in great detail what he was seeing and doing. The letters, which were directed principally to his mother, must have pleased his parents immensely. They do not contain much in the way of personal disclosure of feeling toward his parents, but such reticence was common among young Englishmen of the time. Lawrence wanted very much to please his parents and often felt he was disappointing them or would eventually do so.

In 1911, when Lawrence was doing archeological field work near Carchemish, in Turkey, he wrote home: "Poor Father! his sons are not going to support his years by the gain of their professions and trades. One a missionary: one an artist of sorts and a wanderer after sensations; one thinking of lay education work: one in the army, and one too small to think. None of us can ever afford to keep a wife: still the product of fairly healthy brains and tolerable bodies will not be all worthless in this world. One of us must surely get something of the unattainable we are all feeling after. That's a comfort: and we are all going for the same thing under different shapes: Do you know we illustrate the verse about heart, soul, mind, body? Will Arnie prove the strength that will make it all perfect and effective?"[37]

In another letter the following month Lawrence emphasized further the antimaterialistic idealism of the Lawrence brothers: "I fear father is right about us and our careers: but this idealistic disregard for the good things of the world has its bright side. And to say that he had 5 sons, none making money, would be a glorious boast — from my point of view at least."[38]

TWO

YOUTH

Introduction

After the war, when Lawrence looked back over a decade of involvement in what he came to regard as an alien cause, he warned of "the dreamers of the day."[1] He called them dangerous men, "for they may act their dream with open eyes to make it possible." His own dreaming of the day, his preoccupation with a personal crusade, with the liberation of a people in bondage, began during his schoolboy days. "I had dreamed, at the City School in Oxford, of hustling into form, while I lived, the new Asia which time was inexorably bringing upon us," he says in the epilogue to *Seven Pillars of Wisdom*, his epic account of the events of the Arab Revolt.[2] Later, after a series of interviews with him, Basil Liddell Hart wrote: "The idea of a crusade, the idea underlying it, revolved in his mind, giving rise to a dream crusade, which implied a leader with whom in a sense he identified himself yet remained as . . . a sympathetic observer. Naturally, it would be a crusade in the modern form — the freeing of a race from bondage. Where, however, was he to find a race in need of release and at the same time of *sufficient* appeal to him? The Arabs seemed the only suitable one left, and they fitted in with the trend of his interests."[3] Lawrence, given this passage by Liddell Hart for critical review, changed only the word "*sufficient*" to "historical." Schoolboys who dream of performing heroic deeds, even perhaps of leading an oppressed people out of bondage, are not unusual. What is unusual and perhaps unique in Lawrence's case is the particular confluence of personal history, psychological need, extraordinary capabilities, and historical opportunity that made it possible for these dreams to be enacted in reality.

As we have seen, Lawrence began in early childhood to lead expeditions, to study soldiery and to read of warfare. At nine and a half he was making his first brass rubbings of knights in armor,[4] and at fifteen he was reading treatises on techniques of warfare and military castle building.

During the years in which he was an Oxford undergraduate, he prepared himself further for the major acts and events of his life. He traveled in France, and studied its castles and military architecture. He became imbued with the military, psychological and philosophical themes of the Crusades, and above all with the romantic literature of medieval France.

This literature supplied the Crusaders with an ideology that could ennoble, if not the deeds themselves, at least what motivated them, and could help to rationalize the excesses of their behavior. These works were the principal literary sustenance of Lawrence's youth. E. M. Forster's comments, in an unpublished passage that was to introduce an edition of Lawrence's letters, provide an appropriate introduction to this period, in which a romantic quest begins to take shape:

> From eighteen onwards he extended his holiday range to France — circled there more and more widely until, at Aigues-Mortes, he was stopped by the Mediterranean. By the time he was twenty he had picked up medieval military architecture, and seen every twelfth century castle of importance in England, Wales, France. The notion of a Crusade, of a body of men leaving one country to do noble deeds in another, possessed him, and I think never left him, though the locality of the country varied: at one time it was Arabia, later it was the air. Had he been a Christian, his medieval equipment would have been complete and thought-proof: he would have possessed a positive faith and been happier: he would have been the "parfait gentil knight," the defender of orthodoxy, instead of the troubled and troublous genius who fascinated his generation and failed to fit into it. He would have been much smaller. In the Aigues-Mortes letter the imperfections of his armour already appear. He longs to set sail, like St. Louis; but for where? And he longs, like Wordsworth, to be at peace.[5]

Complementing his absorption with the Crusades, in both their military and romantic aspects, Lawrence's personal preparations for the deeds he believed he would someday be called upon to accomplish were thorough and extensive during these years. He applied his intellectual powers to learning all he could about military strategy and began to become acquainted with the Arab lands and people during his first trip to the East in 1909. He applied also his manual dexterity and physical endurance to testing his short but sturdy frame for the ordeals that lay ahead. He undertook extraordinary feats of climbing and walking in France and Syria under conditions of personal privation.

The time he spent at Jesus College may also be looked upon as a period of intellectual, physical and emotional preparation, unusual for an undergraduate in its singleminded concentration upon the study of medieval society, architecture, warfare and literature. Oxford was a time of greater freedom for Lawrence than his schoolboy days, but the work of inuring himself for some great task ahead continued unabated. While at Oxford he came to know David Hogarth, the archeologist and traveler to the East, whose fatherly interest was to be decisive for Lawrence's career. It was also during these years that Lawrence made what was, to my knowledge, the only serious attempt to become close to a young woman. His reaction to the rejection he received seems to have had a lasting effect upon the direction of his emotional attachments.

Soon after Lawrence's graduation from Oxford, Hogarth arranged for him to join Hogarth's British Museum archeological explorations at the site of the ancient Hittite city of Carchemish in Asia Minor. Strategically located at a crossing that commanded the upper Euphrates, it appeared as a great mound rising a steep one hundred feet out of the river, a ruin set in a windswept treeless land. The village of Jerablus, some forty houses built on rising ground, was about half a mile away. "Very magnificent must Carchemish have been," his archeological companion, Leonard Woolley wrote, "when its sculptures were gay with colour, when the sunlight glistened on its enamelled walls, and its sombre brick was overlaid with panels of cedar and plates of bronze; when the plumed horses rattled their chariots along its streets, and the great lords, with long embroidered robes and girdles of black and gold, passed in and out of the carved gates of its palaces; but even now, when it lies deserted.and in heaps, it has perhaps in the melancholy of its ruin found a subtler charm to offset the glory of its prime."[6]

The three years at Carchemish afforded Lawrence, then in his early twenties, an excellent opportunity to live and travel in the Middle East and to study its people and cultures under conditions of relative personal and political stability.

These years were, for the most part, full and happy ones for Lawrence. A psychoanalyst presented only with the history of Lawrence's life during this period of his youth would find little that would lead him to anticipate the tortured and tormented soul that emerged from the campaigns of World War I. It is true that Lawrence turned away from civilized bourgeois English society to a world of fellowship among men in a foreign culture. But many Englishmen, many men of other civilized nations, have left a conventional course to find another life truer to the demands of their own natures, and Lawrence's archeological interests took him naturally to the Carchemish site when the opportunity arose.

Indeed, there was nothing in Lawrence's behavior or writings to indicate conflict about his choice. "Till the war swallowed up everything," he commented on the manuscript of Graves's biography, "I wanted nothing better than Carchemish, which was a perfect life."[7] Half the letters Lawrence ever wrote to his family, at least of those that have been preserved, were written in this period of less than four years. They are full, rich accounts, eagerly drafted, of a life that seemed satisfying in every respect. We get from them a picture of an unusually gifted young man, learning and mastering a hundred skills, pursuing what his friend Ernest Altounyan called "the exquisite realization of self."[8]

It was as if Lawrence were converting himself into an instrument of achievement, in dedication to an abstract conception of self. He seems to have given little thought to the ends that he would later strive to attain. For while he remained in many ways boyish and emotionally immature, Lawrence was becoming increasingly perceptive about other people, sensitive to their psychology and personal needs, and paradoxically mature beyond his years in the experience of life and the handling of men. His own emotional involvements remained selective and highly controlled, and account for the intense sense of loneliness so many of his friends observed.

The most significant skill Lawrence developed during these years was his capacity to use his knowledge of other peoples to move out of his own cultural framework. The exploration of the consequences for Lawrence of this identification with the Arab peoples is a major theme of later chapters of this book.

4

Literary Influences

Too little attention, it seems to me, has been paid to the literary influences on Lawrence during his youth. In these years reading may provide much stimulation for the growth of ideas and dreams, and, ultimately, the impetus for action and the form the action takes. Its effect is often lasting.

Although Lawrence read widely, his reading was dominated by medieval romantic works, especially French, and the ideas of medieval romanticism came to fill his consciousness.[1] Arnold Lawrence is of the opinion that his brother's medieval researches were "a dream way of escape from Bourgeois England," and that neither medieval history nor archeology continued to hold his attention when he ceased to need them for the benefit of his own personality.[2] Earlier, Lawrence had shown an interest in epic tales, such as the *Kalevala* of Finland; *Huon de Bordeaux,* the French fairy-tale epic of the early thirteenth century; and Lucian's *True History,* a satire on the *Odyssey*. He told Robert Graves that although at Jesus College he "read history, officially," he "actually spent nearly three years reading Provençal poetry, and mediaeval French chansons de geste. When time came for degree wasn't prepared for exam."[3] Later, to Liddell Hart, he wrote that in addition to "the usual school boy stuff. . . . I also read nearly every manual of chivalry. Remember that my period was the Middle Ages, always."[4]

The intensity of Lawrence's interest in medieval epic poetry and the depth of his identification with the world it depicted is conveyed in the recollection of a college friend: "I remember a rare occasion when he came to a meeting of the College Literary Society: a paper was read on the *Chanson de Roland*. When it was over Lawrence spoke for about twenty minutes in his clear, quiet voice, ranging serenely about the epic poetry of several languages. It was all first hand: *you felt that he had 'been there.'* "[5] (Italics added.)

At twenty-two Lawrence wrote his mother that he was reading with pleasure *Le Petit Jehan de Saintré,* a fifteenth-century manual of chivalric manners, which describes the education and tutelage from early childhood, chiefly at the hands of women of the court, of a budding knight.[6] The romance of Tristan and Iseult and thirteenth-century *fabliaux* (droll stories concerned with adultery, wantonness, and the corruption of the clergy) are other readings that Lawrence mentions specifically.[7]

The romantic revivals in epic form of Norse, Icelandic, Arthurian, and other legends and tales of heroism by the nineteenth-century English medievalist William Morris were always favorites of Lawrence. He also read with pleasure the works of other romantic Victorians, among them Christina Rossetti, Maurice Hewlett and Tennyson. Lawrence's interest in the revival of handicrafts and in printing was inspired by medieval influences, especially by Morris, who had elaborately printed Chaucer and other medieval works at his Kelmscott Press. In addition, Lawrence read Froissart and other chroniclers of the world of the Middle Ages,[8] and had in his collection at home such modern works as the Everyman's Library *Medieval Stories and Romances,* which contained a popular exposition of chivalry, including "what Sir Guy says to Saladin about the Rule of Chivalry."[9]

Lawrence's devotion to Sir Thomas Malory and the Arthurian legends which, like himself, were born in Wales and developed in France, epitomized his medievalism. At eighteen, as he sat gazing out over the sea off Brittany, he quoted rapturously to his mother, in a manner which would embarrass a youth of today, Tennyson's *Idylls of the King* (in which Queen Victoria's poet laureate popularized and chastened for his sovereign's readers the lusty legends of King Arthur's Court).[10] Malory's *Morte d'Arthur* was one of three books Lawrence carried with him throughout the Arabian campaign.

The original *chansons de geste* were poetic, sometimes epic narratives, composed by the trouvères of eleventh-century France to commemorate the deeds of Charlemagne and other legendary heroes. The *Chanson de Roland,* an epic, is the most famous. The *chansons de geste* set down in verse the heroic values of feudal society. Noble deeds are performed by knights and barons, whose special qualities and virtues appear in their early childhood, against less worthy enemies and rivals. Actual historical events are related, though distorted by legend. Manly virtues of sacrifice, bravery, and loyalty to the king and country are depicted. The most important human relationship in these epic tales of adventure is that between men (Oliver and Roland, for instance) and is characterized by close Christian comradeship and love; little is said of romantic love between men and women.

By the end of the eleventh century the Muslims had taken possession of the Holy Land and the Church summoned the nobility of Western Europe to the rescue. The *chansons de geste* which arose before the Crusades, would, in their original form, have had little to offer the Crusaders. Their rough heroes were concerned chiefly with local and largely nonreligious wars, whose limited purposes did not contain much to inspire the Crusaders. But several developments in the latter part of the eleventh century served to create a literature that became intimately associated with the Crusades and furnished in poetic form their inspiration and rationale. There arose in the warmer atmosphere of Provence the poetry of the troubadours, who, as servitors of their feudal lords, sang the praises of the ladies of the court in poems and lyrics of romantic love. Within the Church the idealization of the Virgin Mary, which eventually became a cult, contributed richly to the new image of women as beings to be worshipped. Furthermore, the castles built in Europe in the twelfth century provided courts and a more settled society, in which romantic interests could flourish, refinements of life could develop, and the value of women might be appreciated. The position of women of the upper class improved as "the castle became a court where feminine graces might shine, and the Virgin, the Mother of God and the Queen of Heaven, took powerful hold on human hearts."[11]

Late in the twelfth century in France there arose a new literary form, the *romans d'aventure*, attributable to a specific author. These tales added another dimension to the knightly ideal: the cult of courtly love. New materials, less tied to the actualities of local French wars than the *chansons de geste*, were found in the "Matière de Bretagne" (derived from the Arthurian romances brought into Brittany from Wales in the twelfth century), and in Ovidian and other classical themes of love which were brought from the south. In the court of Eleanor of Aquitaine, mother of Richard I, the writers of *romans d'aventure*, the most famous of whom was Chrétien de Troyes, told of Tristan and Iseult, of Lancelot, Arthur and Guinevere, of Percivale, Galahad and the quest for the Holy Grail.

Following the inspiration of the trouvères of northern France, the troubadours of Provence and the *romans d'aventure*, the ideal of courtly love developed. Whereas before the twelfth century women had been subjugated and seen as inferior, or as instruments of the devil to tempt men into evil, now the knight's lady was placed on a pedestal. He went off to reclaim the Holy Land from the infidels, not for God alone (the Church had an ambivalent attitude toward this diversion of the knight's energies from his holy struggle), but for love of his lady, and his valorous deeds were performed for her as acts of worship.[12] Romantic gallantry combined with the older elements of chivalry contained in the *chansons de geste* brought to flower the ideals of the medieval chivalric code, which was to evolve ultimately into our rituals and stereotypes of gentle-manly behavior. "Whatever may have been his true reason for fighting, his only avowed motive was the love of his lady, which was the formula which usually accompanied the challenge to combat. All the heroes of the age have a mistress in the background, who uplifts them to acts of valour."[13] Usually this relationship was outside marriage, for marriage was considered incompatible with love, but any other lady, any other man's wife, would do.[14]

What is most striking about the chivalric ideal, as it developed in twelfth-century France, is the contrast it presented to the actualities of medieval court life and the Crusades themselves. Henry Adams pointed out that at the social level "while the Virgin was miraculously using the power of spiritual love to elevate and purify the people, Eleanor [of Aquitaine] and her daughters were using the power of earthly love to discipline and refine the courts. Side by side with the crude realities about them, they insisted on teaching and enforcing an ideal that contra-dicted the realities, and had no value for them or for us except in the contradiction."[15] Similarly, the elevation of women in the chivalric ideal did little to raise the position of women in medieval society.[16] From the social standpoint it was a veneer, furnishing the men of the period with a psychologically useful ideology. Similar contrasts existed among the ideals of courtly love themselves. On the one hand they are curiously platonic and virtuous, while in some of the tales, especially those derived from Arthurian legends, the knights are heavily engaged in romantic liaisons that are filled with lust, adultery, incest, and the murder of rivals, and that result in the birth of illegitimate children, King Arthur himself being a prime example.

But these social and emotional contradictions pale in significance when compared with the extraordinary discrepancies between the lofty faith and heroic idealism of the Crusaders and their actual performance. As Steven Runciman put it: "There was so much courage and so little honour, so much devotion and so little understanding. High ideals were besmirched by cruelty and greed, enterprise and endurance by a blind and narrow self-righteousness; and the Holy War itself was nothing more than a long act of intolerance in the name of God, which is the sin against the Holy Ghost."[17]

I myself cannot help but believe that the inspiration for the chivalric ideal, and the strong investment in an ideal of romantic love, came in part from the awareness in the courts of Europe of the acts of cruelty, aggres-sion and hatred in which the knights of Europe were engaged. For the chevalier of twelfth-century Europe, the illusions of ideal love and epic heroism offset in secular terms his actual behavior just as the Church's concept of a Holy War counterbalanced the crimes against religious faith in which Christendom was engaged. The literature of the nobility drew its materials not principally from the Crusades themselves, but from the nobler legends of the continent and the magical stories of the Knights of the Round Table.

These discrepancies, as we shall see, have striking parallels with the contrasts in Lawrence's psychology, and with the gulf which came to separate his own romantic ideals, much influenced by the medieval concepts that inspired his actions, from the realities which he encountered in their execution. But there is little evidence that he paid much attention to the seamy side of the Crusades, despite the fact that he read widely in medieval history, had medieval history scholars as tutors, and wrote his thesis after making several trips to France and Syria for the purpose of studying Crusader castles. In fact, in his stress on the military, technical, strategic and tactical aspects of the Crusader castles he seemed to avoid considering in detail the purposes to which these structures were put or the real purposes of the Crusaders in the East. In the thesis he wrote at Oxford based on these researches, he does discuss the differences between the military orders of knighthood, the Templars and Hospitalers, and the different sorts of castles they built, but says little about the range of their activities.[18]

Lawrence wrote his mother of his admiration for Richard I after visiting Richard's castle, Château-Gaillard: "The whole construction bears the unmistakeable stamp of genius. Richard I must have been a far greater man than we usually consider him: he must have been a great strategist and a great engineer, as well as a great man-at-arms. I hope Mr. Jane [one of Lawrence's tutors] will emphasize this in his book. It is time Richard had justice done to his talents."[19]

Yet in his admiration for Richard as a military strategist, Lawrence seems to overlook the cruelties of this Crusader, of which he must have been aware (for one, Richard butchered more than two thousand Saracen prisoners at Acre when his negotiations with Saladin hit a snag).[20] In one passage only, in a letter to his mother during his travels, does Lawrence indicate his awareness of the excesses of the Crusaders, and this concerned a "civil" campaign, the Albigensian Crusade against the heretics of southern France. "The town had been taken, and the Crusaders wanted to kill the heretics," Lawrence wrote his mother, "but there were many Catholics in the town as well. 'What shall we do?' they asked the Legate, Peter of Castelnau. 'Kill them all,' said he. 'God will recognize his own,' and some 8000 were butchered in cold blood. Pleasant people those 13th Century Crusaders."[21] Much later, Lawrence wrote Liddell Hart that he had no general interest in the Crusades as a religious enterprise, and evidently told him that his sympathies were more with the Crusaders' opponents than with them.[22]

Lawrence's apparent unconcern with the true behavior of the Crusaders does not, in my opinion, reflect cruelty or unconcern with suffering

on his part, but rather, his need to isolate the technical aspect of a problem from its meaning and to sustain an ideal conception even when
certain facts would otherwise challenge it. Lawrence's medieval reading
helped him to build a myth of the absolute contest of the forces of good
against evil. When the actual events of the Arab campaigns made it impossible for him to maintain this myth he became deeply troubled.

Lawrence's attraction to medieval romanticism has other, more personal
psychological determinants. He was beginning to develop within himself
a heroic ego ideal which he could counterpose to the threat to his self-
regard that the childhood discoveries concerning his parents' situation had
brought about. The medieval romances suited him ideally. The world
they depicted was one in which men of noble birth acted as proper
heroes, were not drawn down in station by their ladies, and engaged in
noble deeds on an epic scale, having been, like himself, chosen for this
purpose in childhood. Although the romances of the court were an
exciting diversion, and the images of romantic love inspiring, the business
of war and the close comradeship among men loyal to one another was
perhaps more important.

Women in this literature represent many of the ambiguities with which
Lawrence wrestled in his perceptions of his mother. Beautiful, sublime
and sexual on the one hand, they were worshipped in an idealized,
ritualized and platonic fashion on the other. True to their true lovers,
they frequently betrayed their husbands, while the husbands themselves
regularly betrayed their wives. Although the medieval noblewoman dominated her knight through the demands she made for worshipful devotion
and the accomplishment of extraordinary tasks, she also inspired in him
the sense of her own value. To please her he strove to bring·back to her
accounts of great deeds she could admire. In the rollicking Arthurian
romances women are consistently adulterous, though some are remarkably steadfast in their loyalty to the object of their infidelity. Yet simultaneously the chaste figure of the Virgin, the Mother of God, accompanies
the warrior, and in some medieval tales substitutes for the knight in
tournaments when he is delayed because of devotion to her.[23] For
Lawrence the redemption of the fallen woman, whose value is inextricably bound to his own worth, was a compelling need. Unable to sustain
an idealized view of women, he ultimately abandoned the effort, and his
view of women in their sexual functioning became, as we shall see,
debased in his later years.

It is difficult to see how this medieval literature, had it not served
strong personal needs in Lawrence's psychology, could have compelled so
fully the attention of someone of his critical ability. For no matter how
fine the style, beautiful the poetry, or lyrical the imagery, it is essentially
a literature of fantasy, of make-believe. The *chansons de geste,* the
romans d'aventure and the Arthurian romances and myths are fairy

stories, often lovely ones, that appeal to the childlike and unrealistic mind, a mind that needs to be nourished on a glorious and idealistic conception of the world that is not bound by the limitations of actuality. That Lawrence could for three years and more be so preoccupied with this literature that he claimed he was unprepared for his examinations supports the view that major aspects of his personal development were arrested during the years of childhood. Yet it is a testimony to his genius that he was able later to adapt heroic fantasies, that seemed to draw upon the myths of these youthful readings, effectively in the pursuit of positive historical objectives.

Lawrence's literary medievalism bears an indirect connection with his later attraction to Arab culture. The poetry of the troubadours and the literature of medieval courtly love contain many of the themes to be found in the popular Arab poetry that reached Spain and France after the Arab conquests in the eighth century. As E. Lévi-Provençal has pointed out, the figures of the lovers, the situations in which they find themselves, and the impediments to their fulfillment are similar in both literatures.[24] The degree of Lawrence's exposure to Arab literature is not known, although his mentor Charles Doughty, the traveler in Arabia, encouraged him to read early Bedouin poetry.[25] It does, however, seem likely that he found in the Arab world romantic aspects that appealed to the same needs in his personality as had the romantic literature of medieval Europe, which so dominated the readings of his youth. In any event, once Lawrence became immersed in Arab society, whose tribal structure resembled in many ways the feudal society of medieval Europe, his interest in the world of the Middle Ages and its literature subsided.[26]

5

Crusader Castles

At thirteen Lawrence began to go on bicycle trips in England to visit medieval castles and churches. Often he went alone, but sometimes he would be accompanied by his father and other family members, or by his friend C. F. C. Beeson. According to Beeson, Lawrence was interested in the design of military buildings as early as 1905. Toward the end of that year the two friends had exhausted the accessible examples in England, and they read during the winter of 1905–1906 in the Radcliffe and Ashmolean libraries in preparation for the investigation of the ruins and restorations of France.[1]

The Lawrence family had kept in touch with French friends in Dinard, especially with a family named Chaignon. Lawrence spoke competent though not elegant French. The Chaignons' home seemed often to have served as a kind of base for Lawrence's travels during his summer trips. In all, six trips to France are documented during the years 1906–1910 in the *Letters*, although Lawrence wrote Graves that he made eight such tours during his school and university vacations.[2] According to Beeson, Lawrence was in France during a summer before 1906, but he did not know any details. Mrs. Lawrence was aware of her adventurous son's tendency to take somewhat reckless chances and to be accident-prone, so she was eager for Beeson to accompany Ned in France in order to watch out for him.

The trips to France that concern us here are the bicycle tours Lawrence made during the summer holidays of 1906, 1907 and 1908 when he was eighteen, nineteen and twenty. On the 1906 trip, which lasted four weeks, he was accompanied by Beeson. In April 1907, during his Easter holiday, he visited the medieval castles of North Wales, not far from his birthplace.[3] In August 1907, Lawrence traveled with his father for part of the month, and their shared interest in photography stimulated Lawrence's picture-taking. On the 1908 trip, which lasted six weeks, he was alone.

Lawrence traveled on the latest model of high-speed bicycle, with dropped handles and an unusually high top-gear ratio, specially built to his order in a shop in Oxford.[4] During 1906 Lawrence and Beeson ("Scroggs") confined themselves to the parts of Brittany near Dinard, Saint-Malo and the Channel coast. In 1907 Lawrence reached the Loire. In 1908 he traveled the length and breadth of France, reaching Champagne, the Mediterranean, the Pyrenees and the western part of the country. The plan to undertake eventually a detailed study of the military architecture of the Crusades may have begun to take shape during the 1906 and 1907 trips, both made before Lawrence began his studies at Jesus College, but only the 1908 tour was specifically devoted to this purpose.

The published accounts do not bring out the extent to which these travels, like so many of the ventures of Lawrence's youth, were a personal preparation, a testing of his body and his spirit for future trials. Beeson noted how his friend, whom he had known for about two years before their trip to France, "had to prove himself." Lawrence was "always making himself tough, always climbing, always testing the limits of his powers."[5] Beeson also felt strongly Lawrence's leadership qualities. Once in Brittany they visited a castle ruin with a moat that was crossed by a bridge. According to Beeson, Lawrence had to jump the moat instead of using the bridge. Lawrence seemed to the more cautious man to take unusual, even reckless, chances when climbing about old walls with loose stones. An image has stayed in Beeson's mind of Lawrence atop some rocks in France with his foot trembling as he tried to find a footing. Beeson warned, "You'll fall," and offered to help. But Lawrence would not let him.[6] Beeson was also impressed with his friend's resourcefulness. On one occasion when his tire was punctured, he became quite troubled about the possible delay in the trip. But Lawrence was not frustrated or irritated. He knew someone "around the corner" who could fix it. Lawrence frequently repaired his own tires.

Beraud Villars, a Frenchman who has written a good biography of Lawrence, has criticized him, correctly I think, for failing in his travels in France to understand the "soul" of the country.[7] But Villars did not realize Lawrence's determination and singlemindedness of purpose, this preparation of himself, of his mental and physical equipment, for a great task.

Lawrence's letters home, especially on the first (1906) trip, contain several proud statements of how fit and strong he was becoming, with a fine physique, which he attributed to not eating too much, certainly not as much as his hosts: "The Chaignons told me yesterday that the English ate all too much. I was rather amused and told them that they ate too

much for strength: I said that Mr. Chaignon might possibly be nearly as
strong as I was if he ate as little as I did: it wasn't a bit too personal, they
talk very freely about each other and myself. It rather surprised Mr.
Chaignon — was a new idea for him. He had just acknowledged that I
was the stronger of the two. I told them that Bob was weaker than I
because he ate too much; they think I am très original; they don't know if
I'm in earnest or not."[8] A few days earlier he had written that Mme
Chaignon "got a shock when she saw my 'biceps' while bathing. She
thinks I am Hercules."[9]

On his trips Lawrence wrote proudly home of how lightly he could
travel, how little he could get by with eating, and how cheaply he could
live in the most meager of surroundings. His letters contain long accounts
of his thrift. For instance, in 1906: "My silk shirt was a blessing. It took
up no space, and every day I used to roll it tightly around my other
articles, and it used to hold them all in place. Thus my luggage was never
larger or longer than my carrier. Father will be very interested to learn
this, for the carrier is a small one. It went through the trip excellently and
gave absolutely no trouble. I carried two pairs of socks and wore a third.
Next time I would only carry one pair and would not trouble to bring a
sponge. A spare pair of trousers is useful and in fact necessary: also a
spare shirt. A coat is quite useless if a cape is carried: by this means the
weight can be reduced to practically nil."[10]

According to Beeson, his friend was not fastidious about food and
would eat most of what was available in the countryside. When they
went to a farmhouse for a meal, T.E. would be greeted as a familiar
friend (which suggests that he had made at least one previous visit to
Brittany since his early childhood years in Dinard). When the food in
France was really unfamiliar or bad, Lawrence could complain colorfully.
He once described the food of the Tarn district of the south: "Their food
is weird and wonderful (*omelette aux pommes de terre* yesterday and
other articles unspecified and indescribable), the bread tastes like . . . can
you imagine leather soaked in brine, and then boiled till soft: with an
iron crust, and a flavour like a brandy-snap? It takes me considerable
mental and physical effort to 'degust' a mouthful: milk has not been
heard of lately, butter has a smell like cream cheese, but a taste like
Gruyère (thank goodness for the Roquefort, 'tis the district, and its
strength would make palatable (or indiscoverable) a cesspool), and in fact
a dinner for me is like an expedition into Spain, Naples, the North and
Antarctic regions, Central Australia, Japan, etc."[11]

Lawrence's letters from France, though pedantic with detail at times
(especially the long descriptions of churches and castles), are suffused
with the excitement and pleasure of discovery. They show an enormous
range of interests, from the position of the grandmother in the French
family ("she is all powerful . . . an affront to her usually causes a 'conseil

de famille' ") to tipping (or not tipping) castle guides. Lawrence begins here to show the descriptive powers that were later to characterize his literary work. Little of the cynicism that embittered his spirit after the war is evident in these enthusiastic, sometimes joyous and frequently poetic accounts. He found "a special joy" in Carcassonne: "One does not need a guide with one, all is free and open except some of the towers: there are guides, but no fees."[12] His ecstatic reverence for the beauties of Chartres gave his mother special pleasure, although she misinterpreted his aesthetic raptures. George Bernard Shaw appreciated Lawrence's description of Chartres, which Lord Carlow had privately printed in an elaborate edition after Lawrence's death. But Shaw chided Lawrence for omitting the stained-glass windows, and characteristically goes him one better in his own account:

> In this example of the first attempts of the late Lord Carlow to rival Jenson, Caxton, Morris, Ashendene Acland, and Count Kessler as an artist-printer, we find E. T. [sic] Lawrence, Quondam Prince of Damascus, a boy writing to his mother, already showing symptoms of the itch for description which at the end of his life developed into a mania, and broke through every convention. . . .
> . . . Lawrence describes it all indiscriminately with one amazing exception. He does not mention its transcendant glory: the stained glass windows. True, they are indescribable. But why did he not say so?[13]

Suspecting that Robert Lawrence, who edited *The Home Letters of T. E. Lawrence and His Brothers*, might, with his need to deny any discord or problem within the family, have omitted passages that in his view would blemish its image, I decided to read the original letters, which are preserved in the Bodleian Library.[14] I discovered that indeed Dr. Lawrence had omitted numerous passages, particularly from the earliest letters, which show the most youthful exuberance and irreverence on the part of his younger, less inhibited and less restrained brother. The omitted passages, which give the letters considerably more humanity and make them less pedantic, are those which express anything critical or insulting about other persons or places, negative or discordant comments, some complaints, boyish accounts of politics, and various small kindnesses or expressions of concern or affection toward other members of the family that Dr. Lawrence thought too trivial to print. In his way, Dr. Lawrence seemed to be attempting to maintain his own version of a family myth, one of sanctity and purity.

The omitted passages contain in particular long descriptions of the crudeness of the lives and habits of the people of Brittany, which contrasted sharply with the Arthurian "Matière de Bretagne" and other romantic French medieval literature in which Lawrence was simultaneously steeping himself. He was disparaging of the drunkenness, poor manners, overeating and ignorance of the Bretons, although he showed an understanding and fondness for particular individuals. "A child is always the person to ask for directions as to the road, or distances; they know better than their elders here," he wrote in irritation.[15]

Lawrence grew extremely impatient with the Chaignons' timidity, conventionality and exaggerated concern for his safety. They seem to have been acting *in loco parentis*, especially during the earlier trips. "At seven at night," he wrote, "no one of them except Madame Chaignon will go a step beyond the door without some sort of cap; it is quite a fetish with them and the other French: they used to cry out all manner of extraordinary things as I rode past: one would think they were badly off for a sensation. They ask where you lost your hat! The best reply I think is that one has just swum across the channel, and had lost the hat half way."[16] There are also several youthful discussions of politics, including Lawrence's first disparagement of traditional military generals, whom he here called (just after the Boer War) "of the Winston Churchill type."[17]

Although these letters do not reveal much of Lawrence's inmost feelings, they are filled with conscientious and affectionate concern for each member of the family, and inquiries about Oxford neighbors. He shares a great deal about his interests with his family and considerately selects particular topics that he knows will match the interests of each one. For his mother, in addition to the poetic sharing of lines of Tennyson and the raptures over Chartres Cathedral, Lawrence seems to go to endless pains to find a petticoat of the type she has asked for. To his father, to whom only two letters are specifically addressed, he writes of politics, of cycling (a beach for doing "a little speed work on the sands"), of false teeth and medieval architecture. Will, who was starting out in archeology at the Ashmolean Museum in Oxford, receives gently reproving words about his archeological errors and advice on how to proceed. Finally, with Arnie, who was six to eight years old during this period, he shares his delight in small things: "Tell Arnie I saw a brown squirrel run up the wall, and he went right up the keep to where Scroggs was sketching: when Scroggs moved he jumped to the main well. He was a very good jumper. The squirrels about here are very large and carry their tails like the foxes do theirs, straight out behind."[18] Or later: "Accept my best worms Arnie and have all ready to hug me on Tuesday."[19] To his friend Beeson, in addition to providing details about medieval towns and architecture, Lawrence compared the women of Arles ("glorious") and Tarascon ("hideous, exactly like grey horses").[20]

Lawrence took advantage of a new university regulation that allowed him to submit a thesis as an additional part of his final examinations for his degree.[21] He chose as his topic the influence of the Crusades on European military architecture to the end of the twelfth century, not an unexpected choice. We have seen already how extensively Lawrence traveled in England, Wales and France from 1905 to 1908 visiting the important castles. He felt that it was essential to examine and photograph their architectural features at first hand in order to establish the influence of one form of building upon another, to determine by comparisons the periods in which particular developments occurred, and to fix the dates of various transitions. He now needed to study the castles of Syria and Palestine "from their own evidence" and accordingly visited the Middle East for the first time in the summer of 1909.[22] But his keen desire to go there had been awakened the previous summer when he reached the Mediterranean and wrote to his mother in excitement: "I felt that at last I had reached the way to the South, and all the glorious East. Greece, Carthage, Egypt, Tyre, Syria, Italy, Spain, Sicily, Crete . . . they were all there, and all within reach . . . of me. I fancy I know now better than Keats what Cortes felt like, 'silent upon a peak in Darien.' Oh I must go down here, — farther out — again! Really this getting to the sea has almost overturned my mental balance: I would accept a passage for Greece tomorrow."[23]

Lawrence's travels gradually made him doubt the traditional view, propounded particularly by the nineteenth-century authorities C. W. C. Oman and E. G. Rey, that the Crusaders drew their excellence in castle building from the East, and that Syrian workmen were imported even to build Château-Gaillard, the masterpiece of Richard I.[24] Particularly "in treating of Latin Fortresses in Syria itself," Lawrence insisted that "documentary evidence of building is absolutely valueless. Medieval fortresses must in every case be dated from their own evidence."[25]

In the limited time available to him he scrambled over endless fortifications, steps, towers and ruins making notes and plans and taking photographs for his thesis. Mosquitoes, indigestible food, snakes and assault by suspicious natives were among the obstacles he encountered. In the course of his personal examinations of castles and cathedrals (his need was always, as his friend E. F. Hall phrased it, "to see for himself"),[26] Lawrence would delight in finding errors in the guidebooks ("Mondoubleau which the guidebooks called ix cent. Really it was an enormous keep of the latest xii").[27] And he gave way to a boyish delight in the discovery of a "beautiful" latrine at a castle in Brittany during one of the earlier explorations, and chided his prudish older brother for not appreciating it when he visited there: "By the way, did not Bob, (many thanks for the post card) go and see the castle? What could he have been thinking about not to mention these most attractive domestic conveniences?"[28]

The excitement of discovery comes through vividly in Lawrence's letters, as his suspicions regarding the castle builders of Southern Europe are confirmed by his own findings. " 'Eureka,' " he wrote Beeson, from France in 1908, "I've got it at last for the thesis: the transition from the square keep form:* really it's too great for words."[29]

* A traditional Norman tower structure.

The need to come to startling conclusions — what he called "my rather knight-errant style of tilting against all comers in the subject,"[30] — or, more importantly, to overturn the position of the "regulars," Oman and Rey, led Lawrence to overstate somewhat the implications of his findings. "There is no evidence," he wrote, "that Richard* borrowed anything great or small, from any fortress which he saw in the Holy Land: it is not likely that he would do so, since he would find better examples of everything in the South of France, which he knew so well. There is not a trace of anything Byzantine in the ordinary French castle, or in an English one: while there are evident signs that all that was good in Crusading architecture hailed from France and Italy. A summing up of the whole matter would be the statement that 'the Crusading architects were for many years copyists of the Western builders.'"[31]

Yet Lawrence himself acknowledges the possibility of mutual influence, "the transfer of trifling detail," because East-West interchange among the upper classes was constant.[32]

The actual writing of the thesis was done in the winter of 1909–1910 and completed by the end of March. Despite its somewhat overly sweeping conclusion, his tutor was so impressed with the work that he gave a dinner for the examiners to celebrate it.[33]

According to Lawrence he refused to have his thesis printed because it was only a preliminary study, "not good enough to publish."[34] In 1929 he wrote of it: "An elementary performance, and I think it has been destroyed or left behind somewhere, in the course of my life. At any rate, I haven't a notion where it is — but a strong memory that it was worthless."[35] This self-disparaging view of the work, so characteristic of Lawrence, was directly contradicted by the statement of Professor Ernest Barker, one of Lawrence's medieval history teachers, who had studied and written about various aspects of the Crusades himself. Barker read the thesis when Lawrence submitted it and concluded: "It proved conclusively, so far as I could judge, that the old theory of the influence of the castles of Palestine on western military architecture must be abandoned, and that instead of the East affecting the West, it was the West that had affected the East."[36]

Lawrence's fundamental point, that the early Crusaders from Southern Europe took a lot of knowledge about military castle building with them when they went to the East, and did not learn the art from Byzantine examples, has been largely sustained by subsequent writers. These writers also agree that there was more interchange and mutual influence between East and West than Lawrence acknowledges, that there is much that is not known about who influenced whom, and that more firsthand comparisons, based on direct examinations of the evidence from the castles

* Lawrence does not mention the French or other European Crusaders.

themselves, is needed to achieve accurate dating and to learn fully the history of military castle building.[37]

A letter to his parents of January 24, 1911, indicates that Lawrence was then contemplating writing a "monumental work on the Crusades." If he had done such a book, it would have included further considerations of these questions, and he wrote later to his biographers that his "basic intention in exploring Syria" during his youth "was always to write a strategic study of the Crusades" or to write a history of the Crusades.[38]

One unhappy byproduct of these years of exploration was malaria. Lawrence was subject to recurrent bouts of it through most of his life. He probably contracted the disease in 1908 in the south of France when he was nearly twenty. "I have however forgotten what a mosquito bites like, since I left the marshes of the coast. Aigues-Mortes is celebrated for the ague in winter," he wrote home from there in August of 1908.[39] Lawrence's statement to Graves, "I got malaria in France, when I was sixteen," is almost surely an exaggeration "youthwards."[40]

6

Lawrence at Jesus College, 1907–1910

Oxford was still a place of the hansom cab and the horse-drawn carriage in the first decade of the twentieth century, and life at Jesus College was not atypical of the university community as a whole:

> Freshmen were photographed with the distraction of a shower of lumps of sugar thrown by their seniors. Terms were kept by attending chapel at 8 A.M. or by "keeping a roller," i.e. putting a mark against one's name on a sheet at 7:40 A.M. in Hall. A short "choir practice" on Sundays, attended by most men living in college, counted as a "roller" or chapel if one subsequently went to chapel on Sunday evening. Thus with careful management it was possible to score three out of the required seven appearances in a single day.
>
> Breakfast, taken in one's room, might be a considerable meal and it was not uncommon to give breakfast parties. Luncheon on the other hand, was usually frugal. Before going out to play games it might be bread and cheese, Cooper's marmalade, and college ale. Tea was also taken in one's rooms or ordered perhaps from the stores and brought up by the "boy." Dinner, always well attended, was the only meal in the hall.[1]

The prizes and distinctions Lawrence received as a schoolboy in ancient history, English language and literature, and scriptures enabled him to receive in January 1907 a Meyricke Exhibition in Modern History to Jesus College, which provided £40 toward his tuition.[2] He failed to receive a history "scholarship" at St. John's College, which would have brought him £100. He told one biographer that he had studied too much mathematics before he switched to a concentration in history in his last year at the Oxford City High School.[3] He entered Jesus College in October 1907, when he was nineteen. He was nearly twenty-two when he completed his studies.[4]

His interest in medieval history and antiquities provided a unifying force to Lawrence's college years. He was observed by many of his friends to be odd in certain ways, "utterly unlike anyone else," but in no way did he seem more unusual to his classmates than in the degree to which he "knew what he wanted"[5] and devoted his time to the intense pursuit of knowledge of "medieval poetry and buildings, and of a multitude of strange places."[6]

Lawrence lived in the college for only one term (the summer of 1908). His parents had a well-equipped, sturdy two-room bungalow built for him at the back of the garden behind their house in order that he might pursue his studies in privacy and quiet.[7] One friend has described his visits with Lawrence there, and the atmosphere in this little house. Lawrence maintained the rooms in the austere and simple fashion that best expressed his personality; the walls were draped with a green workshop cloth to keep out the noise. "It was the most silent place I have ever been in. The silence was almost palpable and as we lay on cushions, or rather I lay uncomfortably and he squatted, we agreed that only in silence can the soul hear its own accents, and that only a withdrawal from the world can ensure a man the honesty and integrity of his purpose — and we went on to consider what we could do in life."[8]

Even though Lawrence lived at home rather than at the college and rarely, if ever ("never," Lawrence insisted), appeared in the dining hall, he made an intense impact upon those classmates who came to know him. One classmate, T. P. Fielden, wrote that he and a friend of his, A. T. P. Williams, would "raid" Lawrence at times in his room, and would usually find him on the floor with three or four books, reading them concurrently, page by page.[9] Williams (a history scholar who later became head of Winchester and then dean of Christ Church) wrote of Lawrence:

> I have never since felt anything like the extraordinary fascination which Lawrence's curious penetrating knowledge of medieval poetry and building, and of a multitude of strange places, had for me. Even then, when he was only nineteen or twenty, he had wandered all over France on his bicycle, living on milk and apples; there and elsewhere he had explored, and seemed to remember everything. Probably he talked much more freely then than later, but it was not merely or mainly what he said, endlessly interesting as it was, that made him a wonderful companion: there was a sureness and completeness about his whole being which matched the depth and steadiness of his eyes.[10]

Lawrence's mother confirmed his assertion that during this period he was a vegetarian. "For about three years," she wrote, "he gave up eating meat, and lived on a vegetable, milk and egg diet. For breakfast he always had porridge and milk, never touched tea or coffee; sometimes if he was going for a long ride he would ask us to have porridge ready for him on his return. Cakes and fruits he liked."[11]

Although Lawrence had no interest in group athletics, he was a keen participant in the Oxford Officers' Training Corps, "the territorials," and was a member of the signal detachment. His pleasure in this may have stemmed from the fact that this group functioned as a bicycle corps, military style.[12] Sometimes the signal corps slept out in tents. Lawrence, according to Sir Basil Blackwell (a fellow signal-corps member) was "quirky" and would never, despite his living later as an Arab in the Middle East, stick his head out of the tent during the night. Another friend and classmate, E. F. Hall, attributes this to a literal following of the orders forbidding "sleeping out": Lawrence "kept the letter of the law by sleeping with his legs inside the tent, and his head among the guyropes; and if I remember rightly it was a copy of the *Odyssey* carried inside his tunic pocket that was his constant companion."[13]

Hall observed, as Beeson had, the intensity with which Lawrence seemed to be preparing himself for some future role. Lawrence had known Hall (later to become an archdeacon in Devon) since the fourth form at the City of Oxford High School and frequently came into his rooms in college. Hall noticed there were times when his young friend's eyes "appeared to burn with the intensity of a soul in pain — they could be positively terrifying after overstrain of work."[14] On one such occasion Lawrence surprised Hall by firing a revolver out of the window of a house on an Oxford street (the cartridges, to Hall's relief, proved to be blanks). "One glance at his eyes left no doubt at all that he told the truth when he said that he had been working for forty-five hours at a stretch without food, to test his powers of endurance. I did not realize that he was, in his own later words, 'hardening for a great endeavor.' . . . I thought it was that other side of him — the consuming power of the 'desire to know' — in this case, how much the human frame could stand."[15]

Another student remembered thinking that Lawrence "had the mind of a medieval monk: his values were quite different than ours, the games of the average undergraduate meant little to him and of ambition or dreams in the usual worldly sense he had none. To be self-sufficient in the Platonic or perhaps the Stoic sense was his ideal."[16]

The most important adult figure for Lawrence in Oxford from 1908 on, and the person who helped him to focus his archeological interest, was David Hogarth. In 1908 Hogarth succeeded Sir Arthur Evans, the pioneer discoverer of the Minoan civilization, as keeper of the Ashmolean Museum, and it was at this time that he took an interest in Lawrence, whom he discovered helping the assistant keeper arrange the medieval pottery at the museum. He soon gave Lawrence a part-time job sorting the pottery fragments.[17]

The son of a country clergyman, Hogarth had traveled widely in Greece, Asia Minor, Syria, and the Levant before settling in Oxford. He remained a man of the world, knowledgeable in its ways and places, deft and sensitive in the handling of men. He was an excellent scholar of the Middle East, and a careful, creative archeologist, who could have been a great one had he possessed the patience for its endless details and had had less protean interests and capabilities.[18] Several of his books on travel in the Middle East inspired a generation of travelers and were classics of their time. In his writings and conversation Hogarth made the Middle East seem alive and real to Lawrence, and its attraction for him, stimulated by the older man (they were separated in age by twenty-six years), soon became irresistible. By the time Lawrence made his first trip to Syria and Palestine in 1909, although he had known Hogarth for only a year (Lawrence tends to overstate how young he was when they met), he had already come to depend upon Hogarth's kindness, understanding and gentle strength. Hogarth was, Lawrence wrote to Mrs. Shaw in 1924, "a very kind, very wise, very loveable man, now in failing health. I'd put him high among the really estimable human beings. All my opportunities, all those I've wasted, came directly or indirectly, out of his trust in me."[19]

The most insightful picture of the relationship between Hogarth and Lawrence was provided by Hogarth's only son, William, in an interview. William, who until his death was head of the Athlone Press in London, remembered with pleasure the familiar figure of Lawrence in the household. Lawrence took a great interest in William, who was a young boy then, and taught him to paddle a canoe and to shoot. The elder Hogarth, according to William, represented the academic and worldly life of Oxford more than T.E.'s own father could. David Hogarth was also the first of Lawrence's friends who belonged to the intellectual world, and was in full standing in that world.[20]

Hogarth was affected by Lawrence's brilliance and charm, and came to treat him somewhat like an adopted son. Lawrence in turn became his disciple. Hogarth, in William's view, was a calm, unexcitable, though tolerant person — "if he had a fault he was too unemotional" — who provided shape and stability to Lawrence's life. He understood his young friend and could deal firmly with Lawrence's psychological extravagances, telling him directly when he thought he was being silly or when "his behavior was a bloody nuisance" (as it was when Lawrence created problems for himself later in the writing of *Seven Pillars of Wisdom*).[21]

Hogarth was, Lawrence wrote after his death, "the parent I could trust, without qualification, to understand what bothered me," and "the only person to whom I had never to explain the 'why' of what I was doing."[22] He came to represent what Lawrence valued most in Oxford. Several months after Hogarth's death Lawrence wrote to an artist friend: "Hogarth *shone* in Oxford, because he was humane, and knew the length and breadth of human nature, and understood always, without judging. Oxford seems to me a quite ordinary fire-less town, now he is gone. He was like a great tree, a main part of the background of my life: and till he fell I hadn't known how much he had served to harbour me."[23] As a friend wrote to Lawrence, Hogarth had been "a tower of strength standing between you and the hateful outer world."[24]

Vivyan W. Richards, a Welsh-American "metaphysician" who was at Jesus College with Lawrence and who was perhaps his closest contemporary friend during those years, has provided an account of their relationship and of Lawrence's activities at that time.[25] Richards's description (like those of so many of Lawrence's friends) is colored by the intensity of his enchantment with Lawrence and his affection which, in Richards's case, was a worshipful devotion. Knightley and Simpson, in their recent book, have elaborated upon Richards's love of Lawrence. The authors imply that Richards would have desired a physical intimacy with Lawrence, but that he received from him only affection and respect of a spiritual sort.[26]

Richards shared with Lawrence a passion and a nostalgia for a medieval, heroic, chivalric world before the advent of gunpowder and printing, a world free of the materialism of contemporary life. Together they were attracted to the medieval cult of William Morris, with his emphasis on personal craftsmanship. They made a pilgrimage to the Cotswold town in which Morris had lived and worked, and planned printing schemes that were inspired by Morris's printed replications of illuminated manuscripts.

Richards described Lawrence's personal habits during these years, especially his enjoyment of hot baths (one of the few pleasures Lawrence never denied himself), and how little he ate and slept. Together, Richards wrote, they explored Oxford at night, and once Lawrence took a dip through a gap in the ice of a frozen river (a feat not confirmed by anyone else).[27] Richards recorded in some detail the many books Lawrence read, especially the works of the Romantic poets, and observed him debating details and dates of medieval history and architecture with other undergraduates. Richards also noted Lawrence's efforts at brass rubbing (especially when the armor interested him), wood carving and photo developing. But Lawrence saw a narrowness in Richards's outlook and interests, which may have discouraged him from committing himself too deeply to any of their projects.

Above all, "it was the intoxication of his dear companionship that I could never resist,"[28] Richards wrote, and he repeatedly referred to himself as Lawrence's pupil, one who was enchanted and inspired by his friend's endlessly fascinating interests, schemes, adventures and knowledge as they sought out the cultural feast that Oxford and its environs could furnish to two sensitive undergraduates. Richards stressed Lawrence's humor and fondness of jokes, and he emphasized the subtle, spontaneous and individual nature of his pranks. Lawrence had no interest, according to Richards, in "crowd fooling," of the kind perpetrated during the Fairs or the Eights Week regatta.

For me the most valuable picture of Lawrence as an Oxford undergraduate came from interviews I had with an American historian, W. O. Ault. Ault came up to Jesus College in 1907 as a Rhodes Scholar from Kansas. His account is of particular value because like Lawrence he was greatly interested in the Middle Ages (he eventually became an eminent medieval historian at Boston University), and he was the only other member of their class to study medieval history with the same tutor as Lawrence, Reginald Lane Poole. For the latter reason alone, Ault came into frequent contact with Lawrence, and they often met with their tutor together throughout the three-year course.

Ault recalls Lawrence as small, with an "insignificant" physique, the head too large for the body, a long face, tow hair and a very quiet manner. His voice was low-pitched and soft, but not effeminate. Ault did not notice the giggle that has been described by some. He confirms that Lawrence took no part in the life of the college, did not eat in the dining halls, lived at home much of the time (somewhat unusual even for local students), and did not turn up for the college photograph of his class. He did not take part in organized athletics, which was, according to Ault, quite rare.

Ault was deeply appreciative of Lawrence's kindness to him: "Lawrence seemed to put himself out. He was very understanding of me as someone from another country. The English young men at Oxford tended to treat the Americans rather contemptuously — like schoolboys — but Lawrence was decidedly a friend and helped me to feel more at home. No other person took the trouble he did to be kind."[29]

Lawrence shared his many hobbies and interests with the midwesterner, taking him on bicycle rides through the countryside surrounding Oxford (Ault was to write his thesis on medieval farming) to visit various churches and discover new brasses. Lawrence introduced Ault to the art of brass rubbing, and Ault still treasures, and has hanging in his home in Newton, Massachusetts, several rubbings they did together. Lawrence showed him that sometimes the brasses in the church floors had different, older, reliefs on the opposite side. He would bring along a screwdriver, and while Ault stood guard at the gate, he would unscrew a brass and turn it over. The assurance that they were doing something sacrilegious lent additional excitement to the discovery.

Lawrence also shared his particular interest in medieval armor with Ault, and several times they visited the shop of a smith who was the local authority on how suits of armor had been made. From his young companion and the smith Ault learned how the suits were fashioned to be thick enough to withstand arrows, and assembled so as to present a glancing surface, yet not so heavy that a knight could not get around.

In their work together with Poole, Ault developed a great respect for Lawrence's intelligence and intellectual inventiveness as well as for his sense of humor. He recalls Poole, a fellow of Magdalen and an eminent historian, as rather stuffy, a view Lawrence shared. "Smoke always came out of the *center* of his mouth," Ault recalled, "and his hands were well manicured. He looked as if he had descended from a long line of maiden aunts." Lawrence confessed to Ault one day that he had decided to stir Poole up by submitting an essay in a colloquial style. During their tutorial, Poole turned to Lawrence and said, "Your essay is good enough but your style is that of a tuppenny-ha'penny newspaper."[30]

In summary, Ault felt Lawrence to be an exceptionally fine, sensitive and perceptive young man. And he thought Lawrence, with his brilliance and humor, would have made an exceptional don had his career not taken a different direction.

Lawrence drew from his relationships with his tutors at Oxford a great deal of the intellectual sustenance upon which his later career as a scholar-leader was based. He admired Poole despite Poole's correctness — "my most unpontifical official tutor at Oxford" — whom he credited with having "read every book, and remembered the best ones."[31] But he respected most and was influenced most strongly by his unofficial tutor or "crammer," the historian L. Cecil Jane.

A tense, spare, rather ascetic person, with a long loping stride, Jane had begun teaching Lawrence privately in history when Lawrence decided to switch from mathematics to history during his last year at the City of Oxford High School.[32] Lawrence continued to be coached by Jane until he took his finals in June 1910, and according to his mother, they arranged during the last year for Lawrence always to be Jane's last pupil so he would have extra time.[33]

Lawrence valued Jane as a thorough historian and was stimulated by his ideas. To Robert Graves he wrote that he would go to Jane nearly every day "and discuss nearly every point of all history." He described Jane admiringly as a "fully-charged personality,"[34] but also as "quite abnormal." In a letter home, Lawrence indicated that Jane could become "morbid" at times and suffered from a "harmless form of insanity" (probably a form of depression).[35] He wrote a fuller view of his former teacher in recommending him as a coach to his brother Will, who was thinking of writing a thesis: "Mr. Jane's tuition would be great joy to you: it is not filling, but intensely stimulating. He will give you the minimum of pertinent facts, and leave you to mould them to your purposes. Don't hesitate to argue with him. He does not know till it is challenged, half the reasons which make up his mind."[36]

Jane's view of his special student is contained in a letter written in 1927 to Robert Graves, which Graves published in part in *Lawrence and*

the Arabs.[37] Here is the complete text of Jane's letter, including passages
omitted by Graves:

> I coached him in his last year at the Oxford City School and saw a great
> deal of him all through his time at Oxford. He would never read the obvious
> books. I found out in the first week or two that the thing was to suggest
> rather out-of-the-way books. He could be relied upon to get more out of a
> suggestive sentence in a book than an ordinary man would get from a volume.
> His work was always on his own lines, even to the hours when he came to
> me. Shortly after midnight to 4 A.M. was a favorite time (living at home he
> had not to bother about College regulations: it was enough for his mother
> to report that he was "home by twelve"). He had the most diverse interests
> historically, though they were mainly medieval. For a long time I could not
> get him to take any interest in late European History — was very startled to
> find that he was absorbed by R. M. Johnston's *French Revolution*. His special
> subject for the history school was the crusades, and I have copies of the
> books which he used, with some very typical notes in the margin — and they
> are interesting for the passages which he underlined. While he was at school
> still I used to be amused [not "surprised" as Graves has it] by his fondness
> for analyzing character: it was a little habit of his to put questions to me in
> order to watch my expression: he would make no comment on my answer
> but I could see that he thought the more. In many ways he resembled his
> father very much, quite one of the most charming men I have known — very
> shy, very kind. Lawrence was not a bookworm, though he read very fast and
> a great deal. I should not call him a scholar by temperament and the main
> characteristic of his work was always that it was unusual without the effort
> to be unusual. He loved [not "liked" as in Graves] anything in the nature
> of satire; guilty of having . . . [several words illegible] beyond me to finish a
> book which was hanging fire by coming to my rooms to read in MS and en-
> joying it — especially the more frivolous parts in it; that is why he appreci-
> ated Gibbon's notes so much. He was very diffident about his own work; he
> never published his really admirable (but small) degree thesis which he
> wrote on the military architecture of the crusades: illustrated by photographs
> and plans made on the spot. His first visit to the East was for . . . [several
> words illegible] of that work.
>
> He took a most brilliant first class, so much so that Mr. R. L. Poole (his
> tutor at Jesus) gave a dinner to the examiners to celebrate it. He was very
> silent [not "robust" as in Graves], a little difficult to know — and always
> unexpected. His study (at home in his garden built by himself) [no, for him,
> by his parents] was typical, slightly oriental in character. When he did talk
> it was always very refreshing and very original with a quiet vein of satire
> in it.[38]

Lawrence responded to Jane's special interest in him with small atten-
tions — he sent Jane photographs of French castles — and with a concern
for Jane's welfare that continued long after Lawrence graduated from
Oxford. The concern was expressed in several letters sent to his family

from the Middle East. In one of these he wrote: "It would be a distinct kindness if Will went down to see him [Mr. Jane] occasionally, on pretexts such as Green's [an Oxford friend] request might afford, or even a letter from me. He lives so much alone, and is so short of money (not his own debts either, but other people's) that he gets very much despondent, and visitors who talk decently encourage him. And he is too interesting for it to be an ordeal."[39] Lawrence visited Jane himself as late as the spring of 1921 at Aberystwyth College in Wales to which his former teacher had transferred for reasons of health in the previous year.[40]

It was during the undergraduate years that Lawrence made his most important effort to establish a serious relationship with a woman. The young woman was Janet Laurie Hallsmith. When I first interviewed Robert Lawrence regarding the details of his younger brother's childhood he referred me to several members of the Laurie family for further information — two sisters and a brother, with whom he had remained in touch. These were the children whose father was the agent of an estate in the New Forest near Langley Lodge, where the Lawrences lived from 1894 to 1896. Lawrence's childhood friendship with Janet and the other Laurie children has already been described. The account that follows was supplied to me in interviews by Mrs. Hallsmith herself. She seemed to me utterly candid within the limits of memory, and I sensed no conscious interest on her part in embellishing her story in order to claim an important association with a famous man.

In 1899 Janet was sent to Oxford to boarding school and to be near the Lawrences. Two years later, her father drowned in Southampton Water and she returned home to be with her mother. She continued to visit the Lawrences in Oxford and sometimes stayed with them. She and T.E. saw each other frequently through his undergraduate years. "I always spent Sunday afternoon at tea with him," she said, "and sort of watched him grow up." Later she visited "Ned" on occasion in the detached bungalow. Although women were not officially allowed in the undergraduate rooms, Lawrence served Janet and her sister breakfast in his room on at least one occasion.

The relationship between Ned and Janet from childhood on was one of ragging and teasing. He would chide the rather tomboyish girl for not being a boy or tease her for not being capable of doing things as well as he could. The teasing, she said, had a tender quality and she never felt hurt by it. At an Oxford breakfast party, she recalled, T.E. dared her to throw a lump of sugar across a court into an open window. She took the challenge and after two misses the third shot went in and hit the occupant. T.E. had ducked out of sight, and there she was, embarrassed to find herself spotted in the window by the irritated don across the way. This childlike, playful quality characterized their relationship. They never discussed their feelings about each other, especially as he seemed unable to, and she had never thought of him seriously as a suitor or mate. On the contrary, he maintained an emotional distance. Once when he was about nineteen she remarked to him, "Ned, you never look me in the eye." He replied, "It gives me a painful sensation to look into your eyes."

Janet was therefore surprised when Lawrence's interest in her took a more serious turn. She had always felt toward him as an older sister toward a clever brother, and he also inspired in her a feeling that he needed to be taken care of. Besides, he was more than two years younger and too short — he was the same height if not shorter than she was. Mrs. Lawrence had wanted her to marry Bob, who was nearer her age. But Bob was "so terribly good," and he once had corrected her for using the word "pub" ("Pub is not a nice word," he had said). Janet's heart was turning to Will despite the more than three years' difference in their ages. He was the tallest and handsomest of the Lawrence boys and in her view the most "dashing."[41]

When T.E. asked her to marry him, she was understandably taken aback. He was about twenty-one at the time, still an undergraduate, when he proposed. She had come to the Lawrences' for dinner, and she and Ned had stayed at the table after the meal was over. He bolted the door so the parlormaid could not come in. "We were joking about his brothers when he suddenly proposed." There had been no warning, no preliminaries, such as a kiss or a revelation of feelings. Though she felt that the proposal was a serious one, in her astonishment she laughed at him. He seemed hurt, but merely said, "Oh, I see," or "All right," and spoke no more about it.

Despite Mrs. Lawrence's objections Janet and Will had hoped to marry, but he was killed in the war in 1915. In 1919 Janet married Guthrie Hallsmith, a war hero who later failed as an artist. Because her father was dead she asked Lawrence to give her away. At first he agreed, but just before the wedding he sent her a note saying he could not go through with it, offering as his reason that he was too short and would look silly walking down the aisle with her. But the two remained friends. He occasionally visited the Hallsmiths at their home in Newquay in Cornwall and was godfather of their first child.

Mrs. Hallsmith was a woman of warmth and charm, and like both T.E. and his mother, a person of indomitable will. At eighty-six, having suffered several bouts of heart failure, she continued to relish her life and the people and things around her.

Nine months after first speaking with Janet Hallsmith of her relationship with Lawrence, I visited Lawrence's childhood friend the Reverend E. F. ("Midge") Hall and his wife on Dartmoor in Devonshire. We were talking of Lawrence's shyness when one of the Halls offered spontaneously, "There was one girl he loved." They seemed reluctant to reveal her identity until I told them I thought I knew, having spoken with Janet Hallsmith several months before. "Oh, you know then," Hall said. "I have never mentioned it to anybody." And went on to tell me that Lawrence as a youth had spoken with him of his love for Janet Laurie.[42]

Once during his undergraduate days, Hall told me, Lawrence arranged for himself, Janet and "Midge" Hall to go boating on the Thames. But instead of taking Janet with him, he fixed it so that Midge and Janet went in a punt and he followed fifty yards behind in a canoe. Afterwards Hall asked Lawrence "what on earth" he had done that for. Lawrence replied that he was "observing" his friend and Janet from afar. He then added, as if to himself, "I'm getting over the disappointment of letting the other man speak for the girl I adore. I don't know." Hall said that he did not think Janet ever really reciprocated Lawrence's love for her.

When he saw Janet Hallsmith at a later time, Hall said to her, "You know Ned Lawrence adored you," and she replied that she had known but could not consider him seriously as a suitor. As if to sum up his memory of the relationship of his two friends, Hall remarked, "She was a lovely girl, a lovely girl. She was a dear. He worshipped from afar."

It is difficult to weigh the importance of Lawrence's relationship with Janet Laurie and the disappointment it contained, for he never wrote about it, and except for Midge Hall, never spoke of it to his friends. There are only sparse references to Janet and the Lauries in the *Home Letters*. Because the relationship had begun in childhood he was able to accept her as a good friend and could allow her to penetrate to a degree his already strong reserve. They had fun and played games together. Yet strong feelings of attraction and love built up in the boy, perhaps without his realizing their intensity. But he was unable to share his emotions, to communicate these feelings to the girl, or to change the relationship to an adult one. Janet was therefore naturally surprised when T.E. proposed so abruptly and did not intend to hurt him when she reacted with anxious laughter. Perhaps she sensed that his conflicts, his essential immaturity, prevented his courting a woman successfully, at least at this time. As the incidents Hall described showed so clearly, Lawrence had to be the observer — to worship from afar.

The Greek OY ΦΡΟΝΤΙΣ (Does Not Care), which he chose to place over the entrance of his cottage, Clouds Hill, after the war, applies to many aspects of Lawrence's life and character, but is particularly appropriate to the way Lawrence handled his feelings of disappointment over the failure with Janet. The expression derives from the story in Herodotus of Hippocleides, who was the successful suitor of the princess Agarista, but drank too much wine and began dancing on a table. He disgraced himself by standing on his head and beating time in the air with his legs (the Greeks wore short skirts). When Agarista's father cried, "You have danced away your wife," Hippocleides replied cheerfully, "I don't care."

We will never know in what way Lawrence's disappointment in love affected his decision to leave England and live in the Middle East, in its predominantly male society, for the better part of the next five years.

Probably it was one factor among several that determined his life plan, a plan not established by a single decision, but by a series of smaller steps that depended always on a variety of personal interests and external circumstances.

Yet I am of the impression that this disappointment played a significant part in Lawrence's turning to Syria and to Carchemish, where a congenial life among men, the archeologist's world of the dig, the camp and the campfire, without the need to relate seriously to women, provided what Lawrence claims were the pleasantest years of his life. Although I am in substantial agreement with Janet Hallsmith and other women who have maintained that it is nonsense to say that Lawrence hated women — he had, after all, a number of social relationships with them that were mutually gratifying — because of his deeply ambivalent attitude toward women as sexual beings, and the intense sexual inhibitions related to this attitude, he never, to my knowledge, ever again attempted to form a serious love bond with a woman. Throughout his life he chose voluntarily the worlds of men — the dig and the military — where the demands of women would be minimized. He remained, according to his brother Arnold, a virgin until his death.

At the end of their college years British students underwent six days of final examinations. The examination essays determined then, as now, graduation, class standing and the possibility of honors, and were circulated among members of a committee that included professors to whom the student had not previously been exposed, possibly from Cambridge University as well as from the various Oxford colleges. The students were then quizzed orally on what they had written. The mark they received on their essays might be raised but not lowered as a result of the oral examination.

Lawrence, as a result of his travels and reading in French poetry, claimed he was unprepared for these examinations and was advised to submit a special thesis (his study of Crusader castles), to supplement the other papers. He received a First Class Honors degree in modern history.

There are five memorials to Lawrence at Jesus College. A bronze tablet greets the visitor at the main entrance. A copy of a portrait by Augustus John (the original is in the Tate Gallery) hangs in the hall. James McBey's pencil sketch of Lawrence, drawn at Damascus in 1918, hangs in the Senior Common Room. More recently a replica of the bust by Eric Kennington (the original is in the crypt of St. Paul's Cathedral) was placed in the chapel by Robert Lawrence. Finally, the Lawrence family established the Lawrence Brothers Memorial Scholarship in memory of T.E., Will and Frank. As J. N. L. Baker has written: "In the long history of the College no member has attracted so much comment and controversy as Lawrence; none has merited greater appreciation."[43]

7

The First Trip to
the Middle East, 1909

Lawrence began his first journey to the Middle East in mid-June 1909 aboard the Pacific and Orient steamship *Mongolia,* which took him by Gibraltar through the Mediterranean to Port Said, Jaffa and Beirut. By the time he returned to Oxford in October his travels, mostly on foot, had taken him through much of northern Palestine, along the Lebanese coast to parts of western Syria, and eastward to the Euphrates region of southern Asia Minor, where he was later to spend three important years working at the site of the ancient Hittite city of Carchemish.

The explicit reason for the trip was his desire to study at first hand the castles of Syria and Palestine as part of the research for his thesis on the military architecture of the Crusades. But his longing to explore the lands of the Middle East, the places where Western civilizations originated, went much deeper. His friend Richards said that the lectures of the Egyptologist Flinders Petrie at Oxford had stimulated it. But Lawrence's letter to his mother on first reaching the Mediterranean the year before reveals a deeper passion. And his developing attachment to David Hogarth influenced his desire to go there himself.

On this trip Lawrence became exposed for the first time to a radically different culture, and began the process of absorption in its way of life out of which his later triumphs and personal torments were to grow. He wrote lightly to his mother that he felt "most inclined to build a tent on Tell el Kadi [one of the mounds in Palestine] and be a hedonistic hermit."[1] Neither his writings on this journey nor those of the Carchemish period reveal evidence of conflict, or of the struggle with personal identity that was to lead him later to warn against the submergence of oneself in an alien culture.

On this first trip Lawrence already shows, however, a remarkable ability to adapt to the ways of life of the Arab cultures, to live, even then, "as an Arab with the Arabs."[2] He was always attracted more to the Bedouins and their renunciation of civilization than to the town Arabs, whose settled lives resembled too much what he wished to reject in bourgeois English society. "The two selves [the Bedouin and the overcivilized European], you see, are mutually destructive," he wrote in 1927 on a typescript of Graves's biography. "So I fall between them into the nihilism which cannot find, in being, even a false God in which to believe."[3]

At Hogarth's suggestion Lawrence wrote early in 1909 to Charles M. Doughty, the famous explorer, to get his "opinion on a walking tour in Northern Syria." Doughty, who had not traveled north of Damascus, discouraged Lawrence from such a journey in summer, calling it "wearisome, hazardous to health and even disappointing," and warned him of the heat, squalor and long distances. "Long daily marches on foot a prudent man who knows the country would I think consider out of the question," Doughty wrote. "The population only knows their own wretched life and look upon any European wandering in their country with at best a veiled ill will. You would have nothing to draw upon but the slight margin of strength which you bring with you from Europe."[4] Lawrence, obviously not dissuaded, answered wryly, "My little pleasure trip appears to be more interesting than I had bargained for: I have fortunately a few months to think about it in."[5] More than two decades later he would write: "Upon each return from the East I would repair to Doughty, a looming giant, white with eighty years, headed and bearded like some renaissance Isaiah."[6]

During those months he consulted C. H. C. Pirie-Gordon, a young archeologist who had recently visited some of the Crusader castles. Pirie-Gordon asserted (in contradiction to Aldington's statements to the contrary nearly fifty years later) that "the guide books were less helpful than at present when dealing with places off the main routes frequented by pilgrims and tourists." He lent Lawrence an annotated map of his own earlier journey to Syria and copies of photographs he had taken of various castles.[7] According to Lawrence's mother, whose memory was admirable, he took with him in addition only a light-weight suit with many pockets in which he carried "all his things": two shirts of thin material, a spare pair of socks, and a camera with many packets of film. A month after his travels began, his *iradehs* arrived. These were official letters of introduction from the Ottoman cabinet to the governors in Syria, which had been obtained for Lawrence by Lord Curzon (then chancellor of Oxford University). They provided him with privileges, protection and assistance while traveling in the Ottoman Empire, "a piquant passport for a tramp to carry," as Lawrence put it.[8] The *iradehs* declared that Lawrence, then not yet twenty-one, was "Professor of University and Artist."[9]

Toward the end of the trip, which he said covered eleven hundred miles, the "noble stockings" had proved to be the weakest link and had "succumbed at last; three holes lately: but I have only the one pair with me (economy!), and they have now done 450 miles: not bad, because they are thin wool. Boots are worn out, but will perhaps last me through. I don't want to have them soled."[10] This was unfortunate or foolish, for two weeks later the boots were walked "to bits" and his feet were covered with "cuts and chafes and blisters," which had rubbed up into sores.[11]

Lawrence's first view of the Middle East in early July at Port Said (then a squalid but rapidly growing seaport teeming with peoples of diverse ethnic groups from all over the earth) was clearly disappointing. The lovely harbor of Beirut, which he reached on the sixth, was an improvement. Leaving Beirut shortly thereafter, Lawrence walked south to Sidon, then southeast to Banias and Safed, and south to the Sea of Galilee. He followed the western shore to Tiberias, took the road west to Nazareth and crossed Carmel to the coast. Turning north he walked up the coast through Haifa, Acre, and Tyre and returned to Beirut at the beginning of August. In August he walked up the coast into northern Syria through Tripoli, Latakia and Antioch, arriving in Aleppo in early September. From Aleppo he went by car to Urfa, and possibly to Harran on the edge of Mesopotamia. He returned to Beirut on September 30 and was at sea on the way home in early October. In a letter home he stated his intention to spend three days in Damascus, and he wrote Liddell Hart more than twenty years later that he did so ("I was also at Damascus, and I forgot how I got there"),[12] but there is no contemporary or later account of this visit. During these wanderings he wrote that he visited thirty-seven of the fifty or so Crusader castles.[13]

In preparation for his trip Lawrence learned some conversational Arabic from a Syrian Protestant clergyman living in Oxford.[14] He probably knew a little more than the eighty words he acknowledged to Graves[15] because he was able to make himself understood even upon arriving in Port Said.[16]

During his wanderings Lawrence often stayed with Syrian families, especially poorer ones, and sometimes he slept in the open air. He was clearly moved by the hospitality of the native people, which contrasted so sharply with the warnings he had received. "This is a glorious country for wandering in," he wrote his father, "for hospitality is something more than a name: setting aside the American and English missionaries, who take care of me in the most fatherly (or motherly) way: — they have all so far [August 15 from Tripoli] been as good as they can be — there are the common people, each one ready to receive one for a night, and allow me to share in their meals: and without a thought of payment from a traveller on foot. It is so pleasant, for they have a very attractive kind of native dignity."[17]

The accounts of Lawrence's travels in Palestine and Syria on this first

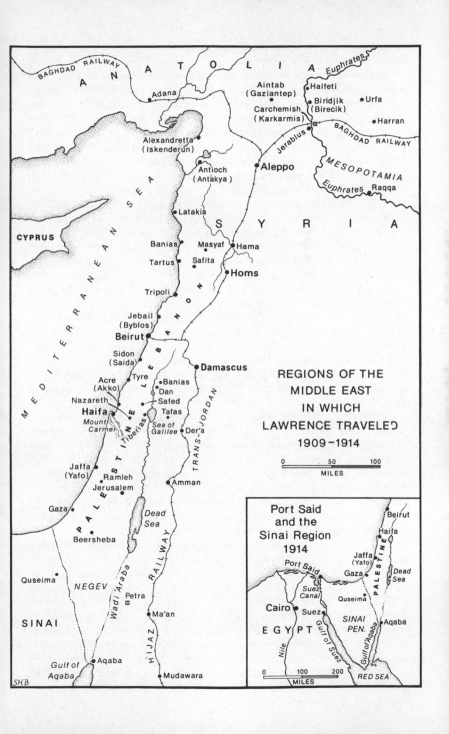

BAGHDAD RAILWAY

A N A T O L I A

Euphrates

Adana

Aintab
(Gaziantep)
Carchemish
(Karkarmis)

Halfeti
Biridjik
(Birecik)
Urfa
Harran

BAGHDAD RAILWAY

Jerablus

Alexandretta
(Iskenderun)

Antioch
(Antakya)

Aleppo

MESOPOTAMIA

Euphrates
Raqqa

MEDITERRANEAN SEA

Latakia

CYPRUS

S Y R I A

Banias
Tartus

Masyaf
Safita

Hama
Homs

Tripoli

Jebail
(Byblos)

Beirut

Sidon
(Saida)

Acre
(Akko)
Nazareth
Haifa
Mount
Carmel

Tyre

Banias
Dan
Safed
Tafas

Sea of
Galilee

Der'a

Damascus

TRANSJORDAN

REGIONS OF THE
MIDDLE EAST
IN WHICH
LAWRENCE TRAVELED
1909–1914

0   50   100
MILES

Jaffa
(Yafo)

Ramleh
Jerusalem

Gaza

Beersheba

Dead
Sea

Amman

Quseima

NEGEV

Petra

Ma'an

SINAI

Wadi 'Araba

HIJAZ RAILWAY

Aqaba

Gulf of
Aqaba

Mudawara

SHB

Port Said
and the
Sinai Region
1914

Beirut
Haifa

Port Said

Jaffa
(Yafo)
Gaza

PALESTINE

Dead
Sea

Cairo
Suez
Canal
Suez

Nile

Gulf of Suez

SINAI
PEN.

Quseima

Aqaba

Gulf of Aqaba

EGYPT

RED SEA

0   100   200
MILES

trip are contained principally in a dozen or so letters he wrote home, in a
few fragments he related to Robert Graves and Basil Liddell Hart, in the
bits and pieces told by his family and friends, and in brief accounts
written to Sir John Rhys, his principal at Jesus College, and to Doughty.
One very rich and detailed letter to his mother, which fills a dozen book
pages even without the minor bowdlerizations of his older brother, provides a full account of the first month of his travels in Palestine. The
letters covering the later part of the trip, especially after Lawrence left
Aleppo, are less frequent and far less complete. During this time, however, he suffered from malaria and was robbed and almost murdered.

These letters provide only sparse, subdued indications of Lawrence's
emotional responses to the many new experiences he was undergoing. But
they are filled with illuminating, meticulous descriptions of the sights and
geography and of the attitudes of the people in the lands he was dis-
covering. They demonstrate, as had the letters from France, Lawrence's
capacity to observe each aspect of the unfamiliar world surrounding him
with such exquisite care that it seems to become his own, and he, as a
consequence, to belong to it. The climate, houses, foods, the way the
foods were cooked and served, the process of hospitality, the beds and
the bedding, are all recorded in great detail. The flora and fauna, friendly
and hostile, are all accounted for down to the fleas, sometimes with good
humor. "The Arabs say that the king of the fleas lives in Tiberias," he
wrote, "but I can guarantee he has summer residences elsewhere as
well."[18]

Although this journey, much of it in settled regions, took Lawrence
among Arabs, he had little opportunity to grasp the tribal relationships,
knowledge of which proved so vital later. He did, though, gain a thorough
introduction to many of the habits, mores, fears, superstitions and other
characteristics of the Arab peoples. He lamented the deterioration of
Palestine and the Palestinians, which had occurred since Roman times,[19]
and the poverty of the Bedouins, remarking prophetically of the thistle-
covered lands around Galilee: "The sooner the Jews farm it all the better:
their colonies are bright spots in a desert."[20]

Lawrence's traveling on foot and alone aroused great curiosity among
the Arabs, which was intensified by his camera on its odd-looking tripod:
"Such a curiosity has never been seen and all the village is summoned to
look at it."[21] Peculiarities of the Ottoman currency and the aggravating
postal system he reserved for his little brother, then nine, who evidently
had a special interest in such matters. Lawrence had particular scorn
for the Baedeker descriptions of castles, his area of expertise: " 'Buildings resembling towers'," wrote Baedeker, "(which are towers)," wrote
Lawrence; " 'small arched apertures resembling loopholes' (and which
are loopholes) and other inanities much worse but too long and childish
to quote."[22]

Lawrence was enthusiastic at this time about the educational and re-forming efforts of the American mission in the Levant and the college in Beirut. At Jebail north of Beirut he was given warm hospitality by Miss Holmes, the American missionary, and met Fareedah el Akle, the Syrian schoolmistress who was to become his Arabic teacher and good friend. In a passage that his zealously Christian older brother omitted from the *Home Letters* he noted the dangers for Muslims of Christian conversion: "It would be equivalent to signing their death sentence, the few converts there have been have all had to go abroad, but there are many secret adherents."[23] Despite the richness of the region in biblical and other ancient lore, Lawrence made, except for occasional references to Scrip-tures that seem aimed at pleasing his mother, few historical references of any kind in these letters. His interest seemed to be absorbed by observa-tions of the life of the present.

During the last weeks of his trip Lawrence had several troublesome and dangerous adventures, which he related to his family as humorously, innocently or incompletely as possible in order not to alarm them. Be-cause of his editing and the further distortions provided by the second-hand dramatizations of others (to which Lawrence may have con-tributed), it is difficult to piece together exactly what happened.

First, Lawrence reveals that late in August at Safita north of Tripoli he had a pistol and was persuaded by a group of Arabs to keep watch with it against "thieves," who turned out to be their landlords after the rent.[24] It appears that he was attacked on two other occasions. At Masyaf, also north of Tripoli, he was shot at from two hundred yards by "an ass with an old gun." Lawrence returned the fire and thinks he may have grazed the horse, which bolted "about half a mile" with its rider.[25]

This is probably the incident described (most likely with a number of distortions) by Fareedah el Akle in an essay she wrote on Lawrence after his death.[26] Here the "ass" has become "a huge cruel-looking Turk," and the grazed horse, a grazed little finger on the Turk, which Lawrence bandages, the two ending up as friends like "David and Goliath." How much of this romanticization is from Lawrence's yarn-telling and how much the embellishments of his admirers is beyond my capacity to determine.

The more serious attack was not described to his family at all. On September 24 he wrote to Sir John Rhys to thank him for his help in obtaining the *iradehs* and said only that the previous week he had been "robbed and rather smashed up" and was not yet "fit for walking again."[27] A fuller account, with Lawrence's editorial corrections, is supplied by Graves.[28] According to this passage, in a village near the Euphrates a Turkoman was led to believe by the villagers that a ten-franc copper watch Lawrence was carrying was gold. He stalked his victim, knocked him down, took his revolver, and tried to shoot him with it, but did not understand the safety latch. He then hit Lawrence with stones, robbed him, and left him hurt. Fortunately, Lawrence's injuries were not so grave that he was unable to make it five miles to the next village. The local authorities and the village elders gave up the thief and returned Lawrence's stolen property, which included the watch, his money, his revolver and Hittite antiquities (including thirty seals which Hogarth had asked him to bring back).[29] To Rhys he wrote: "Lord Curzon's Iradés were invaluable in the matter: they stirred up the local authorities to a semblance of energy, so that the man was caught in 48 hours. Before this I employed them innumerable times: in fact without them there would have been several times unpleasantness."[30]

To his parents he wrote on September 22: "I find an absurd canard in the Aleppo paper of a week ago: my murder near Aintab (where I didn't go). I hope it has not been copied."[31] This may be a reference to the robbery and beating. Pirie-Gordon's account of the incident in *T. E. Lawrence by His Friends* is at some variance with the above; it seems to be based on stories told to him by third parties and should probably be discounted.[32] Lawrence did, however, send him back the map he had borrowed, apologizing for the bloodstains on it.

On his way back from Urfa, Lawrence wrote his parents that his camera had been stolen from his carriage "while the coachman I left on watch was asleep."[33] David Garnett, who edited the *Collected Letters of T. E. Lawrence,* challenges this account on the grounds that Lawrence wrote Sir John Rhys that the camera was stolen when he was robbed and beaten. I can, however, find no reference to the camera in the letter to Sir John. In any event he returned successfully with the photographs and other material for his thesis.

"The stories of his adventures and the hardships he endured on that trip, as he related them to us later, would make the most thrilling reading," wrote Fareedah el Akle, a quarter of a century afterwards. "They would sound like the Arabian Nights. Yet Lawrence made very light of all his sufferings and would joke over them. Many were his narrow escapes from death at the hands of cruel Kurds and Turks."[34] This is a revealing passage, for it conveys the sense of excitement, drama and romance that Lawrence could inspire even in an ordinarily sensible Syrian schoolteacher. It was part of his character to do so, and furnishes the biographer — who attempts to distinguish those distortions of fact which are Lawrence's responsibility from the luxurious myth-making of his audiences — with a challenging assignment. In 1909, when he was just twenty-one, Lawrence was already creating in the substance of his life and his vivid accounts of it material for legends about his adventures and exploits, activities which were, *in reality,* extraordinary.

Toward the end of his trip Lawrence wrote home, "It is remarkable that all these 3 months on most unaccustomed and most changing food and water my stomach has never been upset."³⁵ But, as we have seen, much else was. In addition to being beaten and robbed, and enduring footsores, cuts and blisters, Lawrence also had four attacks of malaria.³⁶ Yet he wished to extend his trip, claiming that Sir John Rhys "won't care if I am early or late." Only lack of money or, more significantly, his poor physical condition required that he return. When he did go back to college in October, Sir Ernest Barker, a family friend who was then of St. John's College, described his face as "thinned to the bone by privation."³⁷ In spite of all his hardships Lawrence succeeded in bringing back with him from Syria jars of Tyrian purple dye for a printing scheme to be carried out with one of his friends.³⁸

Midway in this first journey to the Middle East, Lawrence wrote his mother, "I will have such difficulty in becoming English again, here I am Arab in habits and slip in talking from English to French and Arabic unnoticing."³⁹ Thus, on this first trip of his youth to the Middle East, Lawrence had already started to go beyond the ordinary gathering of knowledge. He had begun to identify himself with Arab ways and Arab life, and to move away from his Anglo-Irish self. It was his knowledge of the Arab world, combined with a deepening of this identification to the point where he could grasp and share with the Bedouin tribesmen their own often dimly appreciated hopes and dreams of change, that enabled him to accomplish his role in the Arab Revolt.

After his return to England, Lawrence wrote to Doughty in November that his tour "has ended happily (I reached Urfa my goal) and the Crusading Fortresses I found are so intensely interesting that I hope to return to the East for some little time."⁴⁰ A meeting (their first) followed which, according to Hogarth, "diminished in no way the disciple's fervour."⁴¹

8

Lawrence at Carchemish

In a letter of May 18, 1911, Gertrude Bell, by that date already an experienced desert explorer, wrote to her stepmother that she had "found . . . a young man called Lawrence," and added parenthetically, "he is going to make a traveller."[1] In fact, during the three and a half years from December 1910, when Lawrence left England bound for Athens, Constantinople and Beirut, to June 1914, when he came back shortly before the outbreak of World War I, he visited England only three times for periods totaling about six months. He spent the bulk of his time during these years in the region of Carchemish, in what is now south-central Turkey, and in northern Syria, but his travels took him into northwestern portions of Mesopotamia and as far south as Aqaba and the Sinai Peninsula. Through comparing his letters, including a large unpublished correspondence with E. T. Leeds of the Ashmolean Museum, it is possible to follow his whereabouts with some accuracy.

A tracing of Lawrence's journeys on a map of the Near East shows his travels to be predominantly in its western and northern regions, among the towns and cities of Syria, Lebanon and southern Anatolia. His contacts were thus as much with the settled Arabs of the towns as with the nomads, and with Circassians, Kurds, Turkomans, Armenians and other peoples of the north as well as with the Bedouin tribesmen.

Following his graduation from Oxford in June 1910, Lawrence had made three trips to France in the summer and fall, visiting churches and cathedrals, and studying the origins and history of medieval pottery in England ("looking at Medieval Pots") for the Ashmolean Museum in Oxford.[2] Meanwhile, the British Museum decided, on the recommendation of David Hogarth, to reopen its excavations at Carchemish. Because of political tensions in the region the Ottoman authorities delayed granting permission until the spring of 1910.[3] Then Hogarth obtained for Lawrence a Magdalen demyship, or four-year travêling scholarship, which enabled him to take part in the project.

In November Lawrence wrote to Leeds: "Mr. Hogarth is going digging: and I am going out to Syria in a fortnight to make plain the valleys and level the mountains for his feet: — also to learn Arabic. The two occupations fit into one another splendidly."[4] He hoped also to continue his studies of the castles and history of the Crusades, to be published as "The Seven Pillars of Wisdom" or "my monumental work on the Crusades"[5] (not to be confused with the *Seven Pillars of Wisdom* which he eventually published).

Lawrence left England in early December and arrived in Beirut three weeks later, having visited en route Athens and Constantinople for the first time. He described these visits to his family meticulously and lyrically. There is indeed a tone of awe and reverence in his letter about Athens, and at the Acropolis he was so moved that "[I] walked through the doorway of the Parthenon, and on into the inner part of it, without really remembering who or where I was. A heaviness in the air made my eyes swim, and wrapped up my senses: I only knew that I, a stranger, was walking on the floor of the place I had most desired to see, the greatest temple of Athene, the palace of art, and that I was counting her columns and finding there what I already knew. The building was familiar, not cold as in the drawings, but complex, irregular, alive with curve and subtlety, and perfectly preserved. Every line of the moldings, every minutest refinement in the sculptures were evident in that light, and inevitable in their place."[6] His descriptions of the bustling Constantinople, which he thought "may well stand for life and activity," are even more thorough.

On board ship Lawrence enjoyed himself arguing about "the infallibility and general excellence of Popes" with three French-Canadian priests on their way to Jerusalem, and also was applauded for his tactful handling in French of a strident debate among them and a French-Egyptian lawyer about French politics.[7]

Lawrence arrived in Beirut shortly before Christmas of 1910 and soon left for the mission school at Jebail (ancient Byblos), a few miles up the Mediterranean coast, where he studied Arabic for the next two months and enjoyed the hospitality and companionship of Miss Holmes, the school's director; Mrs. Rieder, one of the French teachers; and Miss Fareedah el Akle, his Arabic teacher.

Miss Akle, who had first met Lawrence briefly on his 1909 journey, wrote to me her recollections of his visits and of her relationship with him. The minor inaccuracies the letter contains are allowable perhaps when one considers that sixty years had intervened.

Long ago on Christmas Eve, 1909 [actually 1910],[8] I met T.E. for the first time at an American mission school in Jebail . . . where I was teaching. Lawrence had come there as a young man of 21-years [9] to study Arabic, as he had been appointed to work on the excavation of a Hittite city in Jerablus, Carchemish, near the Euphrates, and he needed Arabic to work there.

It was a great pleasure to be chosen to teach him Arabic — which is reckoned to be the second hardest language in the world — but Lawrence picked it up very easily and in a short time he could speak and write a little as he was extremely intelligent and a good linguist. The time I spent as Lawrence's teacher was very pleasant. Every day we would study for an hour on a red sofa in the large hall, Lawrence holding the cat on his lap. T.E. had a nice sense of humor, and the time seemed to pass very quickly. Teaching him gave me the opportunity of understanding him, although sometimes he was difficult to understand. I remember his saying something to me once and I looked puzzled. He said, "Let me explain." After he told me what he meant I thought, "Why didn't I see that straight away." I think that T.E. if he were here, would say to people, "Let me explain!" and we would see clearly what he meant when quite often biographers do not see what he meant at all.

Besides [my] being T.E.'s teacher, we both had common interests: books and authors, archeology and the Arabs. (I felt as keenly as he did about the Arab nation and their history.) All of this helped me to understand Lawrence well. — I don't mean to give a history of T.E. but I should like to speak about what struck me most about him — the spiritual side of his character.

Lawrence did not speak of religion much, but he lived a religious life. He was a man of the spirit and lived rather in the spirit than in the body. I always wondered what was the thing which helped Lawrence lead this wonderful life of service. He did his utmost to use all his gifts, great or small, in the best possible way. Once I remember, he bought an old book from a monastery so old, torn, and worm eaten that no one would have bought it. He wanted to give it to Miss Holmes as a present — she was the president of the American mission school — and he said he must do his best to fix it as no other book was available. He worked on it hours and hours and, when he had finished, I could not believe it was the same book. All his work — great or small — he undertook to do well throughout his life.

Once, talking to Lawrence about an important matter, I asked him a question and he said, "Help comes from within, not from without." This seemed to me to reveal the secret of his inner life. He seemed to be a man guided by a dynamic power in him: the power of the spirit.[10]

I should add that Miss Akle was critical of my view of Lawrence's conflicts, as expressed in an article I had sent her, and wrote to a friend of hers, "Lawrence seems to me to be like an oyster which has, through pain and suffering all through life developed into a pearl which the world is trying to evaluate, taking it to pieces layer by layer, without realizing the true value of the whole."[11]

In February 1911, before beginning work on the dig, Lawrence accompanied Hogarth and Gregori, the Cypriot headman at the site, on a tour by rail and sea — not on foot this time — of cities and sights of northern Palestine. They journeyed to Jerablus via Der'a, Damascus and Aleppo. In March they arrived in Carchemish and the archeological work was begun.

In choosing to work and live at Carchemish and in Syria during these important years of his young manhood, Lawrence removed himself from the burdens of a structured academic life and the confinements of English society. He chose instead an entirely new and self-contained world, one in which he became an important personage, known by everyone throughout the region, and fondly by all but those who crossed him. It was a free world, lived out of doors for the most part. Although women travelers and friends sometimes visited the site, Carchemish was largely a masculine society, free of the burdens of sexual jealousies and commitments.

When away from the dig Lawrence missed "the delicious free intimacy of the men of Carchemish."[12] To his childhood nurse he wrote toward the end of the first spring, "We are having a splendid time out here: not that we are finding very much, but the place is splendid, and the workmen, and the climate."[13] Later he called Carchemish "the jolliest place I've ever seen. A marvelous, unreal, pictured pageant of a life."[14]

He worked first under Hogarth directly and then with R. Campbell-Thompson. "Mr. Hogarth does the writing up of the results," he wrote his family soon after his arrival. "I do the squeezing and drawing the inscriptions and sculptures, and (with the great Gregori of the *Accidents of an Antiquary's Life* [one of Hogarth's books]) direct the men."[15] And a few weeks later: "The most pleasing part of the day is when breakfast hour gets near. From all the villages below us on the plain there come long lines of red and blue women and children, carrying bread in red-check handkerchiefs, and wooden measures full of leben [sour goat's milk] on their heads. The men are not tired then, and the heat is just pleasant, and they chatter about and jest and sing in very delightful style. A few of the men bring shepherd's pipes, and make music of their sort. As a rule, they are not talkative: they will sit for minutes together at the house-door without a word: often coming out in the morning we have found 100 men grouped outside, wanting work, and have not heard a sound through the open window just above! The only time they get talkative is when they are about half-a-mile apart. A little companionable chat across the Euphrates is a job — except to one's ears near by, for sound carries tremendously in this region, and they bawl with their raucous voices."[16]

The digging during the day was arduous labor for the workmen, who earned about eight piastres or fourteen pence a day. The early digging often involved moving large stones and the remains of buried walls and houses. Lawrence wrote of the stones: "Some of them weigh tons, and we have no blasting powder or stone hammers with us. As a result they have to be hauled, prehistoric fashion, by brute force of men on ropes, helped to a small extent by crowbars. At this moment something over 60 men are tugging away above, each man yelling Yallah as he pulls: the row is tremendous, but the stones usually come away. Two men out of three presume to direct operations, and no one listens to any of them, they just obey Gregori's orders, and their shouting is only to employ their spare breath. Now they are raising the 'talul,' the curiously vibrant, resonant wail of the Bedawi [Bedouin]. It is a very penetrating, and very distinct cry; you feel in it some kinship with desert-life, with ghazzus and camel stampedes. (Meanwhile the stone has slipped and fallen back into the trench, and Gregori's Turkish is deserting him.) Whenever he is excited he slips back into Greek in a high falsetto voice, that convulses our hoarse-throated men."[17]

The evenings were "filled up with odd jobs that might have been done in the day, squeezing and copying inscriptions, writing up pottery and object lists, journals, etc. Also it gets cold after sunset, and we go to bed early (about 10 or 11 as a rule), to avoid it. In the matter of food all goes quite easily, except for the Haj's* quite inadvertently emptying a curry tin into a pilaff! It was like eating peppered flames, and the other two are now crying aloud about their livers!"[18]

At night, when it was not too cold and windy, Lawrence often slept out on top of the mound. He enjoyed bathing in the Euphrates, and later brought from Oxford a Canadian canoe for excursions on the river. The canoe was fitted with an outboard motor and Lawrence took great pleasure with the engine, anticipating his gratification in mechanical work with air-sea rescue boats in the RAF many years later.

The digging ceased after some four months, and in July Lawrence began a one-month walking journey of the Euphrates region around Carchemish to study several castles in the area, notably at Harran, "Rum Kalaat" and Aintab (Gaziantep), and to search for engraved Hittite seal stones because, as his brother suggested, "it would lead to strange people and places."[19] He contracted dysentery and had more bouts of malaria, from the last of which he had not yet fully recovered when he returned to England in August. He visited Doughty during that time, and returned to Port Said and Beirut in early December. He spent the next few weeks in and around Jerablus, where the archeologists were engaged in struggles with Salim Tumah, "the local magnate," over the ownership of the site, and with German railroad personnel about the course of the Baghdad Railway, then under construction in the area. The archeologists were also preparing for the new season. Even though embroiled in these activities, Lawrence found time for trips to Aleppo and Damascus. In January 1912 he was sent for a month to Egypt, to excavate a tomb with

---

* Hajj Wahid was the chief guardian of the site. "Hajj" is a title meaning that its bearer has been on a pilgrimage to Mecca.

the famed Egyptologist Flinders Petrie at Kafr Ammar, forty miles south of Cairo. Then he returned to Jerablus, and in March Leonard Woolley, who replaced Campbell-Thompson, arrived.

After more lawsuits related to the struggles over the site (Lawrence was actually imprisoned for a short time, charged with trespassing, "restraint, conveyance and unlawful possession")[20] they were able to resume digging on March 17.

A year had now passed since Lawrence's arrival in Carchemish, and despite the vicissitudes, he was able to write home happily and romantically: "We are all well, very well, and as yet cordial: we have books, and pistachios, and six kinds of soap — if not seven. We eat a lot, and sleep a lot, and talk a lot, and I have for the second time, assimilated [Francis] Thompson's *Mistress of Vision*. It is very good. We sleep by the ropes of the camp, and we rise with the dawn and we tramp with the sun and the moon for our lamp, and the spray of the wind in our hair."[21]

Ernest Altounyan, the son of an Armenian surgeon in Aleppo whose company and hospitality Lawrence frequently enjoyed, recalled Lawrence at Carchemish in 1911 as a "frail, pallid, silent youth," one who was impersonal and curiously isolated from others. His speech was soft and reluctant. "By fall," Altounyan wrote, "he had spun his cocoon, but had not yet the assurance that enables the full-grown man to leave it when required."[22]

Winifred Fontana, the wife of the British consul in Aleppo, with whom Lawrence developed a friendship based on shared literary and aesthetic interests, describes him as looking "about eighteen" in the spring of 1911 and noted that he had cast off "much of his absorbed and discomforting aloofness with his visiting clothes and clad in shorts and a buttonless shirt held together with a gaudy Kurdish belt, looked what he was: a young man of rare power and considerable physical beauty. The belt was fastened on the left hip with a huge bunch of many-coloured tassels, symbol, plain to all Arabs that he was seeking a wife."[23] Woolley confirmed that Lawrence had his tassels made bigger than anyone else's, but observed, more accurately, that they did not necessarily signal that he was looking for a wife, but only that he was yet a bachelor.[24] Woolley also observed that although Lawrence could live and work with the poorest tribesmen under conditions of utmost simplicity, he also "quite appreciated comfort," an appreciation his older colleague seems to have shared.

Seven weeks after Woolley's arrival, Lawrence wrote E. T. Leeds: "We are building a great house, with mosaic floors and beaten copper fittings, Damascus tiles on the walls (including yours!) and much stone carvings. The little relief of doves over our bathroom door is charming and Woolley fancies himself in the bathroom: a gleaming mosaic floor reflecting his shining body against the contrast of the red-stuccoed walls: and the repoussé copper bath to put new tints into the water. Our fireplace is

fine — a good deal of Hittite base and column work, and basalt mould-
ings. We are putting in a burnished copper hood, and polished over
mantel. The whole effect will (I hope) be chaste and yet rich. We really
have no complaint of the way the museum is doing us — or we doing the
museum."[25] In addition Lawrence provided the room with fine rugs, arm-
chairs of black wood and white leather that he had had made in Aleppo,
antique pots, and a piece of Morris tapestry.[26]

As the months went by, Lawrence became better and better known in
the region, and not only because of the notoriety created by the doings
connected with the dig. His growing knowledge of Arabic, his readiness
to involve himself with Arabs and others from all strata of society, his
concern for the people, and his colorful style of handling problems made
him a popular figure. This fact, or phenomenon, was attested to by many
observers who visited the site. "All Syria has heard of me: — and of us,"
he wrote home exuberantly, two months after the digging began.[27] By
June he was writing, "Today I cured a man of compound scorpion-bite
by a few drops of ammonia: for that I have a fame above Thompson's as
a hakim [doctor] and as a magician who can conjure devils into water,
from my mixing a seidlitz powder for the Haj in the kitchen before
visitors."[28]

Lawrence's characteristically ambivalent attitude toward this fame,
which soon extended into the markets of Aleppo, where he had many
dealings in various kinds of antiquities, is reflected in a letter to his family
in June of 1912, written after he had shown a duly impressed Englishman
about the town. The Englishman asked: " 'I was wondering how many
times you have been to Aleppo, and I was wondering how many times
you have been in the bazaar, and I was wondering how many purchases
you have made, and how many people spoke to you:' and when I had
satisfied him on all those points he said: 'When I was trying to buy that
embroidery in the silk bazaar, and wanted all your attention, nine old
acquaintances greeted you with all signs of returning gladness, and six
new ones were presented.' And just as he said so one of the dervishes
[they were watching five dancing dervishes] got up and said: 'Did you
not travel with me in the train last year?' and a muleteer and carriage-
driver called out together 'Salaamat, effendi!' and Haj Wahid's sister,
passing, asked me of the health of his wife. I have not seen that Englishman since, for the consular dragoman [interpreter] drove up just then,
and begged me to come to the government with him. And yet I think not
six people in Aleppo know my name! Baron the hotel keeper told me
laughing at lunch time that nine people had called to see me with antikas
up till then: It is now evening, and I have not seen him to ask for more
modern figures. Such is fame and a famous servant, and the power to
know things in Aleppo."[29]

Lawrence was excited by Aleppo, a great trading center of Western

Asia and one of the "Seven Pillar" cities of his proposed book: "Aleppo is all compact of colour, and sense of line; you inhale Orient in lungloads, and glut your appetite with silks and dyed fantasies of clothes. Today there came in through the busiest vault in the bazaar a long caravan of 100 mules of Baghdad, marching in line rhythmically to the boom of two huge iron bells swaying under the belly of the foremost. Bells nearly two feet high, with wooden clappers, introducing 100 mule-loads of the woven shawls and wine-coloured carpets of Bokhara! Such wealth is intoxicating: and intoxicated I went and bought the bells."[30]

Digging continued into June of 1912, at which time Lawrence made a short trip to the port of Alexandretta to see to the shipment of pottery for the Ashmolean. In June also, with the aid of advice and medicine from his family physician in Oxford, Lawrence struggled to help the local physicians and authorities fight a cholera epidemic in the Aleppo region, where ninety to ninety-five percent of cases were proving fatal. In July he returned to the site, still functioning as a "house physician," got "an attack of fever" himself, and returned to Jebail in August for a visit and to study more Arabic. He seems to have begun wearing Arab dress about this time.

Digging was resumed at Carchemish in September, with somewhat disappointing results, which were compounded by shortages of money from the British Museum, further attacks of fever and two broken ribs for Lawrence himself, and more difficulties with the Germans who were constructing the Baghdad Railway. In mid-November he set off for England, where he remained about six weeks, and returned to Beirut in mid-January of 1913. He found northern Syria snowbound.

There were many serious difficulties, including the disputes over the ownership of the site, during the years at Carchemish, with considerable personal danger at times to Lawrence, Woolley and the others. Woolley seemed willing to resort to strong-arm tactics when the work was impeded by the Ottoman authorities, and more than once threatened the local governor and other officials with a revolver, including a judge in his own courtroom. Woolley's intimidation of the authorities, which seemed at times the only effective way to enable the work to go on, caused such notoriety as to bring about a less than cordial reception for him later from the British ambassador in Constantinople.[31] A body of laws called Capitulations, by the terms of which foreigners in the Ottoman Empire were left to be judged on many important matters by their own courts, encouraged Lawrence and Woolley in an attitude of taking matters into their own hands. "You must be ignorant of our privileges here," Lawrence wrote home in June 1912. "If I murder Haj Wahid in our courtyard before the eyes of all the police of Biridjik [Birecik], no one can legally interfere; they might but I could sue them for it. If I was in a Turkish prison I would get out (of its ruins) double quick."[32] He did not, of course, tell his parents that he had recently spent some time in such a prison.

Lawrence's reports of "incidents" at Carchemish — his letters are filled with them — convey the sense that he was involved in a great adventure, a romantic game in which he played many different parts, an unending lark, a romp. Even the digs were "like a great sport with tangible results at the end of things."[33] Yet at the same time he was teaching classes to Arab adolescents and treating poisonous insect bites, cholera, malaria and other diseases. Mrs. Fontana recalled "the dark-eyed, richly coloured Arabs who came to exhibit their finds on the 'Dig' or to beg quinine for their fevered children (Lawrence seemed to know all by name and their children's names too)" and who "watched him with fascinated affection."[34] He was able in a letter to his brother Arnold, twelve at the time, to make an angry battle between two hundred invading Kurds and as many Arabs sound like comic opera: "Wasn't that a lovely battle? Absolutely no one hurt."[35] The year before, with Fareedah el Akle's help, he had found a jackal's skin for Arnie.

Gunrunning at Beirut was equally amusing. "At Aleppo I stayed five days more than I needed," he wrote early in 1913, "entertaining two naval officers, who became partners in my iniquity of gun-running at Beirut. The consular need of rifles involved myself, the consul-general at Beyrout, Flecker, the Admiral at Malta, our Ambassador at Stanbul, two captains and two lieutenants, besides innumerable cavasses [consular guards], in one common law-breaking. However Fontana [the consul in Aleppo, embattled presumably by Kurds, for whom the gunrunning was being done] got his stuff, and as he was too ill to entertain the porters, I had to trot them over to Aleppo."[36]

By the time Will Lawrence visited the site in September of 1913, Lawrence had become a major local personage, a hakim, "a great Lord in this place."[37] "Ned is known by everyone," Will wrote, "and their enthusiasm over him is quite amusing." He reassured their parents that they "must not think of Ned as leading an uncivilized existence. When I saw him last as the train left the station he was wearing white flannels, socks, and red slippers, with a white Magdalen blazer, and was talking to the Governor of Biridjik in lordly fashion."[38] Lawrence's evening garb, according to Woolley, was even finer. Over his white shirt he would put on "a white and gold embroidered Arab waistcoat and a magnificent cloak of gold and silver thread, a sixty-pound garment which he had picked up cheaply from a thief in the Aleppo market; in the evening too his hair was very carefully brushed: sitting in front of the winter fire reading — generally Homer, or Doughty's poems, or Blake — he would look with his sleek head and air of luxury extraordinarily unlike the Lawrence of the day time."[39]

Luther Fowle, an American missionary who was working at Aintab (Gaziantep) near Carchemish, stayed with the English archeologists late in 1913 and has provided a valuable description of his visit. By the time he arrived, Lawrence and Woolley's house had become as richly appointed as any professor's home in England: "In the center was the delightful living-room with open fireplace, built-in bookcases filled with the well-worn leather-bound volumes of the classics with which a British scholar would naturally surround himself, and a long table covered with the current British papers as well as the archeological journals of all the world." Fowle stressed the good faith and friendship which existed between Lawrence and Woolley and the native people. "They insisted that they were safer on the banks of the Euphrates than if they had been in Piccadilly. The leaders of the two most feared bands of brigands in the region, Kurdish and Arab, were faithful employees of the excavators, one as night watchman, the other in a similar position of trust. Of course there was no stealing and no danger. Had not these men eaten of the Englishmen's salt?"[40]

Woolley, who found Lawrence lovable and unusually able, was sensitive to the "feeling of essential immaturity," the persistent gifted-schoolboy in Lawrence. He teased Woolley with practical jokes, some of which Woolley found quite annoying, and made elaborate preparations for one of Hogarth's visits by decorating Hogarth's normally simple mud-walled room with pink satin curtains trimmed with lace and adorned with big pink bows. A pink cushion, hairpins, cheap scents and other reminders of domestic life were distributed about the room to make Hogarth feel "at home." Hogarth not unexpectedly flew into something of a rage when he discovered the joke, but Lawrence, according to Woolley, grinned over the jest for days.[41] Yet (also according to Woolley) Lawrence was himself unusually sensitive to ridicule and could not tolerate jokes made at his own expense.

In the actual work of the dig Woolley found Lawrence "curiously erratic," and whether he would work steadily or not depended on how much the particular task sustained his interest. Lawrence had responsibility for photography, sculpture and pottery. He could take careful notes but often was impatient with the written record. His memory for the fit of a particular Hittite fragment was extraordinary, and he could describe from memory the stratum and associations of a particular potsherd that had been excavated in a previous season, whether by Woolley or himself.[42] He "would make brilliant suggestions but would seldom argue in support of them," Woolley observed. "They were based on sound enough argument, but he expected you to see these for yourself, and if you did not agree he would relapse into silence and smile."[43]

His valuable contributions to the work at Carchemish notwithstanding, it is doubtful that Lawrence would ever have had the discipline, or the desire, to concentrate with sufficient singlemindedness on a particular academic project to become a professional archeologist. A passage in a letter home makes this clear. "At least," Lawrence wrote, after expressing concern whether he would ever accomplish his printing project with Richards, "I am not going to put all my energies into rubbish like writing history, or becoming an archeologist. I would much rather write a novel even, or become a newspaper correspondent."[44]

In the Carchemish period it becomes evident that Lawrence's central interest was in the *self*, not in himself in the sense of mere selfishness or egotism, for his remarkable generosity and kindness to the Arabs and to his friends, and the pains he undertook on behalf of almost anyone to whom he could be of service, have been testified to repeatedly. Rather, it was in perfecting and preparing himself through mastery. I believe this was as much an end in itself for Lawrence as it was a deliberate preparation for some great future task. Whether he was repairing the flue in the house chimney or perfecting his ability to shoot, or enduring the pain of broken ribs and the discomfort of dysentery, Lawrence was concentrating on making himself a perfected and refined instrument.

Ernest Altounyan is the only one of Lawrence's friends from this time who seems to have understood this quality. "Students of his life," Altounyan wrote, "cannot but be impressed by his persistence as a learner. Nothing could master him, but he proved a brilliant pupil in each successive school; until once more driven to tyranny by his unique sense of proportion. This quality has seldom met with its due regard in human history." Altounyan went on to say that Lawrence's "insistence on equality, running all up and down the human scale, is his finest flower," and that "taken in conjunction with an exquisite realization of self, it could hardly fail to be effective and place great power in the hands of the user."[45]

It was to E. T. Leeds, assistant keeper of antiquities at the Ashmolean, younger and less venerable than Hogarth (although venerable enough for Lawrence to address him frequently as "O Leeds") that Lawrence was able to express a Rabelaisian, bawdy side of his personality and his refusal to take things too seriously. This quality was not evident to the same degree in other letters written in these years — certainly not in those to his straitlaced mother. These letters, because of restrictions Leeds imposed on David Garnett, have not been published. Lawrence sent to Leeds a continuing stream of tiles, seals, pots, statues, sculptures and other antiquities with a running commentary to match. Of a homely statue of a Hittite woman Lawrence wrote, sending a drawing of her stolid form: "Only those like ourselves, who worship the silentness of beauty wrapped in darkness, can taste the full joy of her when she shows us her form stripped of the conventions that garb her in from public gaze. I had a half-hour of pure contemplation in ecstasy."[46] Later in the same vein he wrote: "I send you a lady, who is not steatopygous, stopping short modestly thereof. She is flint-age, from Jebail, in polished clay, and hideously ugly . . . but she will make a bust in your portrait gallery of Eve's more immediate descendants."[47] Another lady was "a goddess of the Hittites — Hittite — a creation O Leeds of a brick-maker I think. She is shaped like a whiskey-bottle, only rougher, with mighty breasts . . . a divinity indeed."[48] When a lion on a slab was damaged he wrote: "You ask us what would have been the effect on a lion of castrating it. . . . Well we didn't know exactly, so have tried on one of ours: all its mane dropped out, and it mews like a cat. The men say this becomes hereditary."[49]

Of the food shortage on a survey expedition Lawrence made equally light: "Our menu is a broad one, we eat bread and eggs: and Turkish delight. Only yesterday we finished the eggs, and nearest hens are three days' journey to the N. if only a camel would start laying we would be in Paradise tomorrow.

We have evolved rather a sporting dinner: Wooley you know likes a many storied edifice.

Hors d'oeuvre

The waiter (Dahoum) brings in on the lid of a petrol box half a dozen squares of Turkish delight,

Soup.
Bread soup.

Then

Turkish delight on toast

Then until yesterday

Eggs

Then, sweet . . .

Turkish delight
Dessert
Turkish delight

Of course bread is ad lib."[50]

When Lawrence heard that C. F. Bell, curator of art at the Ashmolean, was to be operated on for appendicitis, he wrote gently in an archeological motif: "If C. F. B. is really a son of Anak [a stalwart race that lived in Palestine before its conquest by the Israelites] he will be worth digging up. Let me know what they found inside: seriously, I hope all is well: 3 months is a long convalescence."[51]

By the beginning of March 1913, Lawrence's most exciting season of "furious" digging had begun, and he entertained himself and his friends with windy canoeing on the Euphrates. Archaeologically, this spring — the whole year in fact — proved to be very rewarding, with the excavation of many fine slabs and sculptures, "the richest British Museum digs since Layard's,"[52] but it also saw, sadly, the collapse of the mission school in Jebail.

In late June, Lawrence's archeological researches took him into new country down the Euphrates around Rakka in Mesopotamia, and in July he returned to England, bringing with him his two Arab friends from Carchemish: Dahoum, the donkey boy, and Hamoudi, the local foreman at the site. He housed them in his bungalow on Polstead Road. The visit was the cause of some difficulties and humor.[53]

One day when his mother and Janet Laurie were present, Lawrence pointed at Janet and asked Hamoudi, "How much is she worth?"

"No good, no good, no worth," came the forthright answer. ("I was a scrawny and miserable-looking thing," Janet explained to me).

Then, pointing to his mother, Lawrence asked, "How much is Mother worth?"

"Oh, a cow," answered Hamoudi. (In contrast to Janet, Mrs. Lawrence apparently looked better fed and more prosperous.)[54]

Upon their return to Jerablus in August Lawrence wrote home that "the Hoja [Hamoudi] and Dahoum entertain large houses nightly with tales of snakes as long as houses, underground railways, elephants, flying machines, and cold in July. I have not yet had the chance of hearing anything ludicrous. You know these two are too sophisticated to be comic in their relation: — they usually say the just — if unilluminative thing."[55]

In the fall the digging was resumed, the house was expanded and partitioned into twenty-two rooms, and Lawrence received a gift of a leopard from a government official in Aleppo.

If the first Syrian trip introduced Lawrence to the Arab world, it was in the Carchemish years that he learned about the Arab peoples. He became thoroughly conversant with the intricacies of their tribal and family jealousies, rivalries and taboos, their loves and hates, and their strengths and weaknesses. It was this carefully gathered knowledge, together with his remarkable ability to identify with the feelings and personal priorities of individual Arabs, to know the emotions and concerns upon which their self-esteem, security, power and prestige were based, that enabled Lawrence to win the confidence and acceptance of the Arab peoples, both during the Carchemish years and afterwards during the war.

The pages of his correspondence are filled with instances of his handling with tact, subtlety and strength countless disputes among the local Arab workmen, between the local people and various authorities, and of course between the Englishmen themselves and the local Arab and Turkish officials. If anything, Lawrence downplays his personal role in his description of events. Troubles seem to get settled magically since he fails to provide the evidence that would show precisely how he, or anyone else, manipulated people and events.

Shaykh Hamoudi, the chief local foreman at Carchemish, who was to go on to work with Woolley at Ur for more than two decades, was interviewed by Ernest Altounyan at the time of Lawrence's death. Hamoudi said that Lawrence's endurance seemed so great to the local people at Jerablus that they could not believe in his death, for "he could outride, outwalk, outshoot and outlast the best of them."[56]

Lawrence's ability to articulate for the Arabs their purposes and aims better than they could for themselves is attested to by Hamoudi: "While we would twist and turn with our object far away, almost out of sight, he would smile and point out to us what we were after, and make us laugh, ashamed."[57] Hamoudi's devotion to Lawrence was deep and intense, and depended in part upon his young friend's ability to empathize with the Arabs' thoughts and feelings. "Once," said Hamoudi, "he fell sick in my house and when it appeared that he would be very ill, the neighbors came around and advised me to put him out, lest he should die and his family should suspect me and the government put me in prison. I refused to listen; but before he lost consciousness he called me and said, 'Don't be afraid, Hamoudi. See, here on this paper I have written to my father to say that if I die you are not the cause.' So I fed him with milk and nursed him till he was well."[58]

This incident illustrates also how dangerously ill Lawrence was, probably during the 1911 walking journey across the Euphrates. Hamoudi said he grieved for him more than for a son he had lost. Passionately, with biblical phrases, Hamoudi declared to Altounyan ("pacing up and down the Aleppo stone paved hall"): "Tell them in England what I say. Of manhood the man, in freedom free; a mind without equal; I can see no flaw in him."[59]

Woolley and others have attested to Lawrence's rapport with the Arab men (his fluency in Arabic was an important ingredient in his success), but Woolley also says that Lawrence had no great liking for many individual Arabs (Dahoum and Hamoudi were among the exceptions).[60] Woolley observed astutely that Lawrence's ability to get along with the men hinged on a similarity between him and them, a childlike enjoyment in turning "the whole work into a game," the "fun of the thing" appealing to him as much as the scientific interest. In addition Lawrence's "uncanny knowledge of their family history gave Lawrence a peculiar prestige." It was Lawrence, again according to Woolley, who invented the system of saluting a discovery with revolver shots, proportioned to the importance of the discovery.

A streak of nihilism was present in Lawrence, even then. When Woolley would find Lawrence sitting with the men discussing a point of village custom or a question of local dialect and would object that no work was being done, Lawrence would grin and ask what anything mattered.[61]

The archeologists' cultivation of personal relationships with the Arabs and their attention to the individuality of the workmen and their families contrasted sharply with the autocratic way the German engineers handled the groups of Arab workers they employed to build the railroad. To the Germans a particular workman was usually just a number in a gang. This difference in treatment naturally worked to the advantage of the Englishmen in dealing with all sorts of local problems, and resulted for the Germans in endless delays in construction. According to Hubert Young, a young British officer who visited the camp in 1913, Lawrence "by his mere personality . . . had converted the excavation into a miniature British Consulate. His rough native workmen would have done anything for him."[62] Another visitor, Luther Fowle, reported that because "the Teuton could not see why the Arab should not and would not accept his regime of discipline and punishment" the Germans were always needing more laborers, "while the Englishmen a few hundred yards away, were overwhelmed with them."[63]

One practice the Englishmen developed that helped to foster loyalty among the workmen was the custom of giving extra piasters on payday for discoveries that the men brought to their employers. The archeologists would examine the item — a fragment of pottery, for example — and give a bonus according to its value, sometimes paying a small amount for a virtually valueless object in order to encourage the finder. This practice also had the advantage of assuring that the workmen took unusual care of what they found and did not lose, steal or break fragments of pottery and other articles.[64]

Most striking was Lawrence's ability to deal with a situation by applying his knowledge of the psychology of the individuals involved, and the local customs or beliefs to which they subscribed. On one occasion a local shaykh threatened to "ensorcel" Lawrence and his associates Campbell-Thompson and Hajj Wahid when they dismissed the shaykh's son from the dig. Force was recommended, but instead Lawrence suggested fighting local fire with local fire. The English should threaten to make a wax image of the old shaykh, which would be stuck with a pin through its heart at midnight. The ritual involved pulling out one of the last hairs from the shaykh's head. The threat of black magic worked and peace was restored.[65] Lawrence described to Hogarth another example of the use of sorcery, in this case to quell the bullying of a local gendarme.[66]

Lawrence was evidently quite capable of using force or direct intimidation when he thought it necessary. "He had," Woolley wrote, "a cool indomitable courage which showed itself clearly in such troubles as we had with Turks and Germans, its earnestness nearly always disguised by an imprudent enjoyment of the humor of the situation; he did not mind the risk, and the bluff appealed to him immensely."[67] Once Lawrence was stoned by several Kurdish tribesmen when he tried to stop them from

dynamiting fish. By threatening to have the local police inspector removed for incompetence, he browbeat the man into agreeing to punish
them.[68]

In an account written during World War I, Woolley describes
Lawrence's angry response to the flogging one of the German engineers
gave the Englishmen's houseboy for a minor offense. When Lawrence
accosted the director of the railway operation and accused the engineer
of assault, the following exchange took place:

"Herr X never assaulted the man at all; he merely had him flogged."

"Well, don't you call that an assault?"

"Certainly not. You can't use these natives without flogging them. We
have men thrashed every day — it's the only method."

"We've been here longer than you have and have never beaten one of
our men yet, and we don't intend to let you start on them."[69]

By threatening to flog the German engineer in front of the whole village, Lawrence was able to force a public apology from him, to the great
amusement of the villagers.

Lawrence's knowledge of family relationships within the tribes helped
him to prevent bloodshed from the vengeance of blood feuds. "Our people
are very curious and very simple," he wrote his family three months after
reaching Carchemish, "and yet with a fund of directness and child-humor
about them that is very fine. I see much of this, for I sleep on the mound
and start the work every day at sunrise, and the choosing of new men so
falls to my lot. I take great care in the selection, utterly refusing all such
as are solemn or over-polite, and yet we are continually bothered by
blood feuds, by getting into the same trench men who have killed each
other's kin or run off with their wives. They at once prepare to settle up
the score in kind, and we have to come down amid great shouting, and
send one to another pit. There is no desire to kill, and public opinion
does not insist on vengeance, if there is 50 feet of earth between the
offender and the offended."[70] Two years later one such feud broke out
among the workmen from two great families, and "the digs for six days
were two armed camps, not eating together, or speaking, walking the
same path, or labouring in the same gang."[71]

Because of his knowledge Lawrence took increasing responsibility for
arbitrating local disputes, a role he was to execute skillfully and painfully
during the war. Once with fifteen horsemen he retrieved a Kurdish girl
who had been abducted by one of the wealthy local Turks.[72] According
to Lawrence's brother Will, "The Kurds apply to him continually as arbi-
trator in tribal difficulties,"[73] and Fowle reported that "the even-handed
justice of the two Englishmen was so well known and respected that they
had come to be the judges of various issues of all sorts between rival
villages or in personal disagreement."[74]

Lawrence stressed his poverty, and enjoyed, especially on his tramps in Syria, living more roughly than most Westerners could or would consent to do. But this Spartan attitude was assumed more for self-training and because it was a realistic and effective way to live in that region than because of actual poverty, for money was available to him from the demyship and usually from the British Museum and from his family. "In 1914 I was a pocket Hercules," Lawrence wrote later, "as muscularly strong as people twice my size, and more enduring than most."[75] We have seen how comfortably Woolley and Lawrence lived, and how opulently Lawrence sometimes dressed. So it is more accurate to say that it was Lawrence's ability to take on the coloration of the people he was among, to live *as if he were* a poor native, which enabled him to enter the life of the local tribes and come to be so fully accepted.

As early as 1911 he was writing home of his preference for the Arab as compared to the European, and the destructive effect of the latter upon the former: "The perfectly hopeless vulgarity of the half-Europeanized Arab is appalling. Better a thousand times the Arab untouched. The foreigners come out here always to teach, whereas they had much better learn, for in everything but wits and knowledge the Arab is generally the better man of the two."[76] In 1914 his preference for things Arab had not yet extended to riding horses and camels, for according to Stewart Newcombe, "Lawrence at that time hated riding horses and had no love for a camel, preferring to walk."[77] By April 1914, Lawrence's involvement in the Middle East was such that he could write home: "I don't think that I will ever travel in the West again: one cannot tell of course, but this part out here is worth a million of the rest. The Arabs are so different from ourselves."[78]

Prominent in Lawrence during these years was a sense of fun, a joy in life, which, though childlike — or perhaps because it was childlike — his companions found infectious. Accompanied usually by his Arab friends, he thoroughly, and quite innocently, enjoyed himself, canoeing on the Euphrates and "sailing down the Syrian coast, bathing, harvesting, and sight-seeing in the towns. Certainly no hermitry!"[79] Winifred Fontana was referring, I believe, to this quality of innocence, violated and destroyed during the war, when she wrote to Robert Graves, upon reading his biography of Lawrence in 1927: "I am glad you passed on my memory of his youthful beauty and colour. Surely there were others who observed it? It is odd how vividly and how often I remembered that bright hair — all through the war when one wondered if it had been trampled into mud yet — and after, as if it were something significant in itself."[80]

From among the seemingly endless stream of visitors to the site, especially in the last year, from his wanderings, and from visits to Beirut, Smyrna, Jebail, Aleppo, Damascus and Cairo, Lawrence developed many friendships and acquaintances that enriched his life and also were of use to him later during the Revolt. The strength and importance of certain of Lawrence's friendships with other men ("comparable in intensity to sexual love, for which he made them a substitute," his brother Arnold wrote) became apparent during this period.[81]

With his increasing knowledge of the world Lawrence took on more and more the role of mentor to his younger brothers, and his letters were filled with somewhat pedantic advice and information about their schooling, facts of history, books, and the like. Although he was reserved in the expression of intimate feelings to his brothers, he addressed himself to their individuality, supported their right to choose their own course, and did not urge them to be like himself. "Frank, I suppose goes up [to Jesus College, Oxford] in October," he wrote in 1913, "and there will be the usual heartburning as to whether he is to live in or not. As a social being he would probably prefer to, and if so he may like a Phoenician bronze bowl as an ashtray . . . for accept my prophecy as sure that he will begin to smoke soon. It is an imitative vice, like short hair, which insinuates itself. In case he lives at home, he must have my little house: — it is for the reverse reason . . . I had it that I might be quiet: Frank that he may be noisy . . . and it speaks many things for the catholicity of the place, that it is equally adapted for each."[82] Arnold — twelve by this time — Lawrence entertained with accounts of battles and animated descriptions of adventures with Dahoum (who was only fifteen at the time), and of crocodiles, hippopotami, spiders, scorpions, snakes and sepulchers.

Lawrence found R. Campbell-Thompson, the other archeologist who was at Carchemish during the early months at the dig, to be "good fun" and pleasant, but was troubled by his jingoism and his excessive love of guns. "I think Thompson is a little cracked," he wrote home with some concern. "He has brought out two rifles with about 200 cartridges, and some revolvers with hundreds of cartridges, and sabres and fencing masks (stolen at Haifa fortunately) and hundreds of useless stuffs."[83]

Lawrence found much more in common with Woolley, whom he had known at Oxford, and admired, at least at first, his aggressive way of handling difficulties. "You should have seen Woolley," he wrote Leeds. "When the police tried to hold up his donkeys, he charged down upon them, drawing his revolver from his sash with the 126 tassels, and shouting mixed Greek, Arab, Italian, English and Turkish. Arrived at the spot he shouldered aside the Corporal and the guard, and pulled the donkey-line himself. The beast, like all donkeys, wouldn't go without being dragged. However, Woolley dragged him."[84]

But they were not personally close, and although they served together in Cairo during the war, seem not to have corresponded thereafter. Woolley found Lawrence "the best of companions," but also very reserved and detached in spite of their many long talks. Lawrence would undo with ridicule any "sentiment" he expressed. After Lawrence's death Woolley wrote:

> I do not remember his ever admitting to any affection for anybody though I knew perfectly well that in the case of certain people the affection was there and deeply felt; in all matters of the emotions he seemed to have a peculiar distrust of himself. Similarly he never discussed religion, at least in its personal aspects, but he gave to Hamoudi an Arabic version of the synoptic gospels and was very pleased to find that it impressed him; but he hated missionary activities and was vitriolic in his abuse of missions, though one of his best friends in Syria was Miss Holmes of the American mission at Jebail. He was fond of talking to the men about the Moslem faith, but had no admiration for it except for its insistence on the virtue of charity.[85]

Hogarth remained the strongest guiding force in Lawrence's life during these years, although Charles Doughty seemed to have been a kind of spiritual forebear. Hogarth stayed at Carchemish only for two months (March and April) in 1911, supervising the digging thereafter from England. Lawrence's attitude toward his mentor was one of boyish awe. "Mr. Hogarth is a most splendid man," he wrote home in March 1911, and "has read, and still reads most things, and likes talking about them and the people who write."[86]

By the spring of 1914 the awe was no less, though it could be tinged with humor: "A breathless hush of expectation — and the scratching of this pen — relieve the usual clatter of our house," Lawrence wrote Leeds. "This is Sunday, and we are all dressed in our best, sitting in our empty, swept, and garnished rooms, awaiting the coming of the CHIEF. He is expected today: and is coming heavy with importance: Woolley is nervous, and I myself can only exist in scribbling to you."[87]

In November 1911, before returning to the East, Lawrence arranged to see Doughty once again in order to discuss his travels. He wrote beforehand, "I have been a twelve-month in Northern Syria [actually only eight months unless the four months in 1909 are included, but Lawrence had already written Doughty about his first trip], some four months of which I spent with Mr. Hogarth digging up what was left of the Hittites in the ruins of Carchemish on the Euphrates" (actually only two months were spent digging with Hogarth). Soon after returning, Lawrence took a letter from Doughty to one al-Bassam, a former friend of Doughty's who lived in Damascus. Lawrence discovered that memories of Doughty from thirty-five years back remained alive among the Arabs of Syria, and faithfully reported the gratifying fact to the old traveler.[88]

Doughty remained for Lawrence throughout these years and afterwards the inspiration for his travels in Arab countries, and provided him with an outstanding example of how to learn about Arab peoples through living among them. "I am not trying to rival Doughty," Lawrence wrote his family in May of 1912. "You remember that passage that he who has once seen palm-trees and the goat-hair tents is never the same as he had been: that I feel very strongly, and I feel also that Doughty's two years wandering in untainted places made him the man he is, more than all his careful preparation before and since."[89]

It was in the Carchemish period that Lawrence began to cultivate a widening circle of friends who complemented the multiple facets of his personality. Each seemed to lay claim to knowledge of some piece of him, the more uncritical insisting upon the congruence between a shifting part and the whole. Yet his brother Arnold, who knew him well, acknowledged that T.E. "when he had just been with someone or was just going to see someone . . . tended to take on the characteristics of that person,"[90] with the result that each could find an aspect of himself or herself in Lawrence. Sometimes common acquaintanceship with Lawrence brought his friends into new relationships with each other, but more often he kept his relationships isolated — "separated by bulkheads" was the phrase Graves used to describe this quality.[91]

Lawrence began to look among artists and writers for his friends, valuing them often too highly as he valued himself too little. They in turn found in Lawrence, of whom they seemed to have been universally fond, an object of imagination or beauty for their work. Ernest Altounyan, in whose father's Aleppo home Lawrence spent many enjoyable hours, devoted a small book of poetry to Lawrence (to my knowledge Altounyan's only published poetry), and Winifred Fontana, the wife of the Aleppo consul, was moved upon seeing Lawrence at Carchemish — "his fine eyes lost in thought about Doughty's *Arabia Deserta,* open across his knees" — to pull out her sketch pad and start drawing him. Even his brother Will was inspired several months after his visit to Carchemish to write a poem ("To T.E.L.") predicting his potential greatness. Lawrence in turn would sometimes find aspects of himself in the personalities and work of his friends.

Lawrence's friend James Elroy Flecker, who served as the British vice consul in Beirut in 1911 and 1912, died in a sanatorium in Switzerland early in 1915. Lawrence thought highly of Flecker's poetry and called him "the sweetest singer of the war generation." He drafted an essay on Flecker in 1925, and described him as "always embroidering, curling, powdering, painting, his loves and ideals, demonstrative, showy, self advertising, happy."[92]

When Lawrence was fond of someone, he was wont to take unusual pains on their behalf. He provided great support to Fareedah el Akle in her struggles with her employer, the strict Miss Holmes, and wrote to her at length, offering advice and help for which she was very grateful.[93] Lawrence seemed always ready to fulfill requests one might have thought irritating, such as the call for an iron dog collar that interested a lady in England who had four Arab dogs. For his ailing friend Flecker, Lawrence wrote in June 1914, simply to entertain him, a long, satirical account of a "battle" between the Circassians guarding the German railway activities and the Kurdish and Arab railway workmen.[94] When he was unable to keep an appointment he had made with a lady in August 1912, Lawrence wrote on the same day two slightly different letters of apology, sending one by rail and one by post lest one of them fail to reach her in time.[95] Mrs. Fontana has described the extraordinary consideration that Lawrence showed to her and her children when they visited the site. He made sure they had a dry place to sleep, enticed a band of Kurdish musicians to play and sing for them, took her canoeing on the "swirling" Euphrates and then to an island to gather wildflowers, and paddled "the difficult and dangerous return journey against the current with a coolness and skill that fired my imagination."[96] That he could be deliberately inconsiderate and rude like a naughty schoolboy when someone annoyed him, or was acting pompously, is also well known.

Clearly the most valued relationship of all for Lawrence at Carchemish was with Dahoum, the waterboy or donkey boy at Jerablus. He was only fourteen when Lawrence first met him in the spring of 1911. According to Woolley he was nicknamed Dahoum by his mother at birth because he was a very black baby (Dahoum is a form of *tehoum*, which means "the darkness that was on the face of the waters before creation").[97] Other of Lawrence's biographers say he was called Sheikh Ahmed, though Lawrence provides no direct confirmation of this. Thomas Beaumont, who served with Lawrence in the desert but never met Dahoum, said his name was Salim Ahmed, but no substantiating evidence for the "Salim" exists.[98] By Lawrence's description Dahoum was "mixed Hittite and Arab," and Woolley states that his family lived on the *qal'a* (the mound, which had formerly been a fortress or citadel), and thus traced his lineage from the original inhabitants of the area. Woolley saw a resemblance between Dahoum's face and "those rather heavy and fleshy captains who head the sculptured procession at the portal of our Hittite Palace."[99]

Lawrence found Dahoum an immensely appealing boy, more intelligent than most of the local Arab and Kurdish inhabitants, and taught him photography and other skills that were useful in the work. On Lawrence's many trips away from the site, Dahoum was his frequent companion. They swam together often, and talked a great deal to each other and shared many hours of silence. Lawrence admired the way Dahoum spoke Arabic and wrote Miss Fareedah, "If I could talk it like Dahoum . . . you would never be tired of listening to me."[100] When Lawrence became dangerously ill with dysentery during the journey across the Euphrates in the summer of 1911, Dahoum visited Lawrence daily at Hamoudi's home, and Lawrence in turn tended Dahoum the following year when the latter became ill with a malignant form of malaria and nearly died.

The subject of further education for Dahoum, who talked of going to school in Aleppo, came up frequently. But for Lawrence Dahoum represented the pure and natural simplicity of the Arab unspoiled by Western influences, and he was hostile toward the idea of formal education for him. Dahoum's personality supplied, as Arnold Lawrence indicated in a note in the 1911 diary, "the largest element to the figure of S.A.," to whom Lawrence dedicated *Seven Pillars of Wisdom*.[101]

In addition to the close companionship between them, Dahoum represented for Lawrence an aspect of an ideal he sought: the pure descendant of an ancient Eastern race uncorrupted by Western influences. Lawrence called him still in 1912 a savage "who wrestled beautifully."[102] Woolley wrote that Dahoum was "beautifully built and remarkably handsome" and that the village was scandalized by the intimacy of the friendship, especially when Lawrence had Dahoum pose for a naked figure he carved in the soft local limestone and set up on the edge of the house roof. But Woolley denies firmly that there was any sexual relationship between Dahoum and Lawrence, and stresses Lawrence's puritanical nature.[103]

Dahoum's personality was to a great degree "created" by Lawrence to serve as a kind of ideal self stripped of its Western complexities, a self Lawrence sought to achieve. Arnold Lawrence, who was thirteen and a half when T.E. brought Dahoum and Hamoudi to Oxford, observed how like a son Dahoum was to his brother, "made into what he was by the older man." The family became fond of Dahoum, sixteen by this time, and Mrs. Lawrence tried, to her sons' amusement, to break through the language barrier by speaking to him in French during his visit to Oxford.[104]

When Lawrence left Carchemish and returned to England in June 1914, Hajj Wahid and Dahoum were left to dispose of what was left behind at the site. During the war Dahoum was appointed guardian of the site by the Turks and thus exempted from service in the Turkish army,[105] but he died of typhus before the war ended.[106] Lawrence's grief over this loss was strong and deep and probably inspired the dedicatory poem in *Seven Pillars of Wisdom* ("To S.A."), as Dahoum came to embody the joy and innocence which Lawrence lost in the war and felt he had once had at Carchemish. Later, at a time of unhappiness in the Tank Corps, Lawrence wrote to a young friend, with whom he had been able to share in the RAF ranks a companionship somewhat similar to the one he had known with Dahoum: "You and me, we're very unmatched and it took some process as slow and kindly and persistent as the barrack room to weld us comfortably together. People aren't friends till they have said all they can say, and are able to sit together, at work or rest, hour long without speaking. We never got quite to that, but we're nearer it daily . . .

and since S.A. died I haven't experienced any risk of that's happening."[107]
In 1919 when he was working on *Seven Pillars of Wisdom*, Lawrence
wrote on the back flyleaf of a book of poetry the following note, obviously
concerned with his feelings for Dahoum: "A (?) I wrought for him freedom to lighten his sad eyes: but he had died waiting for me. So I threw
my gift away and now not anywhere will I find rest and peace."[108]

9

The Epic Dream
and the Fact of War

In September 1910, three months before Lawrence set off for the Middle East and for Carchemish, he wrote his mother a letter containing the following passage: "It is lovely after you have been wandering in the forest with Percivale or Sagramors le desirous, to open the door, and from the Cherwell to look at the sun glowering through the valley-mists. Why does one not like things if there are other people about? Why cannot one make one's books live except in the night, after hours of straining? and you know they have to be your own books too, and you have to read them more than once. I think they take in something of your personality, and your environment also — you know a second hand book sometimes is so much more flesh and blood than a new one — and it is almost terrible to think that your ideas, yourself in your books may be giving life to generations of readers after you are forgotten. It is that specially which makes one need good books: books that will be worthy of what you are going to put into them. What would you think of a great sculptor who flung away his gifts on modelling clay or sand? Imagination should be put into the most precious caskets, and that is why one can only live in the future or the past, in Utopia, or the Wood Beyond the World. Father won't know all this — but if you can get the right book at the right time you taste joys — not only bodily, physical, but spiritual also, which pass one out above and beyond one's miserable self, as it were through a huge air, following the light of another man's thoughts. And you can never be quite the old self again. You have forgotten a little bit: or rather pushed it out with a little of the inspiration of what is immortal in someone who has gone before you."[1]

The letter is one of the more revealing that Lawrence wrote. It discloses his view that it is his mother with whom he can share the deeper,

spiritual side of himself, that "Father won't know all this." It explains his
interest in printing in order to give great books — whether someone else's
or his own — a form worthy of the quality of their content. Above all it
reveals the degree to which this twentieth-century Percivale, this modern
grail-seeker, lived in the imagination, especially in the imagination of
others. Even at twenty-two he could write of the need to pass out beyond
his "miserable self" and to follow "the light of another man's thought" —
finding "the right book at the right time" — especially by someone he
could regard as immortal. The present would not do, though he would
always live in the present and master its requirements. Lawrence felt he
could "only live in the future or the past, in Utopia." He tried to achieve
this in two ways in the years that followed — through trying to transform
a baser reality into a lofty ideal in a war, and through his own subsequent
effort at writing an epic. For Lawrence present life was measured always
against an ideal of the imagination, particularly a medieval ideal, and his
most important actions, especially during the war years, may be seen as
efforts to impose upon grimmer circumstances, to which he had also to
adapt, his utopian imaginings.

Lawrence recognized that this idealistic questing was to some extent a
family problem shared with his brothers. In a letter to his family, written
soon after arriving at Carchemish, he referred to himself as "an artist of
sorts and a wanderer after sensations," and reassured his parents that "one
of us must surely get something of the unattainable we are all feeling
after."[2] Fareedah el Akle, with whom he found so much in common, seems
to have possessed a feminine counterpart to Lawrence's hero fantasies.
She once wrote to him: "I never told you that my great desire was (when
young) to be an Arab princess. I mean to say to have been born among
them as an Arab princess."[3]

Lawrence's writings during the Carchemish years, so filled with accounts of his learning, of mastery and of the details of his daily life and
adventures, give little evidence of the workings of the epic dream as they
were expressed in his writings after the experiences of the war years. At
Carchemish life itself, celibate, intense and full, was experienced as ideal,
an existence in which the biblical past, freed of the degradations of the
modern world could, with a minimum of stretching of the imagination,
be experienced as a perfection in the present.

It would be fascinating to know the degree to which Lawrence actually
lived out his daily experiences in terms of the imaginative vistas created
for him by the authors he was reading. Unless we know this, it is mere
speculation to attribute significance to the choice of books at a given time.
Yet this choice, probably more than a matter of taste, may have psychological meaning, especially if a pattern can be perceived. At Carchemish
Lawrence's predilection for medieval epic works is still evident, especially early in these years, although he began to show an interest in more

modern French and English literature. Doughty's works, epic in style themselves, continued to be important to him.

On his walking trip in northern Syria in search of castles, seals and "strange people and places," Lawrence had with him "my Rabelais, Holy Grail, Rossetti and Roland."[4] But it is the works of William Morris, especially his Victorian-Icelandic-Anglo-Saxon-German epic poem *Sigurd the Volsung*, that moves and inspires Lawrence most at this time. Over and over he urges this book on his parents and friends with repeated demands to know their opinion of it. He called it "the best poem I know" and was delighted as the members of the family, upon his urging, revealed that they were reading it. He was especially pleased when he learned his mother was reading it, and he related it to his life among the Arab peoples. "So mother reads Sigurd!" he enthused. "I want to know whether it is the most beautiful book any of you have ever seen: and what she thinks of the telling of the tale: remember the tale itself is Norse, and it is perhaps the most near to us of all the Norse tales — the one we can best assimilate and enjoy — better of course, if one knows a simple people, as I happen to know the Arabs."[5]

How one reacts to the "telling" of such a tale is, I suppose, a matter of cultural perspective and literary taste as well as of personal psychology. To a reader of the present age, at least to this reader, the poem seems terribly dated, disjointed — in fact, silly. The Icelandic versions (Morris had traveled in Iceland) of Anglo-Saxon and Teutonic myths of several generations and tribes of barbarian peoples were purified in Morris's Victorian poetry. His *Sigurd* is filled with the familiar medieval glorification of certain loves, lusts, murders, wars and vendettas, and the disparagement of others. What is interesting from the standpoint of Lawrence's psychology in this transparently Oedipal tale is the degree to which the story is dominated, and the action of the male heroes determined, by the loves and wills of passionate beautiful women and demigoddesses, from whom all important knowledge and power derive. Morris depicts a world of jealousy and conflicting loyalties on the part of both men and women, a world in which treachery, betrayal and vengeance abound, and in which powerful women use the instrumentality of love to manipulate their sons, husbands and lovers, and to inspire them to perform deeds of heroism on their behalf and to their greater glory.

Another favorite book of Lawrence's in this period was Maurice Hewlett's *Richard Yea and Nay* ("Read *Richard Yea and Nay* in Egypt for the ninth time. It is a masterpiece"),[6] a turn-of-the-century novel which tells how Richard I's indecisiveness cost him the love of his sweetheart. Perhaps this story recalled for Lawrence the consequences of his own hesitations with Janet Laurie.

It is difficult to appreciate in the 1970's the gulf that separates us — a gulf that Lawrence helped to create — from the pre-World War I generation of educated Englishmen, many of whom could view the approach of war with exhilaration. In April 1915, Churchill could still find in Rupert Brooke's death something glorious and exciting, the embodiment of the "spirit of 1914," a voice "more true, more thrilling, more able to do justice to the nobility of our youth in arms engaged in this present war, than any other — more able to express their thoughts of self-surrender, and with a power to carry comfort to those who watched them so intently from afar."[7] Apart from Lawrence's personal psychology, in his devotion to the heroic romance he was part of this spirit of 1914, for in these tales, as in the idealism of the prewar generation, war appears to have little objectionable reality, and its murder, bloodshed, grief, inanity, cruelty and pain all glow in a hazy light of greatness, of glory and of nobility.

The idea that Lawrence, while at Carchemish, was employed by the British government to spy on the Germans on the railway and to engage in other espionage activity under the guidance of David Hogarth has been stressed recently by Knightley and Simpson.[8] "There can be no doubt," they say, "that the dig had a dual purpose" of espionage and archeology. They assert Lawrence's connection, through a tenuous series of links via Hogarth and Lionel Curtis (whom he did not meet until after the war), to the precepts of the Round Table, an organization of politically minded British intellectuals who were not themselves involved with spy activities.[9]

In 1965 I had the opportunity to discuss this question with Hogarth's son, William. He could, of course, have been incompletely informed about his father's activities, but seemed confident that David Hogarth had been candid with him: there was military intelligence but no official secret service in 1912, and many British subjects, especially consuls and officers working overseas, were spies in an informal sense, that is, subject to being asked by Foreign Office officials upon their return from sensitive areas what they might have seen or heard. In the Ottoman Empire, Hogarth said, every British official was a spy, but that "neither my father nor Lawrence were officially employed as spies." Hogarth and Sir Edward Grey, who was Foreign Secretary from 1905 to 1916, had been to public school together at Winchester and were in frequent contact before the war, and through such informal channels Hogarth kept the Foreign Office informed, to the extent of his knowledge, regarding the activities of the Turks and Germans in Syria, and naturally enlisted the help of Lawrence, who was constantly on the scene at Carchemish, in this service.[10]

Remarks of Lawrence's in his letters have been quoted by Villars and by Knightley and Simpson as evidence of spying; for example, "the strongly-dialectical Arabic of the villagers would be as good as a disguise to me";[11] and, "for some reason Mr. Hogarth is very anxious to make me learn Arabic."[12] These comments suggest that if Lawrence was involved in espionage he was unevenly informed of his leader's purposes.

Lawrence certainly made efforts to keep Hogarth informed about the progress of the Baghdad Railway and was naturally pleased with delays the Germans incurred in its construction. "Can you tell D.G.H.," he wrote Leeds in February 1913, "on the authority of Mr. Contzen [the railway manager] here, that station construction E. of Harran is suspended at least temporarily, and the men sent home? And that yesterday I walked over the wooden bridge and entered Mesopotamia dry-shod? and that they are knocking in the iron piers of the permanent thing? He always asks after the Baghdad railway."[13]

Lawrence hardly behaved like the model secret service agent. According to Hubert Young, Lawrence told him that one of the German engineers suspected him of spying on the railway and causing difficulties with the local labor. However, wrote Young, "he [Lawrence] did not go out of his way to remove this impression," but on the contrary, took a mischievous delight in rousing the German engineer's suspicions: "He even told us that he had gone so far as to drag some large pipes up to the top of the mound, whereupon the German had reported in a frantic telegram, which somehow fell into his hands, that the mad Englishman was mounting guns to command the railway-bridge over the Euphrates."[14] By the summer of 1913 Lawrence had apparently succeeded in rousing the suspicions of the Ottoman authorities, for he wrote, probably to Hogarth: "The old government has life in it yet . . . it is beginning to keep watch on where I go: at least the ombashi came to me this afternoon, grinning, with orders to go down to Abu Galgal [in northwestern Mesopotamia] with me to protect me . . . as he said 'praise God you are already back, I can perform my duty without ceasing.' "[15] Colonel Stewart Newcombe, who was based in Cairo at the time, wrote Ronald Storrs in 1953 that "to suggest that either man [Woolley or Lawrence] was secretly working for M.I. [Military Intelligence] before that date is, to me, ridiculous."[16]

The matter would seem to have been laid to rest by a letter written in 1969 by R. D. Barnett, keeper of Western antiquities at the British Museum, to *The Times Literary Supplement* after reading a review there of Knightley' and Simpson's book. Barnett summarized the archeological interest in Carchemish since at least 1876 and wrote, "There is not the least evidence of ulterior motives in the choice of the site." He reviewed the private (that is, nongovernmental) funding of the work, pointed out that the British Museum was the natural body for administering it, and concluded emphatically: "No suggestion, therefore, of political or sinister purpose whatever can be seen by us to attach to this phase of Lawrence's and Hogarth's career as far as we are aware."[17]

What is more striking from my own point of view than serious intelligence activity is the curious innocence of the archeologists of Carchemish, the lack of serious concern (like most of their generation) about the clouds of war which they could see gathering in the West and in the Middle East from 1912 to 1914, as the Ottoman Empire began to crumble under the attacks of Italy and the Balkan League. Even in 1913 and 1914 seemingly endless streams of visitors of many nationalities came to Carchemish, while the great powers were arming and the preliminary bouts of World War I were being fought. In Lawrence's letters to his family during the 1909 trip to Syria he indicated his awareness of secret native Christian societies in Beirut and Damascus, but the leaders of the political secret societies out of which the Arab nationalist movement grew were drawn from privileged Muslim families.[18] There is no evidence that Lawrence was in touch with these societies.

Lawrence's concerns about Germany and the Germans seem entirely parochial, and he felt that the skirmishes and battles involving the British archeologists and the German railroad managers reflected little more than the working conditions of the railway workers and the route of the railroad bed. Lawrence was aware in the beginning of 1912 of "great rumors of wars and annexations." These were "not to be believed yet, but such a smash is coming out here."[19] Eight weeks later he wrote to Leeds, "Haldane,° according to consul, is negotiating an entente with Germany." But, added Lawrence innocently, "I have anticipated him, in arranging one with the Teutons here. There is nothing but supping and giving to sup. Haj Wahid looks worried, as though in coming to Jerablus he had not anticipated dinner-parties. However, D.G.H. said: 'be very pleasant to the Railway' and we walk about with our arms round each other's necks."[20]

By November Bulgaria had broken with Turkey after a short war and Lawrence observed that she "has every possibility of finishing off Turkey (if the powers let her) because the Turks are such helpless stupids," but they (the archeologists) "will sit out here and look on at what is going to come of Turkey,"[21] despite the fact that Turkey was already frantically levying "every able-bodied man as soldier," thereby causing a problem in finding workers at the site. The following March Lawrence wrote home irritatedly, "Germany is going in for armaments, England for insurances, and all of them for nonsense . . . consider the suffragettes."[22] But despite all of this, 1913 proved to be Lawrence's best year archeologically speaking, and the pleasures of canoeing on the Euphrates continued.

There is little in Lawrence's letters of this period that indicates much enthusiasm for the potentialities for Arab freedom that the destruction of the Ottoman Empire might mean, probably in part because he was aware of the importance of retaining a show of neutrality while working within the Ottoman Empire, and the danger to his position that might result should a politically pro-Arab letter be read by the Turkish authorities. He did, however, write cautiously on April 5, 1913, during the first Balkan War: "As for Turkey, down with the Turks! But I am afraid there is, not life, but stickiness in them yet. Their disappearance would mean a chance

---

° Richard Haldane, the lord chancellor, had been sent by the British cabinet on an official peace mission to Germany early in 1912.

for the Arabs, who were at any rate once not incapable of good government."[23]

In January 1914, Lawrence and Woolley were called on a two months' survey of the eastern Sinai (the region known in the Bible as the Wilderness of Zin) and the region of Wadi 'Araba from Aqaba to Petra, under the sponsorship of the Palestine Exploration Fund. In this expedition, which was initiated by Lord Kitchener and supervised by Stewart Newcombe, an archeological "cover" concealed a political and strategic purpose. During the expedition Lawrence became familiar with the region, especially around Aqaba, knowledge of which was to prove especially valuable during the campaigns of 1917. He was aware of the political nature of the expedition and wrote home that "we are obviously only meant as red herrings, to give an archeological colour to a political job."[24] The purpose of the survey was to complete the mapping of this area, which was of particular importance because it constituted the border region between Egypt and the Ottoman Empire. Nonetheless, Turkey gave permission to survey north of Aqaba, but not around Aqaba itself, which probably accounted for the resistance to mapping, photography and archeologizing Lawrence encountered from the governor there.

It was during this time that Lawrence first met William Yale, a young American who was surveying in the Negev for a road to be built by the Standard Oil Company. Yale recalls coming across Lawrence, Woolley and Newcombe at Beersheba in January 1914. Yale was annoyed because he felt Lawrence "played me for a sucker," revealing nothing of what he was doing in the desert, pretending to be sight-seeing, and asking Yale and his party if they had seen Petra and this or that ruins. Lawrence later told Yale that he had received a telegram from London ordering him to get in touch with Yale's party and find out what "some American oil men" were up to in the desert.[25]

Lawrence's excitement at being "alone in Arabia" (that is, at Aqaba) with no Western companion, and visiting the beautiful ruins of Petra, alternates with arrogant accounts of his struggles with the Ottoman authorities. The Turkish government was understandably "sore" to discover that their permission given to survey for purposes of archeological and biblical research, however foolishly granted, was turned into part of what Lawrence called "a military game." Lawrence returned to the dig in March for a last season, closed the site in June, and returned to England. He then worked on writing up the archeological findings, and the report of the survey was elaborately published by the Palestine Exploration Fund early in 1915 with the title *The Wilderness of Zin,* a kind of archeological whitewash. A shorter report was published by Woolley in the 1914 statement of the Palestine Exploration Fund.[26]

By the time he returned to England, Lawrence had become highly skilled and resourceful, with an extraordinary capacity to adapt himself to a great range of situations and challenges. Though not yet twenty-six he had demonstrated his abilities as a leader of other men through his capacity to do most things better than they could; by his courage and his willingness to do almost anything first before he expected someone else to do it; by his readiness to take responsibility even for matters that were only his concern because he made them so; and above all through his capacity to understand a problem as it was perceived by other people. He was especially effective in leading Arab peoples, whose language he spoke, and they were awed by his knowledge of their ways and by his apparent fearlessness. He could also be as boyish or seemingly innocent as they, and this permitted him to get close to them. When it came to getting the natives in and around Carchemish to be vaccinated against cholera, of which one might think they would be suspicious, he had no difficulty. "I can get that done most easily," he wrote his family doctor, "for the Arabs do as I want most charmingly."[27]

We have seen also that he was well on his way to rejecting his British, his Western, identity and to assuming a new one among the Arabs. At the same time he rejected particularly the Ireland of his origins. "Why go to such a place," he wrote home upon hearing that his father was in Ireland.[28] A few months later he advised his parents, "Don't go to Ireland, even to play golf. I think the whole place repulsive historically: they should not like English people, and we certainly cannot like them."[29]

Lawrence's romantic and somewhat ambivalent asceticism, his longing for a simple life of poverty and renunciation while at the same time enjoying many creature comforts, relates to this same dilemma. His attitudes are beautifully reflected in a short essay he wrote for his college magazine in 1912, which appeared in the 1912–1913 issue. The essay is a description of a trip that Lawrence and Dahoum were taken on by a poor old Arab man and a boy to the ruins of a great palace in the desert between Aleppo and Hama. They passed through a succession of rooms, courts and arcades filled with the rich scents of jasmine and of tropical blossoms until they came to a great hall. Here, "the mingled scents of all the palace . . . combined to slay each other, and all that one felt was the desert sharpness of the air as it swept off the huge uncontaminated plains. 'Among us,' said Dahoum, 'we call this room the sweetest of them all,' therein half-consciously sounding the ideal of the Arab creed, for generations stripping itself of all furniture in the working out of a gospel of simplicity."[30] The piece is signed anonymously "C.J.G."

During the early months at Carchemish Lawrence had planned to build a house on property he owned in Epping Forest and to print on a hand press with his friend Richards fine illuminated works, following the lead of William Morris and his Kelmscott Press. His letters home are full of discussions with and instructions to his father regarding the business aspects of this scheme, much of which has been gratuitously omitted from the published *Home Letters*. Gradually, however, Lawrence came to question Richards's business sense and his own suitability for the project. Finally, recognizing his increasing involvement in the Arab world he backed out uncomfortably in December 1913, writing his friend in conclusion: "Carchemish will not be finished for another four or five years: and I'm afraid that after that I'll probably go after another and another nice thing: it is rather a miserable come down. I haven't any money; can I offer you a carpet? They are about the only things remaining out here that are any good: Arabs have no handicrafts."[31]

His brother Will evidently had confidence that the "another and another nice thing" would include something worthwhile, for two months later he dedicated "To T.E.L." the following lines:

> *I've talked with counsellors and lords*
> *Whose words were as no blunted swords,*
> *Watched two Emperors and five Kings*
> *And three who had men's worshippings,*
> *Ridden with horsemen of the East*
> *And sat with scholars at their feast,*
> *Known some the masters of their hours,*
> *Some to whom years were as pressed flowers:*
> *Still as I go this thought endures*
> *No place too great to be made yours.*[32]

THREE

THE WAR YEARS, 1914–1918

Introduction

Lawrence's five years of travel, study, and work as an archeologist in Syria, Palestine and Anatolia made it natural that he would find his way into the British military service as an intelligence officer at British headquarters in Cairo. He was exceptionally suited for this work. It was perhaps less predictable that in less than two years he would find himself in the role of a leader of a modern guerrilla war in the Arabian desert. For by the end of 1916 he was in the process of galvanizing the flagging Arab Revolt (restricted at that time to the Bedouin of the Hijaz) into a campaign which would carry ultimately to Damascus and beyond.

From the standpoint of both the historian and the psychologist the war years, especially 1917 and 1918 — the two years of his participation in the Revolt — were the most critical of Lawrence's life. Although his public contributions continued after the war, his historical importance grew out of his activities and accomplishments during those two years. Whatever his subsequent opinions of his wartime achievements, without them there would have been no Lawrence of Arabia as a figure of actuality or of legend.

From the personal or psychological standpoint the years of the Revolt were a watershed for Lawrence. Until the war he was an unusual, versatile and reasonably well-balanced genius with a somewhat undisciplined passion for archeology, a long-standing interest in medieval military architecture and literature, and a great capacity for friendship with all sorts of people. The application of his varied gifts in the service of the Arab Revolt, while they resulted in extraordinary accomplishments and furnished the ingredients of a peculiarly contemporary heroic example and legend, included for Lawrence personally a series of shattering experiences, the psychological impact of which he was forced to contend with for most of the remaining years of his life. These psychological changes, and the unusual insights Lawrence brought to bear in trying to understand and deal with his suffering, have provided the psychologically minded biographer with an unusual opportunity to learn something about a person (and to a varying degree we all share some of his characteristics) who is compelled to live out the demands of his inner life in the public domain.

10

The Background of
the Arab Revolt

The revolt of the sharif of Mecca, Husayn Ibn Ali, and his sons against the Ottoman authority in June 1916 provided Lawrence with a unique opportunity to exercise his diverse talents. These abilities, the most important of which was his capacity to enable the fragmented Arab tribesmen of the Hijaz and portions of Syria to translate their passion to be free of Turkish rule into an effective military operation, had to be exercised in the context of British war policy in the Middle Eastern theatre. This dual purpose — of motivating and guiding the Arab Revolt, while at the same time, as a British officer, serving his country's military and political policies — was inescapable, having been built into his situation from the outset. It renders to a large degree futile the arguments, however carefully based on his own dispatches to higher British authorities, that he was really serving British imperial policy rather than the cause of Arab independence. He was, by the very definition of his situation — he played, to be sure, a major part in *choosing* to enact his special role among the Arabs — attempting to do both.

The history of Lawrence's actions and writings during the war years needs to be seen in terms of his struggle to reconcile these two purposes, which at times were in substantial conflict. Although his position in serving two masters was not his only source of torment, it was nevertheless very real. In order to understand his position during the war, it is necessary to explore the background of the situation in which he found himself in Cairo when he arrived there in December 1914 and to review the development of British policy in the Middle East up to the onset of the Arab Revolt.

To the Arab peoples, the conquest by the Ottoman Turks in the early years of the sixteenth century of territories that included what is now

Egypt, Syria, Lebanon, Israel, Iraq, Jordan and the lands of the Arabian Peninsula along the east coast of the Red Sea, represented the substitution of rule by one sultan for rule by another. Not since the tenth century, when the Muslim Empire of the Prophet Muhammad began to disintegrate, had the Arab peoples known any semblance of political unity, and they had never, of course, experienced national unity in our modern sense. From that time until the present day the political history of the Arab world has been marked by political fragmentation and division, and for most of the period, rule by foreign powers. The dream of national political independence, with which Lawrence intoxicated his British and Arab adherents and also, to a degree, himself, represents an ideal which, for most of the previous thousand years, had had little currency among the political realities of the Arab world.

As recently as 1970, P. J. Vatikiotis, an authority on Arab culture, politics and history, could write with justification:

> What, then, can one say about Arab Nationalism as a force for political development in the Arab world today? Without doubt literate, articulate Arabs (especially those in towns and cities) share a sentiment, a feeling of belonging to an entity they call the Arab Nation (al-umma al-'arabiyya). This is the meaning of al-qawmiyya al-'arabiyya, Arab Nationalism, or Arab solidarity. But is this sentiment a determinant of political action and organization? So far, it has not proved to be so. Arab Nationalism has not achieved its goal of making the Arab Nation co-extensive with one Arab State. For the moment, Arabs are at least legally citizens, or subjects, of several sovereign states exhibiting various forms of political organization, different political structures, and disparate levels of economic development. These states exhibit varying degrees of ethnic, religious and communal heterogeneity. The one thing they have in common, with one exception, is that their populations are overwhelmingly Muslim, and all are Arabic-speaking. In one way or another, they also shared a common experience of foreign domination, rule, or tutelage not too long ago. Moreover, most of them had been, at one time or another, in the period of 1517-1918, part of the Ottoman Empire.[1]

I am using the word Arab, not in its original sense of denoting a member of the nomad tribes of the Arabian Peninsula, but with the more modern connotation provided by George Antonius, a Christian Arab. In his definition, "Arab" has come to mean "a citizen of that extensive Arab world — not any inhabitant of it, but that great majority whose racial descent, even when it was not of pure Arab lineage, had become submerged in the tide of arabisation; whose manners and traditions had been shaped in an Arab mould; and most decisive of all, whose mother tongue is Arabic. The term applies to Christians as well as Moslems, and to offshoots of each of these creeds, the criterion being not islamisation but the degree of arabisation."[2]

By this definition Antonius was certainly correct when he wrote that there has been a "lack of anything approaching national solidarity in the Arab world." Although written in 1938, his explanation for this remains current today:

> The unifying force generated by the genius of the Prophet Muhammad had remained a force so long as Arab power had remained supreme. As that power waned, its cohesive influence weakened; and the diverse people it had welded together into a cultural whole fell gradually asunder to form separate entities, regional and sectarian, according to the district, clan or creed to which they belonged. Side by side with that disintegration, a process of religious evolution was going on, which had led not only to the birth of new confessions, among both Moslems and Christians, but also to an increased emphasis on sectarian differences and to the growth of confessional loyalty as a substitute for cultural solidarity.[3]

Recently, Manfred Halpern has formulated this tendency toward "confessional loyalty" in socio-psychological terms. He has seen the political fragmentation as deriving from fundamental aspects of Arab psychology and ways of engaging in human relationships. Halpern has emphasized the tendency of persons reared in Muslim cultures to yield to authority ("subjection"), and to submerge individual identity, essential for mature political self-consciousness, with that of a protective overwhelming authority ("emanation").[4]

It is against this background that one should view Lawrence's actions and writings during the years of World War I and thereafter. "I meant to make a new nation," he wrote in an introduction to *Seven Pillars of Wisdom*, "to restore a lost influence, to give twenty millions of Semites the foundation on which to build an inspired dream-palace of their national thoughts."[5] These lofty aims, whose overreaching grandness Lawrence came to recognize, not only flew directly in the face of the real politik of the Western powers, of which he came increasingly to complain, but also disregarded what George Kirk has called "the fatal Arab tendency to political separatism."[6] The disappointment of Lawrence's unrealistic aims was inevitable. The consequences for history of his having pursued them so passionately and effectively are still unfolding and still being debated.

Until the nineteenth century there was little national consciousness among the Arab peoples in the Ottoman Empire. Local, internal authority in Arab lands tended to be left in the hands of feudal amirs and local Arab chiefs.[7] Largely in response to pressures from the Western European states, the Ottoman Empire made a number of efforts to modernize the imperial administrative and judicial organization. But these reforms, whether successful or inadequate from the administrative standpoint, failed to prevent the emergence of movements for autonomy in various parts of the empire. Contact with the West influenced these movements strongly but in varying ways. For instance, in the Wahhabi movement in the Arabian Peninsula in the eighteenth and nineteenth centuries, the anti-Turkish agitation was an entirely Muslim movement and, in addition, anti-Western. In contrast, the drive of Muhammad Ali and Ibrahim Pasha to unite the Arab lands under their rule in the early decades of the nineteenth century was both motivated by personal ambition and strongly inspired by Western, especially French, nationalistic, political and cultural influences. During the occupation of Syria between 1831 and 1840 by Ibrahim Pasha, European and American missionary activity was encouraged, especially in Lebanon, which became the gateway for the entry of Western influences into the Asiatic provinces of the Ottoman Empire.

Some scholars, especially Zeine N. Zeine and George Kirk, have questioned whether these missionary activities, which were concerned predominately with religious education and conversion, with teaching the population to read and write, and with developing largely nonpolitical curricula in the missionary colleges, were important in the fomenting of the nationalistic movements which grew up in the empire in the decades before World War I.

Although the political repression under the regime of the sultan Abdul Hamid II (1876–1909) intensified the Arabs' desire for independence, it would appear that Arab nationalists feared British, French and Russian colonial expansion, against which the Ottoman government seemed to offer some protection, more than they did the familiar tyrannies of the empire. In 1882 Egypt fell under direct British occupation, and Muslim leaders, in Zeine's words, "were not blind to the ambitions and interests of the Great Powers in the Ottoman Empire and feared lest any further weakening of the Empire should lead to the occupation of the Arab lands in the Near East by one or more of those powers."[8]

Many leading Arab Muslims sought greater political freedom, an extension of civil liberties, and an end to misgovernment, but remained loyal to the Ottoman government. But their desires were shared by Turkish liberals, the most successful of whom were a group called the Young Turks, which had grown up among Turkish expatriates in Europe and was therefore strongly imbued with Western concepts of parliamentary government and constitutional reform. In July 1908 they came to power in a bloodless revolution in Constantinople accompanied by the rejoicing of the populace.

The Young Turks, however, and their ruling Committee of Union and Progress (CUP), were soon engaged in a tyranny of their own which, unlike the rule of Abdul Hamid II, attempted to control not only the political life of the Arab peoples at a local level, but even their religion and education. Promulgating a chauvinistic Turkish nationalism called

Pan-Turanianism, they attempted to "Turkify" the Arab lands. Despite these efforts to exploit Pan-Islamism, the CUP was in many respects anti-Islamic, and sought, against Arab opposition, to translate the Koran into Turkish and to make a sentimental cult of such pagan Turanian conquerors as Genghis Khan.[9] As I wrote some years ago:

> The young Turks attempted to force unity through Turkifying everything, without regard to local customs or differences in race. They imposed the Turkish language on everyone, and even went so far as to forbid the teaching of Albanian in Albanian schools and Arabic in Arabian schools. Compulsory service in the Ottoman army was imposed on Christians and Moslems alike. To a greater extent than under Abdul Hamid the central government interfered with every detail of local administration. Hundreds of local Abdul Hamids appeared all over the Empire and served to encourage racial hatreds. The revived electoral system became the channel of unexampled corruption, violence and murder. In the elections the opposition was not only kept from the polls, but was often shot down in cold blood.[10]

These repressive national and racial policies of the Young Turks fanned the flames of Arab political nationalism, and a number of Arab societies and political parties (the most famous of which was the ultra-secret al-Fatat, created in Paris in 1909) were formed to defend the Arab cause and protect Arab rights. Members of these societies dreamed of a united Arab Empire, which took precedence in their thinking over allegiance to any single Arab or Muslim country.[11] Recent massacres of the Armenians indicated to the Arab leaders what might be in store for them and helped to stimulate Arab political activity. However, despite the intensification of underground political activity by these secret societies between 1909 and 1914 (many of them functioned in Europe), most of the Arabic-speaking Muslims remained loyal to the Ottoman Empire, even during the war. The secret societies, though strongly nationalistic, feared European designs on Arab lands and remained on the side of the empire out of fear of the Western powers. Al-Fatat, for example, was not prepared to support Britain against Turkey.

In contrast to their policy in Egypt, until 1914 the British favored the maintenance of the Ottoman Empire intact, despite its weakened and corrupt state. British economic and political interests had been expanding in the Middle East throughout the nineteenth century, and political tranquillity in the regions of Suez, the Red Sea and the Persian Gulf had a high priority. Britain's prewar aim was to preserve a stable but politically docile Ottoman Empire, which would maintain the favored conditions of the "capitulations," whereby non-Muslims and foreigners within the Empire were exempt from its jurisdiction, and which could also serve as a buffer against Russian expansion.

Until the rise of Germany after 1870, Russia and France were Britain's chief competitors in the Middle East. Various struggles to achieve a balance of power in the region resulted in an understanding between Britain and France in 1904 whereby France agreed to give Britain a free hand in Egypt in return for a free hand in Morocco. The Russian show of might on the steppes of Asia in the latter part of the nineteenth century pressured Britain into an agreement in 1907 that divided Persia into British and Russian spheres of influence. Although Germany had sent a military mission to Turkey as early as 1883 to modernize the Ottoman army, British policy in relation to Germany revealed far greater concern about its power in Europe than in the Middle East. As late as 1913–1914 Britain entered into an agreement with Germany in which it consented to the construction of the Baghdad Railway to Basra in Mesopotamia in return for having two directors on the board of the railway and German recognition of the exclusive rights of the Anglo-Iranian Oil Company to extract oil in the region of the Persian Gulf.[12] In 1904, however, Britain also entered into an entente with France that was aimed at controlling German power in Europe. Russia joined the entente in 1907.

The humiliating Ottoman defeats at the hands of Italy in 1911, and twice at the hands of the Balkan powers in 1912 and 1913, resulted in the loss of Libya and almost all European Turkey. The political instability and hastening disintegration of the Ottoman Empire made the nineteenth century British policy of favoring its reform rather than partition seem increasingly less viable. But as late as July 1913, Sir Edward Grey, the British secretary for foreign affairs, could write, "The only policy to which we can become a party is one directed to avoid collapse and partition of Asiatic Turkey."[13]

On the Ottoman side these defeats led only to a more violently nationalistic and anti-Arab policy, and the further penetration of Pan-Turanian ideas into the Ottoman army. This resulted in a deep antipathy toward the Unionist government among the army officers, many of whom were Arab.[14]

In 1911 Lord Kitchener, who had a long history of distinguished service to Great Britain in Egypt and the Sudan, became British agent and consul general in Egypt. Although he would not act against Turkey when Britain was not at war with her, he did order the survey of the Sinai that Lawrence and Woolley took part in and he became sympathetic to the advice of those in Cairo who advocated a policy of stimulating Arab nationalism and "detaching the Arabs from the Turks."[15] "The liberation of subject races in the Ottoman Empire is a traditional occupation of the British public," David Hogarth wrote shortly after World War I, and "no ministry, forced into hostilities with the Turks, would have been suffered to abstain long from the declaration of a pro-Arab policy, and from measures to enforce it. . . . Kitchener's responsibility [prior to the declaration of war against Turkey, was] not for the adoption of such a policy, but only for the initial measures taken to declare it and put it in action."[16]

There were various movements toward national independence among the Arab peoples during the months preceding the outbreak of World War I. Uprisings occurred in Cyrenaica, Yemen, Iraq and Arabia during 1913 and 1914. But it was the revolutionary activities of the sharif of Mecca and his sons in the Hijaz (the regions of the Arabia Peninsula along the Red Sea) that became in 1914 the focus of British military and political policies, and that ultimately furnished Lawrence with the opportunity to exercise his initiatives.

Husayn Ibn Ali was appointed sharif and amir of Mecca in the summer of 1908 by the Ottoman sultan and the Turkish grand vizier, the appointment having become entangled with the rivalry between the "Old" and the "Young" Turks, the latter favoring the representative of a different Meccan clan.[17] The sharifs of Mecca, all of whom were of the Hashemite family and claimed direct descent from the prophet Muhammad through his daughter Fatimah, had ruled Mecca and the Hijaz since the tenth century, gaining considerable political autonomy from the Ottoman central government. These sharifs, each of whom bore the title "Protector of the Two Holy Cities," had the responsibility of protecting Mecca and Medina and overseeing the annual pilgrimages. Because of their special position and their claim to descent from the Prophet, the Meccan sharifs enjoyed great privilege and prestige throughout the empire. Husayn himself had been brought to Constantinople with his three sons in 1898 because of a disagreement with his uncle, then the reigning amir of Mecca.

The Hashemite family's long association with the old Ottoman regime undoubtedly played a significant part in the struggles between Husayn and the Young Turks, who were attempting to bring him under their authority. Despite powerful Unionist (Young Turk) pressure, however, Husayn remained loyal to the sultan, did not respond to the call of the Arab deputies in Constantinople to lead an Arab national movement, and even assisted the Turks in putting down an uprising of al-Idrisi, a territorial ruler in Yemen. This action earned Husayn the enmity of the Arab nationalists, and until 1914 he was regarded by them as a supporter of the Ottoman state. The Arabs of the Hijaz, especially the Bedouin, opposed the extension of the Hijaz railroad beyond Medina to Mecca: they feared a further loss in the tolls they could levy during the annual pilgrimage. The Ottoman regime's attempt to extend the railroad by military force was opposed by the local Bedouin, and Wahib, the local *vali* (Ottoman representative) in Mecca, advised that Husayn be deposed.

Husayn's second son, Abdullah, negotiated with the Unionist government an agreement, under which, in exchange for permission to construct the railroad, the sharif would receive one third of its revenues and the amirate would be Husayn's for life and then hereditary in his family. But these agreements did not allay his anxiety, and he looked to Great Britain for support. In February of 1914, Abdullah went to Cairo to see Lord Kitchener (they had met a year or two before) and through him to enlist Britain's aid in his family's struggle against the Ottoman government. But Kitchener would give him no definite assurance because Britain was not at war with the Ottoman Empire. Similarly Ronald Storrs, who was sent by Kitchener in April 1914 to visit Abdullah, declined to supply even "a dozen, or even a half-dozen machine guns" on the same grounds.[18] But despite the lack of direct assurance, Abdullah seems to have been convinced that Britain would support Husayn against the Turks, particularly when she intervened in April to have the Arab revolutionist 'Aziz Ali al-Misri released from a Turkish prison, where he had been held since his arrest in February.

On September 24, Kitchener, now secretary of state for war, wrote the famous message to Cairo in which he asked that Storrs send a "secret and carefully chosen messenger" to Abdullah to ascertain whether "he and his father and Arabs of Hejaz would be with us or against us" in the event of German-Turkish aggression against Great Britain.[19] Abdullah and Storrs had become friendly during Storrs's visit in April: Abdullah was impressed with the Englishman's ability to quote the Koran and had enjoyed quoting pre-Islamic poetry himself. When Storrs's messenger turned up, Abdullah arranged for a meeting with his father that resulted in a favorable reply.

The messenger gave a verbal report to Storrs on October 30, the day that Britain declared war on Turkey, and according to Storrs, quoted Husayn and described his behavior as follows:

"The Ottoman Empire has rights over us and we have rights upon her. She has made war upon our rights, and I am not responsible before God if she has made war upon our rights; nor am I responsible before God if we have therefore made war upon hers." He gesticulated with his arms as he spoke, and threw back the long sleeve of his garments, saying "my heart is open to Storrs even as this, and with a gesture, stretch forth to us a helping hand and we shall never at all help these oppressors. On the contrary we shall help those who do good. This is the Commandment of God upon us: Do good to Islam and Moslems — Nor do we fear nor respect any save God. Give him my greeting, fitted to him and to his country."[20]

Kitchener, learning of this recondite but otherwise positive response to his telegram, cabled Abdullah on October 31 that Britain was now at war with Turkey and "if Arab nation assist England in this war England will guarantee that no intervention takes place in Arabia and will give Arabs every assistance against external foreign aggression."[21]

Thus the evolving alliance between Great Britain and the Hashemite sharif of Mecca grew out of the political and military needs of each. Britain sought an ally in Arabia against Turkey, while Husayn and his family sought to enlist British aid in their internal struggle against an Ottoman regime which was attempting to subvert the traditional authority and autonomy of the Meccan sharif.

"Feisul [Husayn's third son] talked to me something about the genesis of the Arab rising," Lawrence wrote during the war. "It was first imagined by his brother, Abdullah, who reckoned that the Hejaz was capable of withstanding Turkey with the aid of the Syrian and Mesopotamian armies, and our diplomatic help. He approached Lord Kitchener to this end, and obtained satisfactory assurances, but the scheme was put off on Feisul's representing that Turkey was too strong for them."[22] Kitchener's cable of October 31, which was received by Abdullah in mid-November, "caused him the liveliest satisfaction," strengthened his argument for revolt with his father, and conveyed to Husayn "an unmistakeable invitation to foment a revolt of all the Arabs."[23] A second messenger was sent to Cairo to Husayn in December, but the sharif was not yet ready to rebel.[24]

The entrance of Turkey into the war against the Allied powers placed the sharif in a difficult position. While Abdullah was encouraging revolution with the evidence of probable British support, the Unionist regime in Constantinople was pressing him for a show of loyalty, and inviting him to join Turkey in a *jihad* or Muslim Holy War, against the Allied infidels — a war which was in fact declared in mid-November. Husayn stalled, feeling "that the Holy War was doctrinally incompatible with an agressive war, and absurd with a Christian ally: Germany."[25] The failure of Turkish attacks upon the Suez Canal early in 1915 brought new demands for loyalty and for the sending of Arab "volunteers" to aid the Unionist cause.

In the last week of January 1915, Husayn received an emissary from al-Fatat, the Arab nationalist secret society, now centered in Damascus, who said that senior Arab officers in the Ottoman army favored revolt to gain independence and asked if the sharif would collaborate and act in concert with them. But the sharif was cautious in his reply and responded by sending his third son, Faisal, to Damascus. Faisal arrived on March 26 and made contact with members of the secret societies al-Fatat and al-'Ahd.[26] In the four weeks he stayed there, he was sworn into both societies and became imbued with their doctrines of militant Arab nationalism.[27] But the designs of the European powers in the Middle East had become clearer by this time, and the secret societies, which contained among their members many Arab officers in the Ottoman army, were reluctant to rebel against the Ottoman Empire lest they merely end in substituting one form of foreign domination for another.

According to Lawrence, "To most of them the word was never given; for those societies were pro-Arab only, willing to fight for nothing but Arab independence; and they could see no advantage in supporting the Allies rather than the Turks, since they did not believe our assurances that we would leave them free. Indeed, many of them preferred an Arabia united by Turkey in miserable subjection, to an Arabia divided up and slothful under easier control of several European powers in spheres of influence."[28] Nevertheless, many Syrians and Iraqis found their way into the Arab forces and served with distinction during the campaigns.[29]

In May Faisal was in Constantinople, where he professed his loyalty to the Ottoman officials and the sultan. He then returned to Damascus, where he received a protocol drawn up by al-Fatat and al-'Ahd to be brought to the sharif. The protocol explained the conditions of independence under which they would cooperate with Britain against Turkey in a revolt to be proclaimed by the sharif of Mecca. Large parts of the Arab world were to be granted independence and the exceptional privileges granted to foreigners under the Capitulations were to be abolished.[30] But a year of negotiations and struggles on Husayn's part with the Ottoman government and rival Arab tribes was to pass before he was ready to proclaim his rebellion, and by this time the repressive measures of Jemal Pasha had destroyed the possibility of an effective revolt in Syria. The failure of the Syrian Arab leaders to rebel at a time when a revolt might have been successful weakened greatly the Arab negotiating position after the war when the political future of Syria was being decided.[31]

Messages sent or inspired by Kitchener to Sharif Husayn in the closing months of 1914 had encouraged an Arab rebellion against the Ottoman authority and implied that British support for this and for eventual Arab independence would be forthcoming. But by the spring of 1915 the "Arab question" had receded from any position of high priority in practical British military and political policy.[32] The overriding importance of the war in Europe and of maintaining cooperative relationships with Britain's two major allies on the continent, France and Russia, was determining British policy. The Allies on the Western Front were stalemated, but with enormous loss of life, while the Russians were pressed in the Caucasus and sought a diversion against Turkey.[33] Sir John Maxwell, the commander-in-chief in Egypt, favored a landing at Alexandretta and urged it upon Kitchener, who seems to have favored it in principle. But the needs of the Western Front led to the decision in London to launch an attack on the Dardanelles and force a landing at Gallipoli in order to capture Constantinople and defeat Turkey in Europe. After the defeat of the British at Gallipoli in the summer of 1915, a landing was again considered at Alexandretta, but French objections to a British invasion so near to their area of interest in the Levant, and their preference for a landing at Salonika, caused the British to abandon their Alexandretta plan.

Meanwhile on the diplomatic front the first half of 1915 was character-ized by the slow evolution of interest in the partition of the Ottoman Empire among the Great Powers in the event of its defeat (a policy which, needless to say, contained potential incompatibilities with the approach being simultaneously evolved of encouraging alliances with Arab leaders in return for postwar independence for their lands).[34] In the event of its fall Constantinople and the Dardanelles were to be ceded to Russia, by an Anglo-Soviet agreement of March 1915. At the same time "the maze of Arabian politics," as Zeine described it, included a variety of assurances and agreements by the Allies with a number of Arab rulers in the Arabian Peninsula, other than Sharif Husayn.

In reviewing the history of this period, one is struck by the juxta-position of philosophies, representing two historical eras, each trying to adapt itself to the fast-changing realities within the Ottoman Empire in 1915 and 1916. The old colonialism of the nineteenth century, represented by Curzon and Cromer, which looked upon Asia and Africa as regions to be manipulated or carved up in accord with the commercial territorial policies of the European empires, and which regarded Asiatics and Africans as largely incapable of self-government, was being challenged by the liberal strain in British politics, represented by men like Hogarth and Storrs, and eventually Lawrence, who dreamed of Arab indepen-dence and unity under British guidance. It was into the center of this clash of policies, philosophy and politics that Lawrence would insert himself so actively in the coming years.

Faisal returned from Damascus to Mecca on June 20, 1915, with reports of Turkish atrocities in Syria. Though a convert to revolution he still urged delay. Abdullah, however, continued to press his father for action, while Sir Reginald Wingate, the sirdar of the Sudan in Khartoum, con-ferred with Sir Gilbert Clayton, the director of civil and military intelli-gence in Cairo. Wingate and Clayton, acting together, conferred in turn with Arab leaders in Cairo and encouraged the Arab rebellion. At this point Abdullah seems, at least to a degree, to have had his way, for on July 14 Husayn sent a note to Henry McMahon, the British high commis-sioner in Cairo, offering the possibility of "joint action" in the war in return for British recognition of the independence of "the entire Arab nation."[35] With the receipt of Husayn's letter in Cairo British and Hashemite policy became joined.

It is beyond the scope of this discussion to analyze fully the political influences that underlay the Husayn-McMahon correspondence and the Sykes-Picot Agreement of 1916, or to attempt to sort out completely the alleged discrepancies and similarities between them. Yet certain points are pertinent and need special mention. The two sets of negotiations — the Husayn-McMahon understandings and the Sykes-Picot Agreement — re-flect very different priorities of policy, priorities which were to a degree

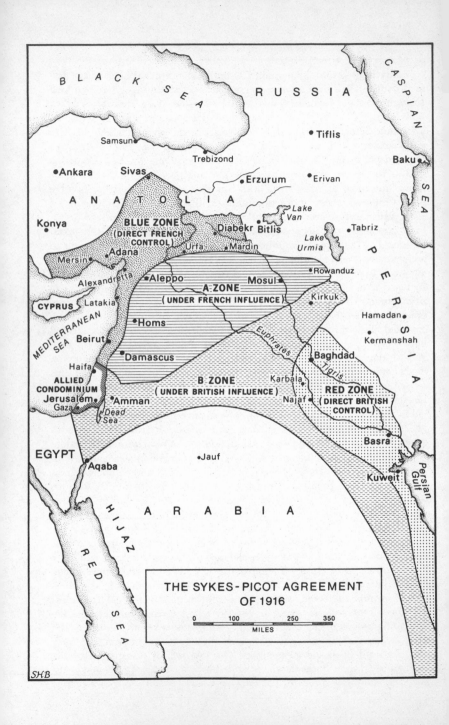

THE SYKES-PICOT AGREEMENT
OF 1916

0   100   250   350
MILES

mutually incompatible. (It is surprising in view of this fact that the agreements dovetailed on as many points as they did.) The important McMahon letters, which were sent to Husayn from October 1915 to March 1916, were formulated under the influence of the "Arabophiles" in Cairo and a nationalistic Arab officer al-Faruqi (a member of al-'Ahd who had defected in October 1915 from the Ottoman army). They were directed primarily toward securing the alliance of the sharif,[36] and were meant "to persuade him, by offers of assistance and guarantees of his future autonomy and independence, to throw off the Turkish supremacy and to keep open the pilgrimage for the Muslim subjects of the Allies."[37] The Sykes-Picot negotiations, which were taking place virtually simultaneously between Britain, France and Russia, were initiated in London, Paris and Petrograd, and represented a typical colonialist approach to anticipated changes wrought by war — the designation of spheres of influence among the Great Powers, and the partition of the territories of a defeated adversary.

Both agreements spoke of the independence of the Arab peoples, but differed on the conditions of this independence and the regions to be included. Both assumed Arab independence in the Arabian Peninsula. Both allowed for French control of a long coastal region on the Mediterranean (now part of Syria and Lebanon) and British control in southern Mesopotamia. McMahon led Husayn to believe that the interior of Syria would be independent, while the Sykes-Picot Agreement divided this large and important region into British and French "zones of influence." McMahon was vague about Palestine, perhaps permitting the Arab view "that Palestine did fall within the area of promised Arab independence."[38] The Sykes-Picot Agreement specified that Palestine would be under international control, except for a small British enclave containing the ports of Haifa and Acre.

The McMahon-Husayn and Sykes-Picot negotiations have taken on great symbolic significance beyond the specific terms that they contain, being the first approaches to the political future of the Arab peoples formerly living within the vast territories of the Ottoman Empire. Although they formed the initial basis for the approach to the problem of the Ottoman lands during the war, events soon made their stipulations largely obsolete. Arab leaders and spokesmen have naturally resented deeply the failure of the British to fulfill the promises of the McMahon letters (Antonius called the Sykes-Picot Agreement "a shocking document"), while British apologists have asserted that no promises were made or binding agreements concluded, that "horse-trading was going on on all sides in the international market," and that, after all, the British did help the Arabs get the Turks out of Arabia and Syria.[39] In balance, truth and justice probably lie somewhere between these positions.

During the same months that he was corresponding with McMahon,

Husayn was simultaneously trying to negotiate his sovereignty with the Ottoman government in return for neutrality, or even alliance with the Ottoman cause.⁴⁰ Furthermore, there was really no basis upon which Husayn, despite his selection by the British as the most likely ally in Arabia or Syria to oppose the Turks, could negotiate as a spokesman for *all* of "the Arabs" in the Ottoman Empire, especially when the Syrian Arab nationalists had forfeited their initiative (and therefore their bargaining strength) by their failure to rebel against Turkey during 1914–1916. Even the sharif himself had not yet revolted in May 1916, when the Sykes-Picot Agreement was signed, and as Hogarth wrote in 1920, as late as April 1916 "the prospect of Arabs taking part in their own liberation was nebulous."⁴¹ There seems little question, however, that the enticements and offers to Husayn and his family that were made in the course of his negotiations with Kitchener and McMahon did much to stimulate the hopes and ambitions of the Hashemite family for political hegemony in Arabia and Syria.

On the other hand the Sykes-Picot Agreement, which divided the Arab lands among the Great Powers, was negotiated without the knowledge of the sharif, or any of the other Arab leaders, who did not know of its contents until May 1917 at the earliest. Although Mark Sykes, Britain's choice to work out the treaty with France and Russia, knew that letters were being exchanged between Cairo and Mecca, it is not clear that *his* negotiations were known in Cairo before 1917. When Liddell Hart asked Lawrence after the war, "When did McMahon know of [the] Sykes-Picot Treaty?" Lawrence answered, "Not until Sykes told him [that is, in 1917], Sykes saying casually, 'Haven't you heard of my Treaty?' Others nearly threw up."⁴²

As Elizabeth Monroe has written (overstating the case to make her point), 1916 was the last year of the "old familiar world of intact empires," the last year in which there could be "secret agreements secretly arrived at, and treatment of whole populations as chattels. It was also the last year of freedom from criticism by anti-imperialist allies."⁴³ Lawrence's role in hastening the end of that familiar world is the subject of the chapters that follow. In 1915 and 1916 he was only beginning to grasp fully the ambiguities of the situation in which he would soon find himself as he moved into his place at the crossroads of British policy and Arab dreams.

In letters of December 1915 and January and February 1916, McMahon and Husayn agreed essentially to disagree on the matter of Syria, leaving the question to be disputed, settled, or otherwise pursued after the war. McMahon reiterated "the interests of our ally France" and Husayn protested that "any concession to give France or any other power possession of a single square foot of territory in those parts is quite out of the question."⁴⁴ The British translation of this last passage is less emphatic: "It is impossible to allow any derogation that gives France or any other

power a span of land in those regions."⁴⁵ The impracticality of an Arab
uprising in Syria, which was altogether ruled out with the arrest by
Jemal Pasha of the Arab nationalist leaders and the transfer of Arab
military units, made Husayn the only logical choice as an ally for Great
Britain in the Arab lands, despite great reluctance in Cairo "to take our
main action upon . . . one of the most barbarous Arab provinces [the
Hijaz] instead of that obviously best fitted to lead in nation-making
[Syria]."⁴⁶ Husayn's reluctance to respond to the call for a Holy War; the
wide prestige of the sharif of Mecca among the Muslim Arabs; the
strategic location of his lands along the Red Sea and flanked by the Hijaz
railroad; and the unsuitability (because of their primarily local interests,
lack of fighting potential or too great distance) of other tribes in Yemen or
the interior of the Arabian Peninsula — all made him the best choice
available as an ally in Arabia. But by the beginning of 1916 he still had
not rebelled.

In January 1916, Husayn sent Faisal to Damascus once again in order
to allay Turkish suspicions. There Faisal stayed in Jemal's headquarters,
where they discussed raising volunteers from the Hijaz for the war
against the Allies. He was taken by his host to see his Syrian friends
hanged, along with various Arab notables, and was shown scenes in films
depicting atrocities presumably committed by Australian troops against
Egyptian men and women.⁴⁷

From January to May, with Faisal still in Damascus, Husayn continued
to negotiate with Jemal for general amnesty for Arab political prisoners
and the recognition of the traditional status and privileges of the amirate
of Mecca. Throughout this time Faisal was asserting his loyalty to the
Ottoman Empire, which naturally caused Jemal considerable bitterness
when he discovered that he had been betrayed.⁴⁸ As Jemal refused the
sharif's terms and as his tone became increasingly menacing, Faisal, who
had been in secret correspondence with his father throughout this period,
determined to leave Damascus and to support the break from Constanti-
nople.⁴⁹ In mid-May he set out for Medina and Mecca in order to help in
the final preparations for the Revolt. He asked permission of Jemal, who
was by now quite suspicious, to go to Medina to accompany a contingent
of Arab "volunteers," led by his older brother Ali, to Jerusalem.⁵⁰ To
Faisal's dismay Jemal replied that Enver Pasha, one of the Ottoman
leaders, was on his way and that they would go to Medina together and
inspect the troops. Faisal had planned to raise his father's crimson banner
as soon as he arrived in Medina and take the Turks unawares, and here
he was to be saddled with "two uninvited Turkish guests to whom, by
the Arab law of hospitality, he could do no harm, and who would probably delay his action so long that the whole secret of the revolt would be
in jeopardy."⁵¹

"The irony of the review was terrible," Lawrence wrote later. "Enver,
Jemal and Feisal watched the troops wheeling and turning in the dusty

plain outside the city gate, rushing up and down in mimic camel-battle, or spurring their horses in the javelin game after the immemorial Arab fashion. 'And are all these volunteers for the Holy War?' asked Enver at last, turning to Feisal. 'Yes,' said Feisal. 'Willing to fight to the death against the enemies of the faithful?' 'Yes,' said Feisal again; and then the Arab chiefs came up to be presented, and Sherif Ali ibn el Hussein, of Modhig, drew him aside whispering, 'My Lord, shall we kill them now?' and Feisal said, 'No, they are our guests.' "[52]

Faisal soon found Medina full of Ottoman troops, for Jemal had decided to reinforce the Medina garrison. Husayn ordered Faisal to Mecca in order that the rebellion could begin. Although Faisal again recommended delay — until August — Husayn feared that his correspondence with the British had become known and that the troops had been sent to deal with him. The visit of a German mission under Baron von Stotzingen along the Hijaz railroad and then to Yenbo on the Red Sea caused additional alarm. The news that the Turks had massacred thousands of Armenians and had abducted Armenian women may also have troubled the sharif.[53]

Word from Syria of a further crop of political executions finally convinced even the reluctant Faisal, and on May 23 a message was telegraphed to McMahon in Cairo (who had continued to correspond with the sharif regarding additional money, supplies and equipment that would be forthcoming from Britain in the event the rebellion was raised): "Sherif's son Abdullah urgently requires Storrs to come to Arabian coast to meet him. Movement will begin as soon as Feisal arrives at Mecca."[54]

In the first days of June, a mission composed of Storrs, Hogarth and Captain Kinahan Cornwallis, among others, met on an Arabian beach with Zayd, the sharif's youngest son, to consider final details of the rebellion.[55] On June 4 Storrs received this message from the high commissioner, who was reporting the Indian government's concern about the threat of hostilities in Arabia: "India asks whether situation necessitates stoppage of the Haj [annual pilgrimage to Mecca] from India. India is unwilling to offend Moslem feeling by notification of stoppage. Please discuss this with Abdullah."[56] But the next day Faisal and Ali proclaimed the independence of the Arabs from Ottoman rule, and on June 10, 1916, the Revolt began in Mecca, which was wrested from its small Turkish garrison after three days of fierce fighting.[57]

In a flowery proclamation issued at the end of June, Sharif Husayn recounted the executions and other atrocities, treachery and crimes perpetrated against Islam by the Young Turk leaders and declared:

We can leave the judgment [of Turkish misdeeds] to the Moslem world, but we may not leave our religion, and our existence as a people to be the plaything of the Unionists. God (blessed be He) has made open for us the attainment of freedom and independence, and has shown us a way of victory, to cut off the hand of the oppressors, and to cast out their garrison from our midst. We have attained independence, an independence of the rest of the Ottoman Empire, which is still groaning under the tyranny of our enemy. Our independence is complete, absolute, not to be laid hands on by any foreign influence or aggression, and our aim is the preservation of Islam, and the uplifting of its standard in the world.[58]

At the time the rebellion began, Gallipoli had been evacuated and the British garrison in Mesopotamia had surrendered. Great Britain was grateful to have this new ally on the Arabian Peninsula. As Zeine has pointed out, the invitation to rebel which Britain had offered and agreed to support, was extended to Sharif Husayn and limited to the Arabs of the Hijaz region of Arabia. In no way had Great Britain envisaged or planned to support "with men and arms a great Arab Revolt from one end of the Asiatic possessions of the Ottoman Empire to the other."[59] In this shift of policy Lawrence's role was to prove critical. As Hogarth wrote of the Revolt a year or two after the end of the war: "It would not have been begun but for Kitchener's invitation in the first instance, and assurance of British support in the second; it could not have been sustained without the money, food-stuffs, and munitions of war which Great Britain provided; it might never have spread beyond the Hedjaz but for the long sight and audacious action of Lawrence; and it won through to Damascus only as a flying right wing of [General] Allenby's last drive."[60]

Although Arab nationalism played a relatively minor role as we have seen in the inception of the Revolt (Husayn having turned its precepts to his local advantage), the extraordinary success of the rebellion provided a powerful stimulus to Arab nationalistic aspirations, which have had as great if not a greater impact upon the modern world as the immediate military and political results of the campaigns themselves.

11

Two Years in Cairo,
1914–1916

Lawrence was in Oxford when the First World War began in August 1914. The war seemed at first to provide an exciting, even romantic, opportunity for the small stratum of educated young Englishmen. "The whole world was their oyster and seemed sure to go on being so till the end of time," Arnold Lawrence wrote me, and went on to say that "Rupert Brooke's 'Now, God be thanked Who has matched us with His hour'¹ expressed the general relief of [my brother] Frank's friends at having something big enough to do, when the war started."²* And T. E. Lawrence wrote Flecker in December, "Not many dons have taken commissions — but 95% of the undergraduates have taken or applied for them."³

Lawrence wrote that he tried to enlist himself but the War Office "was then glutted with men, and [they] were only taking six-footers."⁴ According to Lawrence, Hogarth made an appointment for him to see Colonel Coote Hedley, head of the Geographical Section of the General Staff (Intelligence) of the War Office. But Hedley states that he had not heard from Hogarth before Lawrence came to see him. In fact, Hedley wrote to Liddell Hart, "I well remember the pleasure and *surprise* with which I saw Lawrence, for I knew all about Lawrence and did not need a recommendation from anyone."⁵ Hedley recalls Lawrence in gray flannels, hatless and looking "about 18." He obtained a commission for him as a second lieutenant, and Lawrence then worked for about three months in London finishing the Sinai maps from the Palestine survey and making other maps of Belgium and France. Hedley knew that intelligence officers would be needed in Egypt and he told the Division of

* Frank, the fourth Lawrence boy, was an undergraduate at Jesus College when the war broke out.

Military Intelligence that he had "the ideal officer for that work in my office."⁶ Because of his effective work with Hedley, and his knowledge of the regions of the Middle East in which Great Britain was becoming engaged with Turkey and Germany, Lawrence was transferred to a rudimentary intelligence section that was being formed in Cairo.

During the less than two years in Cairo, from December 1914 to October 1916, when Lawrence began to take a more active role in the operations of the Arab Revolt, he performed a variety of intelligence functions. But beyond these assigned tasks he began to involve himself in what he was able to do best of all, the influencing of others. This capacity was not, of course, new, but for the first time he became acquainted with important military and political figures who were concerned with formulating British policy — at least at the local level — in the regions of the Egyptian theatre. His ambition was to influence policy beyond the opportunities of his station as a second lieutenant or later as a staff captain. The frustration imposed by his junior status may have caused him to react in ways that only accentuated his immaturity — refusing to look, dress, or carry himself as a good regular military officer was expected to do.

In Cairo Lawrence served at first with Woolley, George Lloyd, and Aubrey Herbert under Stewart Newcombe. The group reported to Sir Gilbert Clayton, who was director of intelligence for the Egyptian army. Lawrence continued to piece together maps of the region, but also put to use his detailed knowledge of the several districts and peoples of Syria and Palestine, and of the various strata of Turkish society, in eliciting information about Turkish prisoners ("I always knew their districts, and asked about my friends in them. Then they told me everything").⁷ Because of his knowledge of the region, Lawrence was the logical person to receive information about the size and movements of the Ottoman army, and various spies and other agents of the Allies in the field funneled information through him to his superiors. He also produced and supported the printing of a handbook on the Ottoman army, gathered information about seditious movements in Egypt, and was sent on intelligence missions to the Western Desert in North Africa and to Greece.

'Abd al-Rahman Shahbandar, a Syrian nationalist and physician who had recently escaped from a Turkish prison in Damascus, talked with Lawrence in Cairo early in March 1916 concerning the Arab movement and the political situation in Syria. His account of his visit gives a perceptive description of Lawrence at this time from the point of view of an Arab nationalist leader. Already, it seems, Lawrence held a position of considerable leadership in the British intelligence effort. Shahbandar was impressed that Lawrence knew the names of the secret societies and much about them. "It appears to me that this man is different from the rest of the Englishmen whom we have seen so far, that he listens attentively to the political organization of the Arabs and that his questions show a depth in the subject which is not present except with one who has in it a pleasure and a passion." Among the British intelligence officers in Cairo whom Shahbandar had met, "Lawrence was at the center of their orbit of movements and the instrument of their execution, although his appearance among the other people was the least."[8]

In addition to these duties and activities Lawrence was the liaison officer to the Survey of Egypt, a civil department of the Egyptian government whose scientific activities, especially geographic and geological, were brought during the war into close collaboration with the activities of military intelligence in Cairo. Ernest Dowson, who was director-general of the Survey, has written of his first impression of Lawrence in Egypt:

> At the outset must be pictured the extremely youthful and, to our unseeing eyes, insignificant figure with well-ruffled light hair, solitary pip on sleeve, minus belt and with peaked cap askew, who in these days and throughout his closest connection with the Survey used to be continuously at Giza [the location of the Survey offices on the west bank of the Nile in Cairo], riding his motorcycle Boanerges with a care which was remarked both there and also later when he visited the Government Press at Bulaq.[9]

Colonel Pierce Joyce, Lawrence's superior officer in the Hijaz, also remembers Lawrence's scruffy, unmilitary appearance in the Cairo years:

> My first and very brief meeting with him was at Port Sudan in 1916 when he accompanied Admiral Wemyss to Khartoum to discuss Arabian affairs with Sir Reginald Wingate. I confess the memory of this meeting merely recalls the intense desire on my part to tell him to get his hair cut and that his uniform and dirty buttons sadly needed the attention of his batman. I should most certainly have done so had he not been surrounded by such distinguished people.[10]

Storrs corroborates Joyce that Lawrence was "utterly careless of his dress" during this period. He has given this description:

> His forehead was high; his face upright and, in proportion to the depth of the head, long. His yellow hair was naturally-growing pre-War hair; that is parted and brushed sideways; not worn immensely long and plastered backwards under a pall of grease. He had a straight nose, piercing gentian-blue eyes, a firm and very full mouth, a strong square chin and fine, careful, and accomplished hands. His Sam-Browne belt was as often as not buckled loose over his unbuttoned shoulder strap, or he would forget to put it on at all. Once at least I had to send my servant Ismain running with it after him into the street. . . . Save for official purposes he hated fixed times and seasons. I would come upon him in my flat, reading always Latin and Greek, with

South Hill, home of Thomas Robert Tighe Chapman in Delvin, County Westmeath, Ireland. Courtesy of the Sisters of Charity of Jesus and Mary, the Belgian Order of nuns occupying the house in 1965

The Lawrence boys, taken when T. E. Lawrence was seven or eight.
Left to right: T.E., Bob, Frank, and Will. Arnold was not yet
born. Courtesy of Arnold Lawrence

The City of Oxford High School
in 1964, shortly before it was
closed. Photograph by the author

2 Polstead Road, Oxford, home of the Lawrence family from the time T. E. Lawrence was eight until after World War I. Photograph by the author

Lawrence at the City of Oxford High School. Courtesy of the Principal and Fellows of Jesus College, Oxford, and the Headmaster of the Oxford School

Photograph of Carcassonne by Lawrence from *Crusader Castles II: The Letters*. Courtesy of the Harvard College Library

The cottage built for Ned Lawrence in the garden behind the house at 2 Polstead Road. Photograph by the author

Lawrence and his
brothers during the
Jesus College years.
Left to right: T.E.,
Frank, Arnold, Bob
and Will. Courtesy
of Arnold Lawrence

Brass rubbing of Thomas Cranley,
Archbishop of Dublin (1477–1517) by
Lawrence and W. O. Ault. Courtesy of
Professor Ault; photograph by the author

David George Hogarth,
about 1910. Courtesy of
Mrs. Caroline Barron

Portrait of Charles Montagu
Doughty by Eric Kennington,
1921. From the National
Portrait Gallery, London

Pen-and-ink sketch of Sahyun by Lawrence, in *Crusader Castles I: The Thesis*. Courtesy of the Harvard College Library

Entrance to the citadel at Aleppo, in *Crusader Castles, II: The Letters*. Courtesy of the Harvard College Library

Workmen at the Carchemish dig, spring of 1912. Lawrence is second
from left in the front row and Woolley is beside him in the safari
hat. Courtesy of the Trustees of the British Museum

Exterior and living room of the expedition house at Carchemish. Lawrence and Woolley had it constructed in the spring of 1913 for the use of the archeologists. Courtesy of the Trustees of the British Museum

Lawrence and Woolley at Carchemish with a Hittite slab. From the Imperial War Museum, London

Dahoum at Carchemish. From the Bodleian Library, Oxford

Lawrence during the desert campaigns.
From the Imperial War Museum, London

Lawrence with his bodyguards, March 1917.
From the Imperial War Museum, London

'Awdah abu-Tayyi. From the Bodleian
Library, Oxford

Faisal (French official
photo). From the Bodleian
Library, Oxford

Abdullah. From the Bodleian
Library, Oxford

Photograph by Lawrence of
children sitting on a beach at
Aqaba, 1917. Courtesy of the
Harvard College Library

Faisal's camp at Quweira, 1917.
From the Bodleian Library, Oxford

Portrait of General Allenby by Eric Kennington.
From the National Portrait Gallery, London

Prisoners defile at Tafila, 1918.
From the Bodleian Library, Oxford

corresponding gaps in my shelves. But he put back in their places the books he did not take away; of those he took he left a list, and never failed to return them reasonably soon, in perfect condition.[11]

Storrs recalls that "as a colleague his quickness and instantaneous grasp of essentials was astonishing. 'What does he want?' he would ask as we examined an Arab, or an Arabic document. For what he wanted usually proved to be something very different from the demand expressed."[12] Storrs recalled that Lawrence seemed to "gulp down all I could shed for him of Arabic knowledge, then bounded for him by the western bank of the Suez Canal; yet never by the 'pumping' of crude cross-examination. I told him things sometimes for the mere interest of his commentary. He was eager and unfatigued in bazaar-walking and mosque-hunting. I found him from the beginning an arresting and an intentionally provocative talker, liking nonsense to be treated as nonsense, and not civilly or dully accepted or dismissed. He could flame into sudden anger at a story of pettiness, particularly official pettiness or injustice."[13]

The most complete picture of Lawrence in his professional role during these years is provided by Dowson.[14] I offer it in some detail, for the qualities he displayed in this description "foreshadowed," as Dowson noted, "those displayed in the wider and more exacting arena of Arabia later." Dowson has captured better than anyone else the qualities of Lawrence's personality, his determination to deflate pomposity, expose inefficiency, and explode pretension. Naturally this irritated at times those who were the objects of his challenges or who found him threatening to their established postures or positions.

Dowson has described how Lawrence criticized severely the system of transliteration of Arabic place names into Roman characters that was being followed by two map officers, considerably older than himself, who had spent many months studying the subject. They naturally resented "having to take orders from such a boy, and felt that the War Office had acted in accordance with the ineptitude traditionally pertaining to it in burlesque in putting such a youngster in charge of anything."

In situations like the Survey, where there was a tradition of efficiency, Lawrence's insistence upon performance of high quality was appreciated and respected, and no one was perturbed, but other officers who were less sure of themselves resented Lawrence's effrontery. Although Lawrence had access to all the offices of the Survey and its craftsmen, Dowson "never received a grouse about him: and I never heard of an instance of misunderstanding or friction being created by him either through faulty human contact."

Dowson attributed "the elasticity of response to military requirements" that his office achieved to "a remarkable combination of qualities in Lawrence." These included "a rare capacity to regard an operation of any

sort objectively, and in the process to get inside the skin of the participants," the concentration of his vast ambition upon "achievement (large
or small) rather than for approbation of his personal performance"; the
capacity to leave men "to the utmost extent possible to do their own
work"; and the ability to avoid any belittlement of the work of others.
"His tremendous keenness," Dowson noted, "about anything to do with
the work was remarkable and infectious, with the consequence that his
frequent walks round the various offices and workshops had a most
stimulating effect on the men."

Dowson was impressed also with Lawrence's "extraordinary capacity to
get his own way quietly," working with or around the apparatuses of
government and administration "when this seemed of critical importance
to a necessary end," and recalled also his "extraordinary resourcefulness
and his versatile competence." Dowson describes a small crisis in which
there was an urgent need for a particular intricate spare part which
existed only under seal at the depot of a hostile firm. GHQ could do
nothing without referring the matter to London, which might produce no
results, or at best an intolerable delay. When Lawrence was told of the
problem he asked for an exact description of the article and the precise
location of the premises. The following morning he brought the article
along, saying without explanation that there had been "no difficulty."

Dowson noted that "the diversity of Lawrence's capacity was so remarkable that one only slowly and skeptically accepted its genuineness.
It sprang, I think, from unusual clarity of mind working on an unusual
catholicity of knowledge. This enabled him to seize and apply essentials
even in technical processes with which he was quite unfamiliar." Having
in mind the uses to which he would put this ability later, Dowson
stressed Lawrence's "visualization and photographic memory of topo-
graphical features of any ground which he had traversed" that he drew
upon in the compilation of new territories, which he could then integrate
with pieces of information about a locale he was receiving from other
sources. Finally, Dowson noted as many others have, Lawrence's puckish
humor, "his irrepressible fooling," which, more than his abilities or
achievements, "[we] keep in our hearts and memories."

The weeks in London after the war started, particularly after Turkey's
entry at the end of October 1914, seemed to drag for Lawrence. Once he
knew he was to be transferred to Egypt he looked forward to it eagerly
and resented official delays. Shortly before embarking with Newcombe
from Marseilles on December 9, he sent Leeds a small piece of red tape
affixed to War Office notepaper with the notation, "a sample of official
red tape."[15] Soon after arriving in Cairo, he wrote Leeds, "Today we got
the Office, and we all have the Intelligence: it is only a simple process of
combining the two. Newcombe is Director . . . a magnificent but unpaid

position . . . the Gods alone know what our pay is to be . . . for me I'm broke already, so have only a lack-lustre interest in the thing. Woolley looks after personnel . . . is sweet to callers in many tongues, and keeps lists of persons useful or objectionable. One Lloyd who is an M.P. [member of Parliament] of sorts and otherwise not bad looks after Mesopotamia . . . and Aubrey Herbert who is a quaint person looks after Turkish politics: between them in their spare time they locate the Turkish army, which is a job calling for magnifiers. . . . And I am bottle-washer and office boy pencil-sharpener and pen wiper . . . and I think I have more to do than others of the faculty. If we can get somebody to grapple with the telephone (which burbles continuously) I will be as happy and lazy as I want to be. Perhaps someday there will be work to do . . . but Carchemish seems a most doleful way away."[16]

Lawrence had written Hogarth after arriving, "It promises to be good fun," but soon began to be bored with the map-making, geographical reports and interviewing agents. He turned his attention to Middle Eastern politics — Syria was his greatest interest — and itched for a more active role in the war.

His famous resentment of French colonialism was expressed as early as February 15, 1915, in a letter to his family: "So far as Syria is concerned it is France and not Turkey that is the enemy . . . but I wish I could give it to Germany in some way, for the shameless way in which she dragged Turkey into the war. I don't think any nation has ever done in high politics anything quite so ——— [word illegible]."[17]

In March Lawrence pressed on Hogarth his views of the advantages of a landing at Alexandretta on the North Syrian coast, and as early as March 22 was demonstrating his knowledge of the politics of the various tribes of the Arabian Peninsula, and his desire to "pull them all together, and roll up Syria by way of the Hedjaz in the name of the Sherif."[18] His hopes for a landing at Alexandretta were disappointed in April when a British expeditionary force was sent to Gallipoli "beastly ill-prepared, with no knowledge of where it was going, or what it would meet, or what it was going to do."[19]

Lawrence's exasperation with tracking the movements of a Turkish army that he was taking no more active part in defeating was expressed to Leeds: "There are 40 divisions in the Turkish Army, in peace time, and that is doubled now that it is war, and the only one really settled, the one we 'defeat' from time to time on the canal, is located in the Caucasus by the Russians, at Pardirma by the Athens people, in Adrianople by Bulgaria, at Midia by Roumania, and in Baghdad by India. The locations of the other 39 regular, and 40 reserve divisions are less certain."[20] He also expressed to Leeds his exasperation with the influence of the conservative British Indian government on policy in the Arab areas. "Out upon all this show! I'm fed up, and fed up, and fed up: — and yet we have to go on doing it, and indeed we take on new jobs every day, because the W.O. [War Office] handed over this Med-force to our mercies,° with a side-request to keep India (Augean stable) and Basra [in Mesopotamia] up to date. The only branch I want, Arabian politics, they won't give us, but leave in the hands of a juggins in Delhi, whose efforts are to maintain the Aden Hinterland — a cesspit — in its status quo. Pouf —."[21]

In May, Lawrence's brother Frank was killed in France, and Lawrence wrote to his family that they should put a brave face on their loss. He found intolerable his mother's giving way to her grief in a letter to him and replied: "Poor Dear Mother, I got your letter this morning, and it has grieved me very much. You *will* never understand any of us after we are grown up a little. *Don't* you ever feel that we love you without our telling you so? — I feel such a contemptible worm for having to write this way about things. If you only knew that if one thinks deeply about anything one would rather die than say anything about it. You know men do nearly all die laughing, because they know death is very terrible, and a thing to be forgotten till after it has come.

"There, put that aside, and bear a brave face to the world about Frank. In a time of such fearful stress in our country it is one's duty to watch very carefully lest one of the weaker ones be offended: and you know we were always the stronger, and if they see you broken down they will all grow fearful about their ones at the front."[22]

As the Dardanelles campaign dragged on toward its ultimate collapse Lawrence continued to press without success for a landing at Alexandretta. Although he remained disappointed with the incompetence and failure of British policy and operations in the Near East, he saw in this failure an opportunity for the point of view that he shared with others in the Intelligence Office in Cairo. "I am pleased on the whole with things," he wrote home in October. "They have gone against us so far that our government has become more reasonable, and the final settlement out here, though it will take long, will I think be very satisfactory. We have to thank our failures for that: and to me, they are worth it."[23]

In September Lawrence's brother Will was shot down in France. His death was not known officially until the following May, but Lawrence took it for granted. He had been close to Will and was much troubled by his death. He wrote of his feelings to Leeds in an understated way: "I have not written to you for ever so long . . . I think really because there was nothing I had to say. It is partly being so busy here, that one's thoughts are all on the jobs one is doing, and one grudges doing anything

_____

° The Intelligence Office in Cairo, of which Lawrence was a member, was assigned the responsibility of being the "intelligence base" for the Mediterranean Expeditionary Force being sent to Gallipoli and Salonika, and he was therefore in telegraphic communication with Gallipoli, Greece, Russia and London.

else, and has no other interests, and partly because I'm rather low because first one and now another of my brothers has been killed. Of
course, I've been away a lot from them, and so it doesn't come on like a
shock at all . . . but I rather dread Oxford and what it may be like if one
comes back. Also they were both younger than I am, and *it doesn't seem
right, somehow, that I should go on living peacefully in Cairo*" [italics
added].[24]

Thereafter, Lawrence became increasingly impatient to enter more
actively into the military effort.

At Christmas Lawrence wrote home rather awkwardly and sternly,
"I'm afraid that for you it will be no very happy day; however, you have
still Bob and Arnie at home [later Robert Lawrence was to serve with
distinction as a doctor in France] which is far more than many people
have. Look forward all the time."[25] Lawrence's letters to his family
seemed to pick up in tone, principally, it would appear, because the
policy of supporting Arab efforts on the Arabian Peninsula that he and
his associates were pressing for was becoming accepted by the British
government, and he was able to devote his own efforts to studying Arabia.

But as the weeks of 1916 passed without a more active role for him,
Lawrence became increasingly impatient. "We do nothing here except sit
and think out harassing schemes of Arabian policy. My hair is getting
very thin and grey. . . . I'm going to be in Cairo till I die," he wrote.[26]

Those in Cairo, like Lawrence, who sought to advance the British war
effort by capitalizing on Arab independence movements in various parts
of the Ottoman Empire, had hoped that an uprising could be promoted
in Mesopotamia, and that it might be possible to win the Ottoman
Mesopotamian forces to the Allied side. Sayyid Talib, whom Lawrence
described as "vigorous but unscrupulous," was the leader of the movement
in Mesopotamia, and 'Aziz Ali al-Misri, the founder of the secret society
al-'Ahd, was idolized by the Arab army officers there. But the British
military and political authority for Mesopotamia was the Indian government, which was hostile to the aspirations for independence of the Mesopotamian people. Early successes in this theatre by General Charles
Townshend, who defeated with British troops the Turkish forces at the
first battle of Kut-el-Amara in September 1915, could only have confirmed
the Indian government's belief in the correctness of their policies.

A dispatch sent from General Staff (Intelligence) at Kut to the Indian
Foreign Office on November 8, six weeks after this victory, demonstrates
the characteristic British attitude in the Mesopotamian theatre toward the
Arabs and their strivings for independence:

The formation of an autonomous state in Iraq [Mesopotamia] appears to be
impossible and unnecessary. Here in Iraq there is no sign of the slightest am-

bition of the kind among the people, who expect and seem to be quite ready to accept our administration. Other ideas may grow in the course of years as they have in India, but we are of the opinion that from the point of view of Iraq it is highly inexpedient and unnecessary to put into the hands of the backward people of the country what seem to us the visionary and premature notions of the creation of an Arab State, notions which will only tend to make endless difficulties for *Great Britain* [italics added] here and serve no present purpose but to stimulate a small section of ambitious men to turn their activities to *a direction from which it is highly desireable to keep them for many years to come* [italics added]. Moreover, so far as we know, there is no personality who could be called upon to assume the high position of Ruler of an Independent Arab State.[27]

Later in November, Townshend's Indian and British forces ran into stiff Turkish resistance at Ctesiphon on the way to Baghdad and retreated back to Kut, where a five-month siege began early in December. In March 1916, Lawrence was sent by the high commissioner in Egypt, Henry McMahon, on a mission to negotiate with the Turkish commander and "try to ransom from him, on grounds of humanity or interest, those of the garrison of Kut whose health had suffered by the siege, and whom captivity would kill."[28] An additional purpose of his mission was to negotiate "with Arab elements in Turkish army with a view to detaching them from Turks and making afterwards side with Arab movement."[29] McMahon wrote Sir Percy Cox, the chief political officer in Iraq (who, in his report of Lawrence's activities, said of the mission, "I cannot as a political officer of the Government of India afford to be identified with it")[30] that he was sending Lawrence because "he is one of the best of our very able intelligence staff here and has a thorough knowledge of the Arab question in all its bearings."[31] Lawrence, however, has given the additional reason that he was selected because "I had put the Grand Duke Nicholas in touch with certain disaffected Arab officers in Erzurum [a Turkish city on the Caucasian Front which had fallen to the Russians in February]. Did it through the War Office and our Military Attaché in Russia. So the War Office thought I could do the same thing over Mespot."[32]

Both aspects of Lawrence's mission were unsuccessful. The ransom offer (which had reached the sum of £2,000,000 by April 28, the day before the garrison surrendered)[33] failed because the Ottoman commander would not agree to it, and the effort to promote an Arab mutiny was hopeless because no groundwork had been done by local British authorities in Iraq. There had been insufficient planning and time to permit Lawrence's contacts with potential Arab rebels in the area to produce useful results. Furthermore, as Suleiman Mousa, a Jordanian biographer of Lawrence, has suggested, enmity toward the Ottoman Empire among Arabs in Iraq was not on a par with the hatred felt by the Bedouin and Arab nationalists in the Hijaz and Syria.[34]

Some sense of the depth and extent of blundering that went into this campaign — which Lawrence called "a British disgrace, end to end"[35] — is conveyed rather poignantly in one of Townshend's last dispatches to his headquarters two days before he surrendered. He wrote of the great strain he had been under, that he was ill in mind and body, and that he had been given "all responsibility with entire conduct of all operations without a single order having been given me and with not a word of praise or reward."[36] A detailed account of the horror of disease, starvation and death that was Kut in April 1916, and the negotiations for the surrender of Townshend's force (in which Lawrence took part), is contained in the (then) anonymous diary of Aubrey Herbert, a British intelligence officer from Cairo who was present during this period.[37]

Upon his return to Cairo in May, Lawrence wrote a scathing report, criticizing every aspect of the campaign. According to one of Lawrence's fellow officers, it was bowdlerized by the staff in Cairo to protect the commander-in-chief, General Sir Archibald Murray,[38] and seems not to have survived. The dispatches and reports submitted by Lawrence that did survive concern the political tensions and lack of information among the several British commands, and accounts of the surrender terms (and their betrayal) by the Ottoman commander.[39] The first of these goes to the heart of the problem. Lawrence and Cox (whom Lawrence respected but considered "ignorant of Arab societies and Turkish politics," though "very open" to the views of Lawrence and his group)[40] had discussed the situation and had agreed upon the necessity of reconciling the differing views of Egypt, Mesopotamia and India; they recommended that a "round table conference under the presidency of a statesman, who would carry sufficient weight with all three elements," be convened.[41]

The chief significance of the Mesopotamian episode in Lawrence's development as a political and military leader lay in the lesson it contained: the futility, and ultimately the terrible danger, for *all* the population involved, of a Western power's pursuing its national policies on foreign soil with utter disregard for the nature and political aspirations of the local population. Although Townshend's army contained, according to Herbert, five thousand Arabs — half his force — the Mesopotamian and Indian governments had done little work with Arab leaders in the area. Much too late, and after the fact, Lawrence, the Arab expert, was sent to Mesopotamia with orders from Egypt to "promise to do all we can to help Arab Independence."[42] As Lawrence wrote in one of his accounts, the Arabs in the Kut region "had shown themselves, in the main, friendly to us, but had not been asked to take any active part in operations."[43] No effort had been made to work with Arab goodwill, to cultivate it in the pursuit of mutually advantageous policies.

This failure was a classic demonstration of the arrogance or ignorance (or both) that Western "great" powers often display when they work with weaker, local governments of differing cultures. Even from a narrowly military point of view, unless the armies or the weaponry are of overwhelming superiority, as they were in Allenby's campaign in Palestine in 1918, it is unusual for an effective result to be achieved by an alien force in a foreign land. This is especially true if there is a hostile, politically well-organized segment of the population that has the sympathy of the local people. None of these actualities of guerrilla warfare was lost on Lawrence, who was decades ahead of his time and his government in grasping their reality. It is a testimony to his persuasiveness that he was able to convince his superiors in the government to allow him a free hand in working with and through native leaders and populations in the pursuit of British national goals during the years of the Arab Revolt.

At the time of the Mesopotamian campaigns Lawrence was evidently tactless in communicating to local British regular army officers his disdain for traditional approaches. Hubert Young has described "the passion of contempt for the regular army" which Lawrence seems not to have suppressed during his mission in Mesopotamia, and claims that the antagonism between Lawrence and the Mesopotamian military authorities was to have "serious [adverse] effects on British policy in the Middle East."[44] I have not found evidence to support this assertion. In any event Lawrence seems to have learned to control his hostility and to pursue his aims more subtly thereafter.

Aboard ship returning to Cairo in mid-May of 1916, Lawrence wrote a voluminous, descriptive letter to his family, giving many details of what he had observed of the lands and peoples of Mesopotamia, but omitting most of his political involvement and his feelings about the Kut disaster. He revealed his preference for the regions of the upper Euphrates, where he had spent more contented years, over the Mesopotamia he had just visited, and revealed in tales and reminiscences his longing for Carchemish.[45] "Hereafter I will again be nailed within that office at Cairo — the most interesting place until the Near East settles down," he wrote, as if he had no inkling of the direction his life would take in but a few months.

Just a few weeks after Lawrence returned from Mesopotamia to Cairo late in May, news came of the revolt of Sharif Husayn and his sons against the Turks. "The Reuter telegram on the revolt of the Sherif of Mecca I hope interested you," Lawrence wrote home cautiously, three weeks after learning of the Revolt. "It has taken a year and a half to do, but now is going very well. It is so good to have helped a bit in making a new nation — and I hate the Turks so much that to see their own people turning on them is very grateful. I hope the movement increases, as it promises to do. You will understand how impossible it is for me to tell you what the work we do really consists of, for it is all this sort of thing.

This revolt, if it succeeds will be the biggest thing in the Near East since 1550" (he is referring, presumably to the conquests by Suleiman the Magnificent).[46] Lawrence seems so often, as in this instance, to write of momentous matters in a boyish and personal way.

At the time the Revolt began, Lawrence suggested supplementing the official bulletins of the Cairo Intelligence Office with summaries of news and other information from the various theatres of war in the Near East. These summaries, which together constitute a collection of documents filling three volumes, were known as *The Arab Bulletin,* of which twenty-six copies were issued under the editorship of Hogarth.[47] Lawrence contributed a number of items.

The *Bulletin* is a valuable source of information concerning the disposition of the various tribes throughout the Middle East toward the Ottoman government and the Allies; the progress of the campaigns; the fortifications, troop strengths and movements, and other information about the Ottoman army; the political situation within the Ottoman central and local governments; and the activities of their German allies. The *Bulletin* also contains much data about the personalities and relationships of leaders throughout the Arab world. The early issues convey from intelligence reports and journalistic excerpts from North Africa and the Middle East the complex mixture of reactions which greeted the news of the Revolt of the sharif of Mecca against the Ottoman authority.[48]

The Revolt itself proceeded hesitantly during the early months. After the fall of Mecca attacks on the Turkish garrison at Medina failed, and although there were some local successes, Lawrence wrote home in mid-September, "Things in Arabia are not going too well."[49] In August Sir Reginald Wingate, the sirdar of the Sudan (under whose command the military operations in the Hijaz fell at this time), sent Colonel C. E. Wilson to take residence in Jidda (the port for Mecca on the Red Sea), and at the end of the month Faisal complained to Wilson of the lack of military support from Great Britain, which had yet to acclaim the Revolt publicly.[50] Wilson considered the situation of the sharifian forces to be desperate and the Arab movement in danger of collapse. He recommended that a brigade of troops be sent to Rabegh on the Red Sea coast to support Faisal.[51] But the War Office in London, influenced by the India Office's opposition to supporting the Arab movement, considered that such an effort would be futile and wired to Cairo, "Gallipoli and Mesopotamia should have given quite sufficient proof of such futility."[52]

The indifferent success of the Revolt at this time was also due to the reluctance of some of the local tribes in the Hijaz to become allied with a losing cause and thereby risk Turkish reprisal. The absence of proper liaison for the Arab forces in the field, and of military information for the sharif and his sons, were additional factors. All this was compounded by a confusion among the various British authorities in Cairo and the Sudan on how to proceed, to which were added the intrigues of a French mission which reached Jidda in September. "The Arab Revolt became discredited; and Staff Officers in Egypt gleefully prophesied to us its near failure and the stretching of Sherif Hussein's neck on a Turkish scaffold," Lawrence wrote afterwards.[53]

In the meantime, if one were to go by Lawrence's letters to his family, he seems to have had nothing better to do over the summer of 1916 than to design new Hijaz postage stamps for Sharif Husayn, which were to replace the Turkish issues then in use. "I'm going to have flavoured gum on the back," Lawrence wrote in late July, "so that one may lick without unpleasantness."[54] (The red ones were flavored with strawberry essence and the green ones with pineapple, Lawrence told a friend many years later, but the Arabs liked the taste so well that they sucked it all away so that the stamps fell off in the post.)[55] His personal position became more difficult in the summer of 1916, when Sir Gilbert Clayton, who had been a sympathetic and flexible supporter of Lawrence's irregular ways and strong advocacy of the Arab Revolt, was replaced by Thomas Holdich as director of the intelligence section in which Lawrence was serving.[56] Holdich, whom Lawrence described as "excellent in O. [Operations] and fatal in I. [Intelligence],"[57] took his orders from Sir Archibald Murray, the general in charge in Egypt, who had little interest in supporting the Arab uprising. Lawrence found his enthusiasm for, and efforts to help, the fledgling Arab Revolt increasingly stifled by unsympathetic superiors.

Having determined that Holdich was "keeping me away from the Arab affair," Lawrence states in *Seven Pillars*, "I decided that I must escape at once, if ever. A straight request was refused; so I took to stratagems. I became, on the telephone (G.H.Q. were at Ismailia, and I in Cairo) quite intolerable to the Staff on the Canal. I took every opportunity to rub into them their comparative ignorance and inefficiency in the department of intelligence (not difficult!) and irritated them yet further by literary airs, correcting Shavian split infinitives and tautologies in their reports."[58]

One may question whether Lawrence's insubordination was really as tactless as this sounds, as he hardly would have avoided disciplinary action if it had been. In any event, in October he succeeded in wangling leave to accompany Storrs, whom Abdullah had been urgently begging to come to Jidda for consultation regarding a crisis with the Turks on the Red Sea coast.[59] Lawrence states that officials were only too glad to get rid of him; Storrs reports more soberly that he applied for Lawrence because of "gratitude for his assistance in the Hedjaz stamp issue and in other matters, the high value I attached to his judgment on any question, and his admirable company."[60]

At about this time Lawrence applied for a transfer to the Arab Bureau and joined the group in November. The Arab Bureau, formed in February

1916, consisted of a small group of Arab experts, most notably Hogarth and Clayton, who were particularly concerned with political intelligence and the sharifian cause, and from the time of its formation acted as a staff and intelligence office for the Arab campaign. In contrast, the intelligence section that Lawrence was then serving in was under the War Office and more preoccupied with conventional military operations in the Sinai and Palestine. With his departure for Jidda on October 13, 1916, Lawrence embarked upon the two-year period of his life from which his principal fame and notoriety have derived.

It is very difficult to assess Lawrence's role during his two years in Cairo, or to gauge his influence during this period upon the development of British military and political policies and strategies in relation to the Arab peoples. His letters demonstrate his impatience, his intense frustration at policies and decisions of which he disapproved, and his frustration at not having a more active part. To Leeds early in 1916 he described himself as "a miserable grain of faith trying to move mountains."[61] Gertrude Bell provides a contemporary glimpse of the enormity of his youthful ambitions for achievement in a letter written after she had visited with Lawrence during his mission to Mesopotamia. "This week has been greatly enlivened by the appearance of Mr. Lawrence sent out as liaison officer from Egypt," Miss Bell wrote. "We have had great talks and made vast schemes for the government of the universe."[62]

Yet if he was as insolent as he claims he was (which I doubt), or consistently as "thoroughly spoilt and posing" as Young found him to be in Mesopotamia,[63] it is doubtful that he would have got very far in influencing anyone. The contemporary evidence of McMahon, Storrs, Dowson and Hogarth attest to the high regard in which Lawrence was held at this time and the extraordinary depth and range of his abilities. Hogarth wrote in 1920 of Lawrence's "singular persuasiveness" and that when he "was still a second lieutenant in the Cairo military intelligence, but with a purpose more clearly foreseen than perhaps that of any one else, he was already pulling the wires."[64] To pull these wires Lawrence as a second lieutenant or staff captain worked largely through men like Hogarth, Clayton and Storrs, who had closer access than he did to those who actually formulated policy.

But in what direction was he trying to pull? Lawrence's antagonism toward French colonial ambitions in Syria is well known, and his 1915 letters to Hogarth arguing for Arab revolts in order to "biff the French out of all hope of Syria" are also well known and often quoted.[65] In 1915, Lawrence's hopes for an Arab uprising lay at first with al-Idrisi in Yemen[66] rather than with Husayn (although he recognized the sharif's prestige in Syria), and it is possible that he was unaware during 1915 of the negotiations his government was then carrying on with the sharif. In two reports found in the Public Record Office written by Lawrence early in 1916 he set forth his views concerning the anticipated partition of the Ottoman Empire. They are written in a tone of British chauvinism and hard political realism of which any old colonial hand might be proud. In one of these essays he advocated the British conquest of all Syria on strategic grounds, or, should that prove economically, politically and militarily impractical, an agreement and a division of "our spoils with France." (Lawrence would probably have had at that time no knowledge of the McMahon-Husayn correspondence or the Sykes-Picot negotiations which were then in progress.) After the reduction of the Ottoman Empire to holdings in Anatolia, "the most probable claimant — barring the Sultan — to the Khalifate would be the Sherif of Mecca, who has been active in the last few years in Arabia and Syria, asserting himself as an arbiter of morals. He is held down by Turkish money — which we, via Egypt or India could replace with interest — and by a Turkish Army Corps."[67]

Lawrence advocated cutting the Hijaz railroad (as he would later lead the Bedouin in doing), in order to prevent supplies from reaching the Turkish garrisons, and to disrupt local Ottoman administrations by severing their communications with the central Ottoman government. With the Ottoman army in the Hijaz divided into "an assembly of fearful Syrian peasants and incompetent alien officers," the Arab chiefs in the Hijaz "would make their own hay: and for our pilgrims sake one can only hope quickly." This approach, Lawrence predicted, would render the Ottoman government helpless in the Hijaz, and would enlist the help of the Bedouin because the railroad had reduced their annual tolls during the pilgrimages.[68]

In the other paper, written in January 1916, Lawrence wrote that Husayn's activity would be useful to the British government in disrupting and defeating the Ottoman Empire, and also because "the states he would set up to succeed the Turks would be as harmless to ourselves as Turkey was before she became a tool in German hands." He feared colonization by another European power and wrote that "if properly handled [the Arabs] would remain in a state of political mosaic, a tissue of small jealous principalities incapable of cohesion, and yet always ready to combine against an outside force." Husayn, Lawrence wrote further, had "a mind some day to taking the place of the Turkish Government in the Hedjaz himself. If we can only arrange that this political change shall be a violent one, we will have abolished the threat of Islam, by dividing it against itself, in its very heart. There will then be a Khalifa in Turkey and a Khalifa in Arabia, in theological warfare, and Islam will be as little formidable as the Papacy when the Popes lived in Avignon."[69]

These are cynical, coldly written documents. Although they anticipate policies that Lawrence would personally implement, they indicate no sympathy with or interest in Arab freedom, independence or nationalism. On the contrary they advocate using attitudes and ambitions of the Arabs

and their leaders in the pursuit of British military and political policies —
policies of conquest and occupation at that. He seems to have written in
this hard tone with youthful relish, as if to show he was "one of the boys."
Yet it is difficult to interpret Lawrence's personal motives in writing these
papers. We do not know for whom in particular they were intended, or
even to whom they were immediately addressed. "The Politics of Mecca"
found its way to the high commissioner and to Sir Edward Grey, the
foreign secretary in London, and Lawrence may well have been trying to
present the kinds of arguments which could influence or change the views
of superiors who were fundamentally hostile to or at least unsympathetic
to supporting the Bedouin and Husayn on the grounds of traditional
English imperialistic policies and opinions. Most of these officials would
not have wished to hear arguments favoring the formation of cohesive,
free, independent and potentially anti-British Arab states. Lawrence may
have thought that once his government had begun to pursue a policy of
supporting the sharif and the Arabs of the Hijaz, he could, with his
knowledge of the Arab world, then influence policy in his own direction.
Finally, it must be kept in mind that these papers were written in the
beginning of 1916, when Lawrence was not yet twenty-eight, at a time
when the destructive consequences of manipulating other peoples' minds
and lives were not yet fully evident to him. They need to be seen from
the perspective of his subsequent personal and political development.

Looking back to these years after the war Lawrence had some tendency
to exaggerate his role and importance in specific policy decisions. In 1915,
for example, in his letters to Hogarth (and possibly in other papers and
reports that have not survived) he urged strenuously a landing at Alexandretta as the strategic "key of the whole place" (Syria), and provided
extensive justifications for his position. It is not known what Hogarth did
with this information: whether he in turn argued for the Alexandretta
scheme with higher British authorities on the basis of Lawrence's justifications. In 1929 Lawrence wrote to Liddell Hart, "I am unrepentant about
the Alexandretta scheme which was, from beginning to end, my invention,
put forward necessarily through my chiefs. (I was a 2nd Lieutenant of
3 months seniority!) Actually K. [Kitchener] accepted it, and ordered it,
for the Australian and N.Z. forces: and then was met by a French
ultimatum."[70] But there apparently were extensive high-level discussions
of the possibility of a landing at Alexandretta, "which Kitchener had more
than once discussed with Maxwell before the War, and to which he
steadily adhered,"[71] and it is unlikely that Lawrence could have exerted
more than a minor influence, however agilely he could skip through or
leap over channels. In any event the scheme, which might have shortened
the war in the Middle East, was repeatedly rejected.

Lawrence seems also to have been less than completely accurate in
what he told his biographers about the role of Cairo Intelligence in the

Russian capture of Erzurum in Anatolia in February 1916, although this is more difficult to substantiate. It will be recalled that Lawrence told Liddell Hart that the reason he was selected for the Mesopotamian mission the following month was that he had put the Grand Duke Nicholas, who was in charge of the Russian forces in the Caucasus, in touch with disaffected Arab officers in Erzurum. But to Graves he had written in 1927 that the capture of Erzurum had been "arranged."[72] Now it is true that Lawrence, who had had an important intelligence hand in the Dardanelles operations and the evacuation of Gallipoli in January, may have supplied useful information to the Russians on the whereabouts of Turkish troops that were being removed from the Gallipoli campaign; and it is also true that the Arab Bureau may have influenced the results of the battle at Erzurum through the propaganda activity. But all this is quite different from an "arranged" capture, and the available evidence indicates that Erzurum fell only after severe fighting.

These apparent distortions seem to have been made by Lawrence "offhand" and only when his involvement was relatively minor. And he made them long after the fact. They apparently relate to problems of self-esteem, which came to the surface after his war experiences. He seems never to have made similarly distorted statements regarding his influence in bringing about the Arab Revolt, or in persuading British officials to encourage and support the sharifian rebellion during late 1915 and early 1916, although his influence in these events seems to have been of considerable importance. Hogarth, in fact, called Lawrence "a moving spirit in the negotiations leading to an Arab Revolt and organizing the Arab Bureau."[73]

12

The Course of
the Arab Revolt

I am going off tomorrow for a few days. I hope to be back in about
a fortnight or less," Lawrence wrote on October 12, 1916.¹ With these
casual words Lawrence announced his first trip to Arabia, a trip which
would begin his active involvement in the desert campaigns.° When
Lawrence went with Ronald Storrs to Jidda in response to Abdullah's
distress call, the Arab forces under Husayn's four sons had captured most
of the towns in the vicinity of Mecca, but were unable to capture Medina,
which was held by a strong Turkish garrison. Until the Arab forces were
strengthened, they were in danger of losing from Turkish counterattacks
what they had gained during the summer, and the Turkish army would
continue to be able to move supplies freely down the Hijaz railroad from
Damascus.²

Lawrence soon left Storrs and went by sea to Rabegh, up the coast
from Jidda. He then journeyed inland by camel and met on October 23
with Amir Faisal for the first time. "I felt at first glance that this was the
man I had come to Arabia to seek — the leader who would bring the
Arab Revolt to full glory," Lawrence wrote dramatically of this meeting.³
He learned from Faisal what the Arabs needed, and persuaded British
officials in Cairo to provide sufficient supplies, ammunition, modern
weapons and money to enable Faisal to develop an effective fighting

---

° This chapter is written as much as possible from contemporary sources in order
to avoid the transformations of later hindsights. I will not attempt here to provide a
detailed narrative of the *military* operations of the Arab Revolt or of the Palestine
campaigns. These have been described many times in writings by Lawrence himself;
by Liddell Hart, Young, Antonius, Birdwood, Stirling, and Mousa; in the British
official history of the war; and in many other works by officers and officials who took
a personal part in one or another aspect of the operations. Rather, this chapter will
summarize the general course of the Arab campaigns and Lawrence's part in them.

force. These materials soon began arriving through the coastal base at Yenbo.

Lawrence was successful in discouraging the plan favored by Colonel Edouard Brémond, head of the French mission in the Hijaz, and others of sending large numbers of British, French, Egyptian or Indian troops into battle: the Bedouins would not have tolerated this kind of direct intervention "and would certainly scatter to their tents again as soon as they heard of the landing of foreigners in force."[4] In any event, as Lord Hankey wrote, at this stage of the war "the question that arose about Egypt was not one of sending reinforcements, but solely of how many divisions could be drawn from there to France."[5] Even so, in November Hogarth was able to write with some optimism to his sister: "All round, however, the coast is clearing and my own particular little war is going quite well in its own strange way. It is 'the Asian Mystery that it has lived till now'! December will make six months and I hardly dared to give it three."[6]

The strategy that Lawrence and other officers evolved — of working through the Arab forces in the Hijaz while utilizing a small number of British officers, such as Newcombe, Garland, Joyce, Hornby and Davenport, in an advisory and planning capacity — suited well the relatively weakened state of the Allied forces in the Middle Eastern theatre at that time. It also kept British casualties to a minimum, an important objective for Lawrence. He became the principal intermediary between the British and French commands and Faisal's forces in Arabia, and also to a degree among the Arab tribes ("I see myself as primarily Intelligence Officer, or liaison with Feisal," he wrote in a dispatch to Cairo in December).[7] But he was or became, as we will see, much more than a liaison officer. By his powerful influence on Faisal (and on Faisal's brothers and father as well), and through Faisal's dependence upon him for weaponry, supplies, money, advice and technological help, Lawrence placed himself in a position to have a correspondingly strong influence upon the course of British-Arab relations in the years to come.

Lawrence recognized that a direct assault upon the railroad head of Medina, with its strong garrison (eleven thousand men according to the estimate he made in September 1916 from his interviews of Turkish prisoners),[8] would, to be successful, require more numerous forces than were available to the Arabs and would also cause many casualties, which might discourage the Arab effort altogether.

He evolved instead, during a ten-day period of illness in Abdullah's camp in March, a strategy that he summarized concisely in an essay called "Evolution of a Revolt," which he wrote after the war.[9] His plan was to use the mobile Arab forces, familiar with the desert terrain, to break up the communications of the more conventional, static Turkish forces. The large garrisons, especially Medina, would not be assaulted

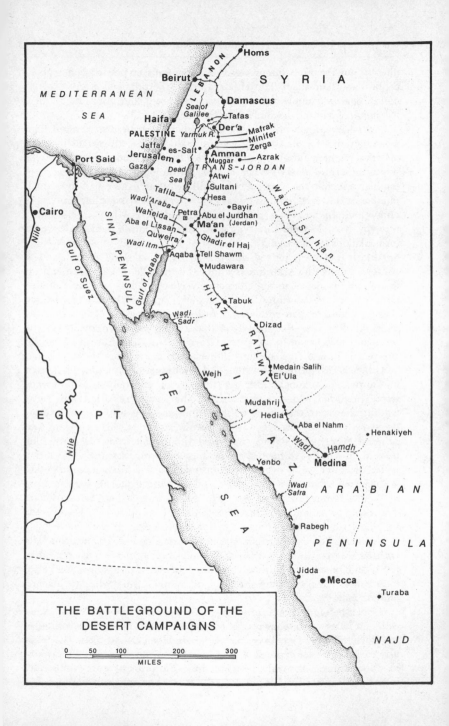

THE BATTLEGROUND OF THE
DESERT CAMPAIGNS

0   50   100   200   300
MILES

directly, for the Arab forces were not numerous or powerful enough to capture and hold them. The Hijaz railroad, the principal artery of communication and supply, would be kept working, "but only just," with a maximum of loss and discomfort for the enemy.[10]

Lawrence was concerned more with what the tribesmen thought than what they did, for his strategy was founded on the advantages inherent in a sympathetic local population. He has expounded clearly in his writings (*Seven Pillars of Wisdom* and "Evolution of a Revolt") the now-familiar principle that success in guerrilla warfare can be had by a small number of active, committed rebels in an otherwise passive but supportive population. In the Hijaz, Trans-Jordan and Syria, the various tribes, brought psychologically into sympathy with the aims of the Revolt, would form a ladder to Damascus.

Turkish traffic was indeed interrupted by demolishing the railroad at strategic points; the Arab forces under the tutelage of Lawrence and his fellow officers began to fight effectively as guerrillas, and the valuable port of Wejh was captured in January of 1917 by a British naval force acting in collaboration with the Arab forces. Seeing these successes, the tribes in the Hijaz that had hesitated to declare their loyalty to the sharifian cause began to join Faisal's army. The Arab forces enjoyed, in Lawrence's phrase, "the constant affluence of newcomers."[11]

As the success of the Revolt took hold in the desert, it also gained favor in Cairo. "Sir Archibald Murray [the British commander]," Lawrence wrote, "realized with a sudden shock that more Turkish troops were fighting the Arabs than were fighting him, and began to remember how he had always favoured the Arab revolt."[12] Others, like Wingate and Admiral Wemyss, who had supported the Revolt from the start, took pride in its success. In his dispatches Lawrence revealed the gratification he felt at Faisal's pride over the achievements of the tribes acting together in their own behalf. In a report sent to headquarters just after the capture of Wejh Lawrence wrote: " 'Yes, we [Faisal is speaking] are no longer Arabs, but a nation.' He was proud, for the advance on Wejh of the Juheina [tribe] was the biggest moral achievement of the new Hedjaz government. For the first time the entire manhood of a tribe, complete with its transport and food for a 200 mile march, has left its own diva [sic], and proceeded (without the hope of plunder or the stimulus of inter-tribal feuds) into the territory of another tribe with a detached military aim."[13]

A week before the capture of Wejh, Lawrence wrote to Stewart Newcombe a letter which conveys his exhilaration with the early successes of the Revolt and the schoolboy spirit he maintained at that time. The letter also contains a clear expression of his view that the British would do best to work through the Arabs, leaving them the primary responsibility for their own destinies.

"This show is splendid: you cannot imagine greater fun for us, greater vexation and fury for the Turks. We win hands down if we keep the Arabs simple . . . to add to them heavy luxuries will only wreck this show, and guerrilla does it. It's a sort of guerre de course, with the courses all reversed. But the life and fun and movement of it are extreme. . . .

"After all it's an Arab war, and we are only contributing materials — and the Arabs have the right to go their own way and run things as they please. We are only guests."[14]

Two weeks later Lawrence wrote to his family: "The job I have is a rather responsible one, and sometimes it is a little heavy to see which way one ought to act. I am getting rather old with it all, I think! However it is very nice to be out of the office, with some field work in hand, and the position I have is such a queer one — I do not suppose that any Englishman before ever had such a place."[15]

As the tribes of the Hijaz came forth to join Faisal, Lawrence wrote to his family enthusiastically in mid-February, "The Arabs of the Hedjaz are all for the Sherif, some keenly enough to volunteer, others less keen, but all well wishers." He continued: "The Arab Movement is a curious thing. It is really very small and weak in its beginning, and anybody who had command of the sea could put an end to it in three or four days. It has, however, capacity for expansion — in some degree — over a very wide area. It is as though you imagine a nation or agitation that may be very wide, but never very deep, since all the Arab countries are agricultural or pastoral, and all poor today, as a result of Turkish efforts in the past.

"On the other hand the Arab movement is shallow, not because the Arabs do not care, but because they are few — and in their smallness of number (which is imposed by their poverty of country) lies a good deal of their strength, for they are perhaps the most elusive enemy an army ever had, and inhabit one of the most trying countries in the world for civilized warfare. So that on the whole you may write me down a reasonable optimist. I hope that the show may go as we wish, and that the Turkish flag may disappear from Arabia. It is indiscreet only to ask what Arabia is. It has an East and a West and a South border — *but where or what it is on the top no man knoweth. I fancy myself it is up to the Arabs to find out!*"[16] (Italics added)

Lawrence's determination to leave open-ended the question of where the northern border of Arabia was, and his plan of helping "the Arabs to find out," was to bring him into constant struggles with Colonel Edouard Brémond. Brémond had the responsibility not only of helping in the military struggle against Turkey but also of representing the French government, which may have been just as unsure about where the top of Arabia was but certain that far enough north there should be a French lid in Syria on Arab national expansion.[17]

Although Lawrence was becoming, as he put it, "a monomaniac about the job at hand," he managed to find time to send his younger brother, now nearly seventeen, some stamps newly printed for the Hijaz, and to ask him what other kinds he wished.[18]

In February 1917, from his base at Wejh, Faisal made contact with the Howeitat and other nomadic tribes of what is now Jordan and northern Saudi Arabia, and obtained their assurances of loyalty. In a dispatch in mid-February Lawrence wrote: "Feisal swore the Abu Tayi Sheikhs* on the Koran to wait while he waited, march when he marched, to show mercy to no Turks, but to everyone who spoke Arabic, whether Baghdadi, Aleppine, or Syrian, and to put the needs of Arab Independence above their lives, their goods or their families. He also began to confront them with their tribal enemies, and force them to swear internal peace for the duration of the war."[19]

In March Lawrence met 'Awdah abu-Tayyi, "the greatest fighting man in northern Arabia," whose support would be necessary for the advance on Aqaba and for "swinging" the tribes north as far as Ma'an.[20] In the spring of 1917, in the tents of the Bedouin leaders and in consultation with Clayton, Wingate and other British officers in Egypt, the plan to take Aqaba by land was developed. Lawrence, 'Awdah and Nasir (the sharif of Medina) set off early in May from Wejh toward the Wadi Sirhan, a famous roadway, camping ground and chain of wells in the desert northeast of Aqaba, with the plan of cutting back to the southwest and taking the important port by land from the rear.

At the beginning of June, Lawrence started from the Sirhan with two men on a secret and dangerous mission to Baalbek (now in Lebanon) and Damascus to confer with Arab nationalists in Syria and to seek out the opportunities for an uprising there.[21] The value of this mission is described in a letter found among General Wingate's personal papers: "Lawrence's exploit in the Syrian Hinterland was really splendid and I hope you will have an opportunity of putting in a word that will help him to get the V.C., which in my opinion he has so thoroughly earned. Clayton and G.H.Q. are now digesting the information he has collected with a view to working out a scheme of cooperation from Sinai, Baghdad and the Hedjaz. There are at any rate the makings of a useful diversion against the railway line north of Maan."[22]

After returning to the Wadi Sirhan, Lawrence, 'Awdah, and several hundred Bedouin from various tribes of the region moved back in a south-westerly direction, taking the Turkish forces by surprise. They moved through Bayr, Al-Jafr, Aba el Lissan, Quweira, and down the narrow and rugged defile in the Wadi Itm to Aqaba, where the Turkish garrison surrendered on July 6.

* The Abu Tayi was a branch of the Howeitat tribe of southern Jordan.

With the capture of Aqaba — it was taken almost without casualties — the war in the Hijaz ended. Faisal could move his base there from Wejh, Sinai was secure, and the British were provided with a vital seaport for supplying their armies in Palestine for operations to the north. "After the capture of Akaba," Lawrence wrote a decade later, "things in the field changed so much that I was no longer a witness of the Revolt, but a protagonist in the Revolt."[23]

A contemporary example of how Lawrence's exploits during the previous month were regarded by other British officers is provided in the diary (not accurate in all its details) of an intelligence officer in Cairo, Captain Orlo Williams, who wrote four days after the capture of Aqaba: "Lawrence of I [the corps to which he was attached] has just returned, dressed as an Arab, from a most gallant adventurous sojourn in Arabia. He went up from Maan along the railway to near Tadmor and thence to Damascus, destroying several bridges on the way, thence back down Palestine seeing Arab and Druse chiefs, whom he found politically favourable to the Sherif. Then on July 2nd he set the Arabs about Maan onto the Turks, with the result that a whole Turkish battalion was wiped out and the Arabs now hold the coast."[24]

The following month George Lloyd wrote to Wingate: "[Lawrence] has done wonderfully good work and will some day be able to write a unique book. Generally the kind of men capable of these adventures lack the pen and the wit to record them, adequately. Luckily Lawrence is specially gifted with both."[25]

Lawrence returned to Cairo from Aqaba and was pleased to learn that Edmund Allenby had replaced Archibald Murray as commander-in-chief of Allied forces in Egypt. A relationship of great mutual trust and respect grew between them, and Lawrence persuaded Allenby that Faisal's Arab forces, based now at Aqaba, could, under his (Lawrence's) guidance, be a valuable adjunct on the right or eastern flank of Allenby's armies advancing through Palestine. In order to forestall opposition from "King" Husayn (the sharif had proclaimed himself king early in November), who might see in the transfer some loss of authority, Lawrence visited him in Jidda. The king accepted the transfer of Faisal "from the area of King Hussein to become an army commander of the Allied expedition under Allenby."[26] After the meeting Lawrence described the old man, whom he had not met before, as "pitifully unfit for the rough and tumble of forming a new administration out of the ruins of the Turkish system."[27]

In August, Faisal's army — and Lawrence as his principal liaison — was transferred from Wingate's command to the Egyptian Expeditionary Force under General Allenby, which meant that Lawrence's work was more clearly under Allenby's jurisdiction. Allenby wrote of their working relationship: "After acquainting him with my strategical plan, I gave him

a free hand."[28] As we shall see, this "free hand," which was used to encourage Faisal toward dreams of an Arab empire in Syria, was to have
increasing political significance as the theatre of war moved northward
into territories where the political interests of the Great Powers were to
come into conflict.[29]

Ten years later Lawrence wrote to Charlotte Shaw of his relationship
with Allenby: "All he required of us was a turnover of native opinion from
the Turk to the British: and I took advantage of that need of his, to
make him the stepfather of the Arab National Movement — a movement
which he did not understand and for whose success his instinct had little
sympathy. He is a very large, downright and splendid person, and the
being publicly yoked with a counter-jumping opportunist like me must
often gall him deeply. You and G.B.S. live so much with poets and politi-
cians and artists that human oddness attracts you, almost as much as it
repels. Whereas with the senior officers of the British Army conduct is a
very grave matter."[30] To another officer who had also served under
Allenby, Lawrence observed: "I love him as Petrie loves a pyramid —
not madly, but in proportion."[31]

Over the next three months Lawrence was engaged in moving back and
forth between Cairo and Aqaba, arranging for the countless needs of the
forces based there, planning and participating in train-wrecking and other
raids along the railroad south of the Turkish base at Ma'an (described in
detail in *Seven Pillars of Wisdom*), encouraging Faisal (who at times lost
heart), and attending to endless organizational problems and details that
related to his liaison work with the Arab and British forces. In late August
he wrote to his family that the campaign was "for the moment . . . heavy
and slow, weary work, with no peace for the unfortunate begetter of it
anywhere."[32]

No detail seemed too small to escape Lawrence's attention. When he
returned to Aqaba in mid-August he wrote home: "My milk camel has
run dry: a nuisance this, because it will take me time to find another. I
have too much to do, little patience to do it with, and things are going
tolerably well. It is much more facile doing daily work as a cog of a
machine, than it is running a campaign by yourself."[33]

In his letters Lawrence reflected different attitudes, according to whom
he was writing. To a fellow officer (W. F. Stirling), for example, he wrote
in a schoolboy tone: "The last stunt was the hold up of a train. It had two
locomotives, and we gutted one with an electric mine. This rather
jumbled up the trucks, which were full of Turks shooting at us. We had a
Lewis, and flung bullets through the sides. So they hopped out and took
cover behind the embankment, and shot at us between the wheels, at 50
yards. Then we tried a Stokes gun, and two beautiful shots dropped right
in the middle of them. They couldn't stand that (12 died on the spot) and
bolted away to the East across a 100 yard belt of open sand into some
scrub. Unfortunately for them the Lewis covered the open stretch. The

whole job took ten minutes, and they lost 70 killed, 30 wounded, 80 prisoners and about 25 got away. Of my hundred Howeitat and two British NCO's there was one (Arab) killed, and four (Arabs) wounded.

"The Turks nearly cut us off as we looted the train, and I lost some baggage, and nearly myself. My loot is a superfine red Baluch prayer-rug.

"I hope this sounds the fun it is. The only pity is the sweat to work them up and the wild scramble while it lasts. It's the most amateurish, Buffalo-Billy sort of performance, and the only people who do it well are the Bedouin. Only you will think it heaven, because there aren't any returns, or orders, or superiors, or inferiors; no doctors, no accounts, no meals, and no drinks."[34]

But to E. T. Leeds, perhaps because he was not a military man, Lawrence wrote of the same episodes more candidly, telling more of his troubled feelings, experience of danger and sense of horror. He described the raid more briefly, mentioned getting "a good Baluch prayer-rug," but added, "[I] lost all my kit, and nearly my little self." Lawrence then went on to say: "I'm not going to last out this game much longer: nerves going and temper wearing thin, and one wants an unlimited amount of both . . . on a show so narrow and voracious as this one loses one's past and one's balance and becomes hopelessly self-centered. I don't think I ever think except about shop, and I'm quite certain I never do anything else. That must be my excuse for dropping everyone, and I hope when the nightmare ends that I will wake up and become alive again. This killing and killing of Turks is horrible. When you charge in at the finish and find them all over the place in bits, and still alive many of them, and you know that you have done hundreds in the same way before and must do hundreds more if you can . . ."[35]

Finally, to his family he wrote in a breezy tone, conveying nothing of his true feelings: "I'm now back in Akaba, after having had a little trip up country to the Railway, for the last fortnight. We met all sorts of difficulties, mostly political, but in the end bagged two locomotives and blew them up, after driving out the troops behind them. It was the usual Arab show, done at no cost to us, expensive for the Turks, but not decisive in any way, as it is a raid and not a sustained operation. There are few people alive who have damaged railways as much as I have at any rate. Father may add this to the qualifications that I will possess for employment after the war!"[36]

In October 1917, Lawrence wrote home of his efforts to find a job in Cairo for his younger brother Arnie, who was reaching the age when he was in some danger of being sent to the Western Front. At about the same time, Hogarth wrote to his wife from Cairo:

He [Lawrence] is going out of reach again now for a spell and they [his family] must not expect letters from him; but whenever I have news of him I'll let them know the facts whether through you or direct. But the intervals will be long. Tell his mother he has now five decorations including the C.B. (to qualify for which he had to be promoted to major) and despises and ignores the lot. Says he does not mind what they give him so long as he has not to wear them! He is in this [word not legible] but very hard and his reputation has become overpowering.[37]

Not all the efforts in which Lawrence was involved were so successful. General Allenby's forces had advanced through Palestine and captured Beersheba at the end of October.[38] Lawrence and a group of raiders left Aqaba late in October in order to assist Allenby's armies by cutting the vital railroad that linked Damascus and Der'a with Jerusalem, Gaza and the Mediterranean coast. Lawrence and one party aimed to destroy a vital bridge across the Yarmuk River west of Der'a, but the Howeitat tribesmen were now operating in cultivated and settled lands outside their native areas. The bridge was reached, but the raiders were spotted by the Turkish sentries before they could lay their charge of explosives, and although other less vital bridges south of Der'a were destroyed, the mission ended in failure.[39]

Something of the danger for Lawrence of these missions is conveyed in Hogarth's letters to his wife. "He . . . is away now on a very risky venture, and I'll be more than glad to see him out of it." And a few days later: "I only hope and trust TEL will get back safe. He is out and up against it at this moment. If he comes through it is a V.C. — if not — well, I don't care to think about it! But, of course not a word to his mother." And two weeks after this: "I have been on tenterhooks, as he was on a very dangerous venture, which failed as I feared it must, but without involving him in the worst fate. So far as I know he is unwounded and he says he is very well and cheerful [as of November 14, the date of Lawrence's last communication with Hogarth]. But he is still far away, and has dangerous things to do — is, in fact doing them every day (this last not for Mrs. Lawrence)."[40]

Following these missions Allenby instructed Lawrence to reconnoiter in the vicinity of Der'a. In mid-November Lawrence set out "in this wintry weather to explore the country lying about Deraa"[41] accompanied by Talal, a shaykh of Tafas, a village northwest of the town. (The traumatic attack at the hands of the Turks that awaited him there and its significance for his future is discussed in Chapter 19.) After escaping from Der'a, Lawrence reached Azraq, a palm-shaded oasis west of Amman, on or about November 22 and returned to Aqaba on the twenty-sixth.[42]

On the twenty-ninth, Hogarth wrote his wife that Lawrence had been awarded the Croix de Guerre with palms by the French, "their equivalent of the V.C. . . . Tell his mother, for he won't!"[43] Lawrence's response to this award indicated his attitude toward medals and honors and also the support for his credo of renunciation that he assumed his parents would give him. "The French Government has stuck another medal on to me," he wrote home, "a croix de guerre this time. I wish they would not bother, but they never consult one before doing these things. At least I have never expected one, and will never wear one or allow one to be conferred on me openly. One cannot do more, for these notices are published in the Press first thing, and to counter-announce that one refused it, would create more publicity than the award itself. I am afraid you will be rather disgusted, but it is not my fault, and by lying low and simply not taking the things when given me, I avoid ever really getting them."[44]

On December 9 Jerusalem fell to General Allenby's advancing forces. Hogarth described the capture as "a great, but a very thorny acquisition."[45] Lawrence was among the official group entering the city because Allenby "was good enough, although I had done nothing for the success, to let Clayton take me along as his staff officer for the day."[46] Of the capture Lawrence wrote his family: "It was impressive in its way — no show, but an accompaniment of machine gun and anti-aircraft fire, with aeroplanes circling over us continually. Jerusalem has not been taken for so long; nor has it ever fallen so tamely before. These modern wars of large armies and long-range weapons are quite unfitted for the historic battlefields."[47]

Lawrence was moved by this historic occasion to lecture his seventeen-year-old brother, who was struggling with exams, about his views of history: "I see Arnie is getting slowly up the obstacles of many exams. They are silly things, terrible to the conscientious, but profitable to the one who can display his goods to effect, without leaving holes visible. As real tests they are illusory. So long as you can read good books in the languages they effect, that's enough for education: but it adds greatly to your pleasure if you have memory enough to remember the why and wherefore of the waxing and waning of peoples, and to trace the slow washing up and down of event upon event. In that way I think history is the only knowledge of the easy man. It seems to me that is enough of didactic."[48]

Lawrence also wrote to Leeds after the entry into Jerusalem and described the enormous amount of captured Turkish booty. He wrote then of his concern that he was "getting terribly bound up in Eastern politics, and must keep free," and, prophetically, "I've never been labelled yet, and yet I fear that they are going to call me Arabian now. As soon as war ends I'm going to build a railway in South America, or dig up a South African gold-field, to emancipate myself. Carchemish will either be hostile (Turks will never let me in again) or friendly (Arab), and after being a sort of king-maker one will not be allowed to go digging quietly again."[49]

Hogarth has provided illuminating glimpses of Lawrence at this time to his son, William: "T.E.L. was with me at Gaza [on December 10 or

11] and is now here [Cairo] for a day or two, looking much fitter and better than when I saw him last. He still looks absurdly boyish for 28!"[50] And to his wife a week later: "It was a refreshing contrast to have T.E.L. about for a week. He anyhow only lives for one thing. They put him up at the Residency this time and made much of him. He went about happily in a second lieutenant's tunic and badges somewhere between a lieutenant and a captain, and no decorations and no belt. When he went to Jerusalem with Allenby he is reported to have borrowed from one person and another a regular staff outfit with proper badges and even decorations. I only hope he appears in the cinema pictures taken on that occasion, because, otherwise, an unknown aspect of him will be lost."[51]

The remainder of December was taken up with operations against the Hijaz railroad and the stations east of Aqaba — Ramleh, Tell Shahm and Mudawara. These raids are significant in that Lawrence was accompanied by other British officers, among them Alan Dawnay and Captain L. H. Gilman, who could confirm through firsthand experience his accounts of the operations.[52]

In January 1918, the well-known battle of Tafila, an important center in the region southeast of the Dead Sea, was fought using Arab "regulars," a force under the command of Ja'far Pasha al-'Askari that was composed largely of Turkish prisoners of war who had elected to secure their release by joining the Revolt.[53] The battle, which was actually a defensive engagement that turned into an offensive rout, was described in the official history of the war as "a brilliant feat of arms."[54] Lawrence was awarded the D.S.O. (Distinguished Service Order) for his leadership at Tafila, which was evacuated and then reoccupied by the Arab forces in March. Of the D.S.O. Lawrence wrote his family in his characteristic tone, disavowing pleasure in his awards and recognition: "It's a pity all this good stuff is not sent to someone who would use it! Also I'm apparently a colonel of sorts [he had been recently promoted to lieutenant-colonel]."[55]

In February of 1918, Lawrence evidently became quite despondent, especially following a serious misunderstanding with Zayd, Faisal's youngest brother, who was unable to account satisfactorily for the absence of some funds that Lawrence had been counting on to pay the forty thousand men now on Faisal's payroll. He wished to quit and confessed to Hogarth that he "had made a mess of things: and had come to Allenby to find me some smaller part elsewhere."[56]

An entry by Hogarth in The Arab Bulletin, written in February 1918, reveals a similar discouragement with aspects of the progress of the Revolt. The Arab regular forces were often unreliable and inefficient, while the Bedouin demonstrated "the nomad's acute distaste for sustained action and winter campaigning." The enemy's line of communication was not permanently cut, although the Hijaz railroad had ceased to be of practical service to the Turks. "Nowhere as yet," Hogarth wrote, "have the Arabs held on for more than three days, at the outside, to any station or other point captured on the line, nor have they wrecked any of the larger bridges. . . . Emir Zeid, who is in command of Feisal's advance force, hesitates to advance, deterred partly by the continued cold, partly by nervousness about operating in a new country under conditions unlike those of Arabia proper, but most of all by the natural inertia and weakness of purpose which he shares with some of his brothers."[57] Lawrence's despondency seems to have lifted somewhat when he discovered in Cairo the extent to which the War Cabinet was relying upon Allenby to move to Damascus and, if possible, Aleppo. He decided then that "there was no escape for me."[58]

But at the very time he was feeling despondent and wanting to give up his role in the campaigns, he was becoming increasingly like an amir himself in his dress and prestige in the desert. He wrote his family early in March: "Three of my camels have had babies in the last few weeks. That makes me about thirty riding camels of my own, but then my bodyguard of servants is about 25, so there are not so many to spare."[59] Late in February Hogarth had written his son:

> Major Lawrence is over here at present in full Sheikh's costume, and is sharing my living tent. The first day he was held up twice by the military police and his servant, an old ageyli [an Arab tribesman] from Qasim, definitely arrested, being in possession of a revolver and cartridges and quite unable to explain himself. He took it quite calmly, however, and was soon released. Lawrence's dagger is very pretty — a sherifial present; his *agal* [band for the head garment] is a good gold one and his *aba* [robe] (from Hasa) fair, but not as good as my sherifial one. He wears a long white silk shirt to his ankles underneath, and the sleeves trail on the ground showing below the aba like some undergarment got loose.[60]

William Yale, who was based in the American Diplomatic Agency in Cairo during the war, provides a firsthand picture of Lawrence's work among the Arabs during this period, in his reports to the State Department in February and March of 1918. Yale interviewed Lawrence and read his secret dispatches. The reports are based on information Lawrence gave him regarding the political situation in Syria, tribal attitudes toward the Allies, and the resentment of Palestinian and other Arabs toward the vigorous Zionist effort to reconstruct the Jewish colonies at this time. Yale wrote of Lawrence in his March 11 report: "He has a knowledge of the sentiments and feelings of the Arab tribes that probably no other Westerner has. His knowledge of the true condition of affairs existing, at the present time, among the Arabs should be more accurate than that of any other person." The report continued: "Major Lawrence said that everything had been prepared, and that he and his

Bedouins were ready, when they should receive word from General Allenby, to cut the Hedjaz R.R. North of Ma'an and establish relations with the British right flank."[61]

In the spring of 1918 the Arab forces were able to cut the Hijaz railroad for good between Ma'an and Mudawara to the south, thus isolating the large Turkish garrison at Medina, estimated then at twelve thousand men.[62] Although the Arabs did not have sufficient forces or "staying power" (tending to loot and take booty following raids and then retire to their tents) to seize and hold the major rail points like Ma'an, Abu el Jurdhan [Jerdun], and Mudawara, the large numbers of Turkish troops they killed, wounded, captured or "contained" at Medina and other isolated Turkish garrisons was of great aid to Allenby in preparing his decisive summer offensive.

In June Lawrence began his preparations for the participation of Faisal's armies in Allenby's final drive. Allenby had agreed to transfer the forces of Sharif Ali and Abdullah to the northern army under Faisal's command, but King Husayn would not allow it. Lawrence went to Jidda and talked with Husayn on the telephone, but the king was obstinate and sheltered himself "behind the incompetence of the operators in the Mecca exchange."[63]

The close collaboration of British and Arab forces along the narrowing Northern Front had become a more complex matter. Greater numbers of British officers were working closely with Arab regular and Bedouin forces (including a British-commanded camel corps), which had swelled in numbers. Negotiations with the large Ruwallah tribes and their legendary chief, Nuri Sha'lan, and with the Bani Sakhr and other northern tribes, whose loyalty to the sharifian cause was less clear, added to the difficulties. Misplaced confidence in the willingness of the Bani Sakhr tribesmen to move actively against the Turks may have played a part in the failure of the operations around es-Salt in the spring of 1918, "the Bani Sakhr tribe remaining quiescent at the critical moment."[64] Furthermore, as the Bedouin followers of the Revolt moved northward, they came increasingly to require the collaboration of settled Arabs of the towns of Syria, whose concepts of Arab nationalism and independence were not identical with the rebellion of the sharif of Mecca and his family against the Turkish government, and were not always willing to fight on the side of Faisal and his brothers against the Ottoman forces, which contained many Arab troops.

An additional difficulty for the British command and for Lawrence arose during the summer of 1918, when he discovered that Faisal, in response to an overture of Jemal Pasha early in June, had been negotiating a possible separate settlement of the Revolt.[65] Faisal appears to have been influenced in this direction by Syrian officers in his army, by recent failures of Bedouin raids, and by his concern, natural under the circumstances, that Arab gains in Syrian territory, which the tide of war had by then reached, would be negated by British commitments to the French. The British felt obliged to provide him with fresh assurances that the Arabs would be permitted to hold any territory they themselves liberated (which would later complicate the postwar political situation), and Lawrence apparently influenced Faisal to continue the struggle by letting him know subtly that he was aware of his activities.[66] Further, Hogarth, in a secret report to Storrs in August, indicated clearly his awareness that educated Syrians would oppose a sharifian administration in their territory, and he, Hogarth, even considered a separate peace with Turkey.[67] But Hogarth ended by urging continuing reliance on the sharifian Revolt as the "chief instrument" of British policy, while trying to bring the Revolt increasingly under the control of British officers working with the sharifian forces.[68] This appears to have been the policy that was followed for the remainder of the war.

Lawrence's letters during the summer of 1918 convey the frenetic pace at which he rushed from Cairo to Wejh to Jidda to Aqaba as he prepared for the offensive that was soon to come. Colonel Pierce Joyce, who was commander of the British section of the Arab northern army, has recalled:

> It was during these desert trips that I first realized Lawrence's joy in motion and craze for speed. One memorable day Lawrence rode in from a visit to G.H.Q. all smiles while we were at lunch in our improved mess at Guweira [north of Aqaba]. He could scarcely eat for eagerness and yet his conversation was about a herd of wild ostriches which had crossed his path on the way over, and describing how his Bedouin escort had fled after them in a vain endeavor to make a capture. It was only afterwards, in Feisal's tent that he announced the glad tidings of the gift of 2,000 camels from G.H.Q., the essential link to the goal of his ambition, the Arab drive north and the capture of Damascus. He was like a boy released from school that day and his energy dynamic.[69]

By the summer of 1918 the Turks were offering a stiff reward for Lawrence's capture. One officer wrote in his contemporary notes: "Though a price of £15,000 has been put on his head by the Turks no Arab has, as yet, attempted to betray him. The Sherif of Mecca (King of the Hedjaz) has given him the status of one of his sons, and he is just the finely tempered steel that supports the whole stunt structure of our influence in Arabia. He is a very inspiring gentleman adventurer."[70] The English press received orders from the censor's office "not to publish any photograph of Lieutenant-Colonel T. E. Lawrence, C.B., D.S.O., for this officer is not known by sight to the Turks, who have put a price on his head, and any photograph or personal description of him may endanger his safety."[71]

Lawrence chose to forgo the possibility of disguising himself to the enemy in order to be readily known by Arabs who could be expected to be friendly. "In the desert I shaved daily," he wrote to Liddell Hart. "My burnt red face, clean shaven and startling with my blue eyes against white headcloth and robes, became notorious in the desert. Tribesmen or peasants who had never set eyes on me before would instantly know me, by the report. So my Arab disguise was actually an advertisement. It gave me away instantly, as myself, to all the desert: and to be instantly known was safety, in 99 cases out of the 100.

"The hundredth case was always the eventuality to be feared. If I saw it coming, I would get into a soldier's cap, shirt and shorts, and get away with it, or draw my headcloth over my face, like a visor, and brazen it out. No easterner could ever have taken me for an Arab, for a moment."[72]

An illuminating and amusing account of the extraordinary tactical problems encountered in coordinating the activities of the Arab regular and irregular forces with the British, French, Gurkha and Egyptian units of Allenby's armies is provided by Hubert Young, who had responsibility for transport and supply. At one time, for example, Ja'far, commander of the Arab "regular army," and his officers resigned temporarily because they took offense at a proclamation of King Husayn's in which he insulted the officers and "told Jaafar Pasha that he was not entitled to command the Arab army which acknowledged only Allah as its leader and [that he] was also extremely rude to the Emir Feisal."[73] Even Lawrence himself contributed to the difficulties of planning effective strategy. According to Hubert Young (a regular officer himself), Lawrence was unrealistic about the problems involved in transporting equipment and supplies for conventional troops because his own experience had been chiefly with mobile Bedouin raiders, who traveled light and lived off the land. When it came to planning the attack on Der'a, Lawrence's "first idea" was "that he would mount a thousand Arab regulars on five hundred camels, two men riding each animal, and send them swooping across the three hundred miles which separate Waheida from Deraa with their supplies and ammunition tied on with bits of string, and a roll of apricot paste, or *qamr-ud-din*, as the Turks call their staple ration, snugly stowed in each of the thousand haversacks. How long he thought the ride would take was never quite clear. He probably calculated on about eighty miles a day, a distance which his Bedouin irregulars could easily manage. Say four days for the trip to Deraa, one day for demolitions, and three days to race back in if General Allenby's big push was unsuccessful."[74]

Lawrence's quality of "doing it himself" when something needed doing or when an operation had failed is well illustrated by Young. In mid-September, in preparing for Allenby's offensive, which was to begin a few days later, an Arab force was to cut the line south of Der'a. But at the appointed time the column was still twenty miles away and "not even a body-guard could now move fast enough to cut [it]."[75] Lawrence decided to do it himself:

> Let him have a tender and a machine-gun and he would run down the line and do in a bridge. There was quite a good one at kilometre so-and-so, with a covered approach down the Wadi which the car could manage. There was only a small post on the bridge, and with luck he ought to be able to do the job before the Turks realized what was happening. It would be rather amusing. To one at least of his hearers it did not sound at all amusing, it sounded quite mad. But this was again the Lawrence whose madness had taken Akaba, and his madness on this occasion cut the Deraa-Amman line. Escorted by two armoured cars, and accompanied by Joyce and another officer, Winterton, he drove off that afternoon in the open tender, crammed to the gunwale with gun-cotton and detonators. While the machine-guns of the escort scattered the small Turkish post, the tender was driven right down to the bridge, where Lawrence laid and fired his charge. Then the small gay figure bumped airily away, perched high on the deadly boxes which any chance shot might blow into a thousand pieces.[76]

During the days immediately preceding and following Allenby's attack, which began on September 19, Lawrence and other British officers were engaged in the final destruction of the rail lines around Der'a and in operations against the Turkish forces south of Damascus. These operations successfully isolated Der'a and cut communications between Damascus and the south. They also contributed to the strategy of leading the Turks to believe that the main thrust of Allenby's attack would come in this vicinity. But Allenby attacked instead against the Turkish west wing along the coast and with such force that the enemy troops were soon retreating in disorder.

"Lawrence," said Young, "was of course his own master. I found out afterwards that he thought we were all under his orders, but I did not know this at the time, and still regarded him more as Feisal's liaison officer with General Allenby than as a real Colonel in the army, a position which he gave the impression of holding in great contempt. I had never been taken into his confidence, and knew nothing about his political schemes."[77]

Until this stage of the war the Arab tribes around Der'a and towards Damascus had not come out openly in support of the Revolt. They were "seated on the fence waiting to see which way the cat was going to jump," fearing a slaughter at the hands of the Turks.[78] However, when Allenby's offensive proved victorious in the closing days of September, the Arab tribes and villages south of Damascus rose against the retreating enemy forces.[79] In reprisal, a column of Ottoman troops committed atrocities against the village of Tafas, three miles northwest of Der'a. (The atrocities led to a loss of control on Lawrence's part that was of considerable personal significance and will be discussed in Chapter 19.)

At dawn on the following day, September 28, Lawrence entered Derʻa alone.[80] Later in the morning the regular Arab forces under Nuri al-Saʻid, Ruwallah tribesmen seeking revenge for Turkish atrocities, and General George Barrow in command of the Fourth British Cavalry Division converged upon the town. (General Barrow states he arrived at 9:30 A.M.)[81]

Alec Kirkbride, a young British officer who accompanied Lawrence during a great number of his activities in the closing days of the campaign before Lawrence left Damascus, also entered Derʻa the morning of the twenty-eighth. In his memoirs he wrote: "We [Kirkbride and Lawrence] reached our destination before the cavalry came in sight and we hoisted the flag of the Hedjaz. The place [Derʻa] was a shambles. Dead and wounded Turks, with a few Germans, lay in the shade of the station buildings; while others unhurt, sat or wandered aimlessly about waiting for something to happen. . . . The townspeople of Deraa were looting furniture and stores which had escaped destruction by fires, which still smouldered here and there."[82]

Lord Birdwood's description in his biography of Nuri al-Saʻid is similar, and he states that by the time General Barrow arrived the Ottoman soldiers had left the town "in filth" and that "wild tribesmen were racing around the streets on their ponies in complete disregard of their own safety and that of everyone else."[83]

General Barrow has left his own account of what happened. He describes Arab atrocities against an ambulance train full of sick and wounded Turks that was drawn up in the station. "In the cab of the engine was the dead driver and a mortally wounded fireman. The Arab soldiers were going through the train, tearing off the clothing of the groaning and stricken Turks, regardless of gaping wounds and broken limbs, and cutting their victims' throats. The atrocities which the Turks are said to have inflicted on the Arab people gave cause for vengeance. But it was a sight that no average civilized human being could bear unmoved."[84] Barrow states he asked Lawrence to get the Arabs out of the station area, but Lawrence said he could not because it was "their idea of war." Barrow then told Lawrence he would take the responsibility for doing so and ordered his men to clear the station, which was done, and the station then was picketed by British sentries.

Nuri's version of the meeting, according to Birdwood, was that Barrow attempted to make him withdraw his forces, "whereupon Lawrence produced written instructions from Allenby to the effect that Arabs should be allowed to take over local administration wherever they entered through their own exertions."[85] Lawrence "managed to ease the situation by arranging for the general's immediate material requirements,"[86] but he was troubled over Barrow's performance. In his view the general had delayed unnecessarily in watering the cavalry's horses en route to the town. Also, Barrow had come without orders "as to the status of the Arabs" and, Lawrence believed, thought of them "as a conquered people."[87] Both charges Barrow hotly denied. He accused Lawrence of "being inebriated by the exuberance of his own imagination."[88]

Young, who arrived shortly after Barrow — at "about ten o'clock" — takes a conciliatory approach:

> Until the Sherifian detachment arrived, there was no sign of any organized Arab force, and he [Barrow] naturally hesitated to leave at the mercy of what he regarded as a pack of ragamuffins a town which had been evacuated by the Turks as a result of his own advance. Lawrence had adopted toward him what I am told was his usual attitude towards British Generals, a mixture of schoolboy cheek with an assumption of omniscience and of being in General Allenby's confidence which Barrow found extremely trying. Even when our comparatively orderly force appeared, he was inclined to be a little contemptuous at first, and I have no doubt that we presented an odd spectacle to eyes accustomed to British and Indian units. This passed off, though, and he and his staff were hospitality itself to the rather dishevelled group of British officers.[89]

Thus at Der'a, just hours before the capture of Damascus, the regular and the irregular were merged. The tensions that arose between Lawrence and Barrow represented only the first brush, a minor curtain raiser to the brewing political struggle between East and West, between the Great Powers and their Arab allies, that was to be joined at Damascus.

13

The Capture of
Damascus

The capture of Damascus represented the climax of the Palestinian and desert campaigns and of Lawrence's personal role in the Revolt. As the Ottoman armies retreated from the city, there converged upon it in the opening days of October 1918 the military forces of the Western powers — British, Australian and French — the sharifian forces of King Husayn, and the various Syrian factions for whom Damascus was the spiritual center. For each group the city had political importance, but for the Arabs it had great spiritual significance as one of the historic centers of the Muslim world. For them it was the "capital" of the desert, and the first capital of the caliphs outside the Hijaz. "Damascus," as Gertrude Bell wrote in 1907, "holds and remembers the greatest Arab traditions."[1] W. T. Massey, an official correspondent of the London newspapers with the Egyptian Expeditionary Forces (Allenby's armies), understood this when he wrote with alarm of the fires that the retreating Turkish soldiers and Germans had set: "For four thousand years Damascus had been coveted by martial kings and the tide of battle had often surged round her, but so fair a jewel was the city that barbarian rulers and their hordes had never destroyed her. She was the oldest living city in the world, and when watching the fires we wondered if we were going to witness her first destruction."[2]

There are scores of accounts of the capture of Damascus and the early, confused days of its occupation by the various Allied forces. Many of them are from firsthand witnesses of part if not all the events of those days. These reports, including the official ones, seem to be particularly prone to the subjectivity and attendant distortions that, perhaps inevitably, often accompany accounts of emotionally charged events. Lawrence's descriptions in *Seven Pillars of Wisdom* are not exempt from this criticism. In particular, one would think in reading them that Damascus was captured by Arab armies almost unaided, whereas the Arab entry into Damascus was made possible by the hard-won victories of Allenby's armies. Lawrence's official reports to headquarters and for *The Arab Bulletin* are more objective and less emotional in tone.[3]

The sharifian forces in the closing weeks of the war were operating in the belief that the British government would abide by the "Declaration to the Seven" issued in July 1918, an agreement made in response to the entreaties of seven Syrians in Cairo the previous month.[4] By this declaration Britain, in contradiction to the terms of the Sykes-Picot Agreement, would support the independence of all areas emancipated by the Arabs themselves during the war. The question of "who got to Damascus first" thus took on an additional significance. There is evidence to indicate that British forces were given orders to avoid entering Damacus, when they might have captured the city hours or days earlier than they did, in order to enable the Arab forces to claim that they, not the British armies, liberated the city.[5] And Allenby's readiness to recognize an Arab provisional government immediately following the capture of the city suggests that this was in fact British policy.

According to Lawrence's report to headquarters of October 1, an Arab force left Der'a on September 29 under Sharif Nasir of Medina and Nuri al-Sa'id, "following up on the 4th Cavalry Division on the right flank." After meeting some Turkish resistance and taking six hundred prisoners on the thirtieth, "the Sherif sent a mounted force forward to get contact with his followers in the gardens East of Damascus, to find that his local committee had hoisted the Arab flag and proclaimed the Emirate of Hussein of Mecca at 2:30 P.M."[6] Lawrence states that he himself entered the city at 9 A.M. on October 1 "amid scenes of extraordinary enthusiasm on the part of the local people. The streets were nearly impassable with the crowds, who yelled themselves hoarse, danced, cut themselves with swords and daggers and fired volleys into the air. Nasir, Nuri Shaalan, Auda Abu Tayi and myself were cheered by name, covered with flowers, kissed indefinitely, and splashed with attar of roses from the house-tops."[7]

But in *Seven Pillars* he wrote that there was an initial period in which the crowds were mostly silent and "looked and looked, joy shining in their eyes,"[8] while to his fellow officer W. F. Stirling he wrote in 1924: "My memory of the entry into Damascus was of a quietness and emptiness of street, and of myself crying like a baby with eventual thankfulness, in the Blue Mist [a Rolls-Royce armored car] by your side. It seemed to me that the frenzy of welcome came later, when we drove up and down in inspection."[9]

Elie Kedourie, a Middle East scholar whose hostility toward Lawrence is often transparent, makes much of the fact that in *Seven Pillars of Wisdom* Lawrence does not mention that an Australian light horse brigade entered the city in the early morning hours of October 1 and "it is to them that Damascus may be said to have formally surrendered."[10] Yet later in the same article Kedourie acknowledges that "it seems clear that a number of Sherifial irregulars were in the city by midnight on the 30th September."[11]

It is difficult to understand what is·meant by Damascus being formally surrendered. According to the Australian General Henry Chauvel, the commander in the area, the Ottoman governor and Jemal Pasha had fled the city the day before. In a critique of *Seven Pillars of Wisdom* that Chauvel wrote in 1936, he says that the city was surrendered to "Emir Said Abd-el-Kader ['Abd al Qadir al-Jaza'iri], who, having assumed control of Damascus on the departure of Djemal Pasha on the afternoon of the 30th September, surrendered the City to Major Olden of the 10th Light Horse at 6:30 A.M. on the 1st October, 1918."[12] This is hardly impressive authority, since 'Abd al-Qadir was removed by Sharif Nasir and Lawrence in favor of other local leadership on the same day. Another version of these events is provided in the British official history, which observed rather understatedly as early as 1930: "There has been some controversy as to which troops were the first to enter Damascus."[13] In any event Allenby was prepared to recognize a sharifian government in Damascus as long as the sharifians were present in the city at approximately the time of its capture.

A firsthand Arab view of the events in Damascus and Lawrence's part in securing the authority of the Arab provisional government has been provided by Dr. Ahmad Qadri, a Syrian nationalist who was present with Lawrence in the city on October 1. When Qadri entered the town hall he was surprised to see that "the good-hearted" Shukri al-Ayyubi seemed to be accepting the authority of the Algerian Jaza'iri brothers, 'Abd al-Qadir and Muhammad Sa'id. This surprised Qadri because these two had not been among the nationalists who had worked with Faisal. Rather, they had worked with the Ottoman government and had ties to France. Qadri has written:

> We could not endure this situation after the great victories we had achieved and Lawrence desired to remove them from intervention in the affairs of government. I agreed with him about that, so we entered the hall of the big Serai [town hall] to discuss the situation with Sherif Nasir [leader of the Arab forces until Faisal's arrival on October 3]. There was arguing going on among the Arab leaders and Emir Said invited Sherif Nasir to come to his house. Wise men convinced him not to leave. Nasir told Said that he must stay. Lawrence said to Emir Said, "This is the opinion of those in whose hands the power is — that you must return to your home. If you do not accept this, Sherif Nasir will order the forces under his power to arrest you. And you must know that the British forces are ready to help the Arab forces to secure calmness and law in the city."

Sa'id, according to Qadri, left in anger.[14]

Lawrence was able to persuade Chauvel to recognize Shukri al-Ayyubi, a Damascene who had been a high-ranking officer in the Ottoman army, as the head of the local administration of the city in the name of the sharif of Mecca. Chauvel later regretted that he had done this because he learned that Shukri al-Ayyubi had not, as Chauvel said Lawrence had claimed, been elected by the majority of the inhabitants.[15] The point is hard to credit since it is difficult to conceive how a general election of the citizenry of a just-conquered city of 300,000 in turmoil could have been brought off in just a day.

There does seem to have been an extraordinary release of control in Damascus on the day of its liberation, with outbursts of joy on the part of the populace in welcoming the Australian, British and Arab liberators in the morning, followed by rioting and looting and violent settling of old scores in the afternoon.[16]

The confusion surrounding the question of who quelled the riots and disorder in Damascus on the day of its capture is typical of the controversy that surrounds those days. Lawrence minimizes the degree of looting, rioting, murder and other violence in the town on the part of the Arabs. He implies that disorder was caused largely by the counterrevolutionary activities of the Algerian brothers 'Abd al-Qadir and Muhammad Sa'id and their followers. In his report for *The Arab Bulletin* Lawrence wrote: "We called out the Arab troops, put Hotchkiss [a type of gun] round the central square, and imposed peace in three hours, after inflicting about twenty casualties."[17] But it seems clear from the accounts of Massey, Chauvel and Kirkbride (who used his own strong-arm methods, including shooting troublemakers with his pistol) that the Arab soldiers had great difficulty maintaining order.[18] Kedourie has written indignantly that the reader of *Seven Pillars* "gathers the impression that Damascus was placed out of bounds to the Australian soldiers because they might meet with disagreeable incidents from which Allenby designed the Northern Arab Army to shield them. In view of the exertions of the Australians to restore order in Damascus which the Sherifians could not preserve, Lawrence's account seems an offensive travesty of the facts."[19] But Chauvel also wrote in 1936: "The Hedjaz supporters were out to make as little as possible of the British and were endeavouring to make the populace think that it was the Arabs who had driven out the Turk. That was quite evidently why I had been asked [by whom, Allenby?] to keep my men out of the city and why I had not yet been asked for any police, though Shukri Pasha [al-Ayyubi] knew that I had a whole regiment of Australians standing by for the purpose in the grounds of the Turkish barracks."[20]

Chauvel acknowledges that it was not until the next day (October 2) that he sent a large force through the city (which he says Lawrence opposed) to bring order. "The effect was electrical," he wrote; "the bazaars were opened and the city went about its normal business." Allenby wrote his wife the following day (October 3): "The town is quiet now, but there was a little pillaging and shooting the day before yesterday, quickly repressed by Lawrence."[21] Chauvel makes no mention of Lawrence's restoration of order, which seems to have impressed Allenby more than the efforts of Chauvel and his troops.

Lawrence has written vividly in *Seven Pillars* of his efforts to cope with the enormous problems he faced during his few days in Damascus, problems which included sanitation, fire, starvation and disease. It is difficult at this date to evaluate his role accurately, but it was a crucial one according to eyewitness accounts by such officers as Kirkbride and Stirling. "A thousand and one things had to be thought of, but never once was Lawrence at a loss," Stirling wrote.[22]

General Wavell, one of Allenby's biographers, has written, perhaps with justification, that "Lawrence's story of the events in Damascus after the entry and of his dealings with Chauvel is not the whole truth, and is unjust to Chauvel."[23] The events surrounding the capture of Damascus followed a period of intense emotional strain for Lawrence. Furthermore, as Allenby's letter to his wife suggests, much of the responsibility for maintaining order in the city fell on Lawrence's shoulders. It is not unexpected, therefore, that he would express resentment toward those whom he felt did less than they could, especially those in positions of authority. Lawrence virtually ridicules Chauvel, making him out to be an insensitive army general, more concerned with observing protocol than tending to the suffering around him. The degree to which the imputation is justified is not an issue that I can settle. There is no question that Lawrence was in a deeply wrought-up state during those days in Damascus and his pen (which could be most sharp in criticism of those with whom he differed) may well have been unfairly caustic in letting out his anger as he recalled those gruesome events. Yet it is clear that Lawrence worked intensively and effectively to bring order to Damascus and some rudiment of needed services to the city and its people in these first few days of its liberation, and that in his view Chauvel, who was officially in charge, acted too slowly and did not do enough.

A well-known episode involving the Turkish military hospital seems to have been a matter of particular controversy between Lawrence and Chauvel, although only Lawrence has described it in detail. The two men agreed in their reports that the fleeing Turks had left the hospital in desperate condition and that Turkish prisoners cleaned it up and buried the dead. Chauvel wrote, in contesting Lawrence's account in *Seven Pillars*, that the hospital was "discovered by Lieutenant-Colonel Bouchier of the 4th Light Horse (vide British) Brigade," but Lawrence's complaint was just that: the British and Australians discovered it, but no one did anything about it.

Lawrence's account, similar but less lurid and dramatic than the one in *Seven Pillars,* comes from an unpublished portion of a letter written in 1929 to William Yale, who was in Damascus during the first days of October 1918:

"About the hospital. Some American° (not you, I think: someone Red Cross or Medical at lunch in the hotel on the 2nd day) asked me to improve the hospital. I had not heard of a Turk hospital, but went to the old barracks after lunch, and was refused admittance by the sentry. I was in Arab kit, and the barracks ground occupied by Australians. I surmounted this difficulty, and looked at the charnel house inside, and went to the town hall for help. Nuri lent me one of the four (?) Arab army doctors, and I took Kirkbride, one of my officers. We pressed a working party from the Turkish prisoners at the gate (poor wretches, they should themselves have been in hospital) for the Australians wouldn't help and turned the Turkish doctors, who were skulking in their quarters, back to work. I am very relieved to hear from you they were Armenians. They spoke Turkish, so I took them for that, and was disgusted at their callous neglect. Before night we had buried all the dead, fed all the possible living, and had posted orderlies to serve water etc.: also got lamps in each ward. I rang up the British general [Chauvel] and asked him to take it over, as it was utterly beyond my resources. He would not.

"Next day [October 3] we cleared about six wards, and got the food better. There were no medical stores with the Arabs, and Damascus could supply little. The English would supply none. By evening the place looked good — relatively to what it had been on the day before. I dare say it was all wrong still: but we were making bricks without either straw or clay, almost, and our progress pleased me.

"Next day Allenby arrived and gave Chauvel orders to relieve the Arabs of the hospital. That I expect, ended the difficulty. I had done my utmost to improve it as soon as I knew of its state. The British guard over it for the first two days had prevented the Arab authorities from hearing of it. They did their best to prevent our entering it, when we did hear of it."[24]

Chauvel claims that the cleanup of the hospital and burial of the dead by the Turkish prisoners was done "under the supervision of the Corps Medical Staff,"[25] but Kirkbride, who stayed on after Lawrence had left to make sure the job was completed, disputes this. Kirkbride gives a detailed account of these events in his memoirs but makes no mention of the presence of any helping or supervising British or Australian medical personnel.[26] In fact, the only mention of British or Australians follows his account of the digging of a trench for the corpses by the prisoners: "These proceedings were observed with interest by some Australian troopers whose regiment occupied the adjacent barracks, but they did not offer to help."[27]

° "An Australian doctor" in *Seven Pillars.*

I interviewed Yale in 1966 and we discussed the hospital. He said "an Australian officer" asked him, about October 3, "Have you seen the Turkish barracks?" (that is, the hospital), and they went there together. Yale said he found the conditions at the hospital as bad as Lawrence had described, and felt sorry that he had not done more to help. He was told by the Turkish (or Armenian) doctors that just before his arrival the hospital had been sacked by Arabs, and he criticized Lawrence for failing to report the fact. Yale complained to the British authorities as an officer representing the United States Army but was told to mind his own business as he was not a soldier. Yale confirmed Lawrence's assertion that the British were under orders not to do anything about the hospital. He said that the Australian officer who brought him there told him that he (the Australian) would be court-martialed if Yale told his superiors that he brought him there, as he had *previously been told not to do anything about the hospital.*[28]

Chauvel does not comment on Lawrence's specific assertion that he refused to take over the hospital. He says only that the hospital was handed over to the Arab administration, and "Lawrence wanted me to hand over all the hospitals in Damascus to the Arab administration." He continued: "I could not agree as regards the European hospitals, particularly as we would want them ourselves, but I did hand over the Turkish and Syrian hospitals. Incidentally, we had to take over the big military hospital [the one in question] again some four days later. It was in nearly as bad a condition as when first discovered."[29] Whomever Lawrence may have wished to have "administer" the hospital, it is hard to believe that help from the British authorities for the improvement of its state was not desired and requested. It is not clear what the "again" in Chauvel's assertion "we had to take over again four days later" refers to since British medical personnel seem to have provided little help in these first terrible days.

On October 3 Allenby and Faisal both arrived in Damascus and a meeting between them was arranged at the Victoria Hotel in the afternoon with Lawrence acting as interpreter and other British and Arab officers present.[30] Allenby told Faisal that he would recognize an Arab military administration of occupied territory east of the Jordan from Damascus to Maʻan, but that he would remain in supreme command as long as military operations continued. Allenby also informed Faisal of the terms of the Sykes-Picot Agreement, by which the French were to have the protectorate over the coastal regions of Syria, and the Arab administration would be excluded from Palestine.

Chauvel described the drama that occurred after Faisal received this news:

Feisal objected very strongly. He said that he knew nothing of France
in the matter; that he was prepared to have British assistance; that he understood from the Advisor that Sir Edmund Allenby had sent him [Lawrence
presumably]; that the Arabs were to have the whole of Syria including the
Lebanon but excluding Palestine; that a country without a port was no good
to him; and that he declined to have a French Liaison Officer or to recognize
French guidance in any way.

The Chief turned to Lawrence and said: "But did you not tell him that the
French were to have the Protectorate over Syria?" Lawrence said: "No Sir,
I know nothing about it." The Chief said: "But you knew definitely that he,
Feisal, was to have nothing to do with the Lebanon." Lawrence said: "No
Sir, I did not."

After some discussion the Chief told Feisal that he, Sir Edmund Allenby,
was Commander-in-Chief and that he, Feisal, was at that moment a Lieu-
tenant-General under his command and that he would have to obey orders.
That he must accept the situation as it was and that *the whole matter would
be settled at the conclusion of the war* [italics added]. Feisal accepted this
decision and left with his entourage (less Lawrence) and went out of the City
again to take on his triumphal entry which I am afraid fell flat as the greater
bulk of the people had seen him come in and out already!

After Feisal had gone, Lawrence told the Chief that he would not work
with a French Liaison Officer and that he was due for leave and thought he
had better take it now and go off to England. The Chief said: "Yes. I think
you had!" and Lawrence left the room.[31]

Chauvel wrote that he thought Allenby "had been a little hard on
Lawrence and told him so." Allenby then said, according to Chauvel:
"Very well, send him down to my Headquarters and tell him I will write
to Clive Wigram [assistant private secretary of George V] about him,
asking him to arrange for an audience with the King. I will also give him
a letter to the Foreign Office in order that he might explain the Arab
point of view.' General Allenby then left by car for Tiberias. Lawrence
left Damascus next day in one of my cars for GHQ, having handed over
to Cornwallis."[32]

Although Lawrence was ending his direct military involvement in the
Revolt, and did in fact leave Damascus on October 4, he had already
played a part in setting in motion the several-sided political struggle that
would follow the war. For as Chauvel continues in his 1929 account of
the events of October 3, 1918, "Neither my Chief of Staff nor I knew at
that time that Feisal had already taken steps to proclaim the Hedjaz
authority in the Lebanon and, I presume with Lawrence's knowledge,
had already despatched Shukri Pasha [al-Ayyubi] to Beirut to take over
the administration thereof."[33] Chauvel recalled with some annoyance that
"the fat was in the fire" when Shukri unfurled the Hijaz flag in Beirut, as
one of his (Chauvel's) staff was present and "the whole thing was reported
at once to the French."[34] Yale wrote in 1929: "Many of us at the time

were convinced that it was part of the British scheme to make the French position in Beirut untenable. We thought T.E.L. advised the Arabs to seize Beirut."[35] Lawrence denied to Yale that he had had anything to do with encouraging Shukri to go to Beirut.[36]

There are many reasons why Lawrence left Damascus when he did. He was emotionally and physically spent (he looked thin and wasted).[37] He was disillusioned with the behavior of the Arabs, which had not conformed with the lofty outlines of his dream. Stirling describes Lawrence as "depressed" on the eve of the entrance into Damascus, and when he asked him about it, Lawrence replied, "Ever since we took Deraa the end has been inevitable. Now the zest is gone, and the interest."[38] In his own official report of October 1, the day Damascus was taken, Lawrence wrote, "I would like to return to Palestine as I feel that if I remain here longer, it will be very difficult for my successor."[39] As he later wrote Basil Liddell Hart about his departure, "Never outstay a climax."[40] Learning that he would have to work through a French liaison officer if he were to stay on was certainly a disappointment and probably hastened Lawrence's departure, but it would hardly have come as a surprise.

Finally, I suspect that he recognized that with the fall of Damascus the important struggle in the Middle East would soon become a political one, to be fought in the centers of power in Egypt, England and France rather than in the deserts and towns of Arabia and Syria, and that he wished to pursue his purposes in this new arena. Although the obvious interpretation of Lawrence's closing words of *Seven Pillars*, describing how he felt after Allenby gave him permission to leave ("and then at once I knew how much I was sorry") is that they refer to his sorrow about the whole Arab affair, they also suggest a more immediate regret at leaving Damascus before the job was done.

14

The Achievements of
"Aurens"

No psychologist can account for the appearance in a particular human being of a given set of talents. No historian who chooses to study how a particular person effects historical change can avoid altogether dealing with the proposition: "It was so-and-so's unique ability to do such-and-such that permitted x to happen." In trying to define and describe the "unique ability," one can be tempted into oversimplification, especially if, as was so strikingly true of Lawrence, the subject can undertake a vast array of personal transactions (some simple, some complex) in a fashion that seems easy or even effortless (that is, easy or effortless if the expenditure of energy and the personal toll involved are not examined too closely). In this chapter I am especially concerned with exploring how Lawrence accomplished what he did in the Arab Revolt, what the gifts were that he brought to bear upon it, and how he applied these gifts to the social, military and political realities that obtained in Arabia, Palestine, Trans-Jordan (both Palestine and Jordan were then part of Syria) and Syria during the campaigns.

There has been considerable controversy in both the Western and Arab worlds regarding Lawrence's achievements in the Revolt, and even regarding the importance of the Revolt itself. I have no expectation that my contribution will settle these issues. On the one hand there are the denigrators, the most extreme of whom have been Richard Aldington and the writer Malcolm Muggeridge in England, to whom Lawrence is simply a fraud. Almost as troubling, especially to the Lawrence family, are the blind idolators whose idealization of Lawrence is not open to rational criticism.

As for the importance of the Revolt itself, from the military standpoint it is generally recognized that the Arab operations on the eastern flank of the British armies in the Sinai, Palestine and Syria, which were commanded by Murray and later by Allenby, constituted a front of secondary importance. But secondary does not mean trivial. Allenby called the Arab effort "invaluable," and Field-Marshal Wavell concurred.[1] In the opinion of J. B. Glubb ("Glubb Pasha," who was later to command the Arab Legion in Trans-Jordan), "the Arabs made a valuable contribution to victory . . . the whole Arab campaign provides a remarkable illustration of the extraordinary results which can be achieved by mobile guerrilla tactics. For the Arabs detained tens of thousands of regular Turkish troops with a force scarcely capable of engaging a brigade of infantry in a pitched battle."[2]

Basil Liddell Hart, basing his statements on figures from the British official history of the war, has summarized the impact of the Revolt and Lawrence's achievement:

> On the eve of Allenby's offensive in September, 1918 his troops totalled 250,000 and the Turks had an equal number in that theatre of war. But he was able to attack with a five to one superiority of force because close on 50,000 Turks were pinned down by the Arab force of 3,000 east of the Jordan, operating under Lawrence's immediate direction, while a further 150,000 Turks were spread over the rest of the region in a vain effort to stem the tide of the Arab Revolt so that little more than 50,000 were left to meet Allenby's assault. If it is unlikely that the Arab forces could ever have overcome the Turks without the punch provided by Allenby's forces, the figures make it much clearer that Allenby could not have defeated the Turks without Lawrence.[3]

The official history also concludes: "Prior to the final offensive with its many thousands of prisoners, the Arab campaign killed, wounded, captured or contained well over 25,000 troops. Like the Spanish guerrillas in the Peninsular War, the Arabs gave the British invaluable aid, while largely dependent upon them for their opportunities."[4]

From the political standpoint, the encouragement of the Arab Revolt by the British, followed by its gathering success during the last two years of the war, provided a powerful stimulus to Arab nationalistic aspirations. In the postwar period the forces of Arab nationalism, which had grown in strength during the war, and the drive of the Arabs toward freedom and independence played an important part in the decline of traditional colonialism.

What of Lawrence himself and his role in the Revolt? In recent decades interest has become so focused upon the legendary or sensational aspects of Lawrence's career, especially with the publication of books by Richard Aldington and by Knightley and Simpson, and the film extravaganza *Lawrence of Arabia*, that sober appreciation of his accomplishments has been difficult. Inaccuracies in Lawrence's full narrative of the Revolt, *Seven Pillars of Wisdom*, have been sought so diligently by his critics that the impression has grown that it is full, if not of lies, at least of marked distortions of truth.

There are, of course, distortions and partial truths in *Seven Pillars*, but these have less to do with the facts of Lawrence's accomplishments than with embellishments of their details for dramatic purposes or with the protection of other people. In writing to his biographers Lawrence tried to be explicit about those points where his writing is less than fully accurate. Concerning the passages dealing with the capture of Damascus Lawrence wrote, "I was on thin ice when I wrote the Damascus chapter and anyone who copies me will be through it, if he is not careful. S.P. is full of half-truth: here."[5]

The subscribers' edition of *Seven Pillars*, of which about two hundred copies were printed in 1926, was sent to thirty officers who served in the Revolt, including such men as Allenby, Joyce, Newcombe, Young, Peake, Stirling, and Winterton. Copies were widely circulated and read by many others who had firsthand knowledge of the events of the Revolt. Some of the officers later wrote their own reminiscences or versions of the campaigns in books and articles, most of which are referred to in this book. Stirling, for one, who worked closely with Lawrence in the later months of the campaign, says in *Safety Last* that Lawrence "sent the book to me to review as to fact."[6]

Neither Stirling nor any other of these men ever questioned the veracity of Lawrence's account. Concerning the attack and seizure of Aqaba by land, for example — the single exploit of the campaigns for which Lawrence is best known — he has been accused of undeservedly claiming credit for its strategy. Suleiman Mousa in particular states that "the plan for capturing Aqaba was devised by Faisal and Auda in Wejh."[7] But Colonel Edouard Brémond, the leader of the French mission (who resented Lawrence), confirms that the plan was discussed in conference before 'Awdah abu-Tayyi joined in the Revolt, and Jean Beraud Villars, a French biographer of Lawrence, who spoke with Colonel Stewart Newcombe about it, has stated: "Colonel Newcombe has confirmed that the Aqaba exploit was entirely conceived by Lawrence who was its real leader and animating spirit, although for reasons of diplomacy that are understandable the official command was left in the hands of the Arab chieftains."[8] Theodora Duncan of California has corresponded with scores of men who were involved in the campaigns, many peripherally, but none has challenged Lawrence's account of his role in them.[9]

Allenby, Lawrence's commander through the greater part of the campaigns wrote that Lawrence was "the mainspring of the Arab movement."[10] W. T. Massey, who was a correspondent with Allenby's army, wrote in the closing weeks of the war, before Lawrence had written

Seven Pillars and before the ballyhooing of Lowell Thomas: "The story of the Arab army has not been written, and I doubt if anyone could write it except Colonel Lawrence. Certainly no other British officer knows so much about it, and probably a great deal will remain secret, but if he would tell the world something of the Arab army's operations, and could be persuaded not to efface himself, we should have one of the most fascinating books on the war. I hope we shall see it."[11] Field-Marshal Wavell, who served in Egypt from 1917 to 1920, expressed a view similar to Allenby's: "The quickening of Sherif Hussein's family revolt into the movement that poured into Damascus [was] something that no one else could have achieved, even with unlimited gold: it was a spiritual even more than a physical exploit, the value of which to the Allied cause was great."[12]

When Aldington attacked Lawrence as a charlatan and a fraud he aroused most intensely the ire of Lawrence's fellow officers. The angry reaction of Captain L. H. Gilman, who commanded an armored-car battery in close association with Lawrence until near the end of the campaign, is typical:

> Aldington makes what is tantamount to an insinuation of the basest treachery on the part of Lawrence. He would have us believe that Lawrence was guilty of perpetrating one of the biggest hoaxes in history; of the deception of all his friends and former brother officers; of allocating to himself the honour and glory of exploits which belonged to others. . . .
> All this and more we, who knew and trusted him, are invited to believe. Those of us who are still alive will not easily be taken in by Aldington's glib and costive pen. Our faith in Lawrence is too great to be thus shaken, and we will not rest until the stigma of this foul indictment has been wiped from the slate.
> Aldington's book is so cleverly and plausibly contrived that many who had no first hand knowledge of Lawrence may give credence to a great deal that has been written.[13]

Gilman then proceeds to refute Aldington on specific matters of which he had firsthand knowledge, such as Lawrence's presence and courage in operations against the Hijaz railroad that Aldington had denied.

Gilman wrote me of his association with Lawrence: "It is the duty of a soldier to be courageous, or appear to be so, and Lawrence certainly had a super-abundance of that commodity! . . . I do not believe there was a man alive, at the time of the Arabian campaign, who could have taken on the job Lawrence so successfully and steadfastly accomplished. His knowledge of the country, the people, and their language had fully equipped him. He had no military training but seemed to be a natural exponent of guerrilla warfare, in which the Arabs excelled." Gilman concluded his letter with saying that he would never again read a book that would "sling mud at the honour and memory of one of the most gallant men in military history."[14]

Finally, there are the favorable assessments of C. S. Jarvis and St. John Philby. Though Jarvis did not serve in the Arab campaigns, he worked on the borders of the Hijaz for fourteen years as an Arab administrator, knew the Arabs of the desert well, studied the Arab Revolt, and has written a biography of his friend F. G. Peake ("Peake Pasha"), who served with Lawrence during the campaigns and was later head of the Arab Legion in Trans-Jordan. Jarvis has provided a detailed analysis of Lawrence's accomplishments in the Revolt.[15]

St. John Philby, an outstanding Arabist who spent forty years in Mesopotamia and Arabia, and was to disagree with Lawrence and struggle with him on several political fronts after the war, defended him eloquently from the attacks of his detractors and understood his central role in the campaigns.[16]

A German view of Lawrence has been provided by Franz von Papen. "The British can indeed count themselves fortunate," he wrote, "to have had the services of a man with such understanding and affection for the Islamic world. From the military point of view his activities were probably not of great importance, but politically and economically they were of priceless value."[17] During World War II the Germans attempted to follow Lawrence's tactics, including paying the tribesmen, in efforts to infiltrate the lands along the east coast of the Red Sea. But they were unsuccessful in securing the loyalty of the local population.[18]

The evaluation of Arab assessments of Lawrence, especially by one unfamiliar with the language and with many of the political and cultural forces involved, presents a number of problems. There is clearly no one "Arab view" of Lawrence. Rather, there are many Arab views, and to be fairly assessed each needs to be examined with an eye to the religion, nationality, political background and political beliefs of the Arab writer, exactly when he wrote his book or article, and the sources he used. It is especially important to find out whether he actually witnessed the events he describes (although an eyewitness account by no means guarantees an absence of distortion), and to determine any other influences on his objectivity or point of view. The same may be said about the assessment of Western views of Lawrence, although the directions of distortion and the reasons for it are easier for one trained in the same culture to determine.

Worthy of particular mention here is the understandable reluctance of committed Arab nationalists to credit a foreigner with the leadership of their own war of liberation — and with a leadership both heroic and successful at that. Their attitude came across clearly to me in my talks with residents in Amman and with the Bedouin of the Jordanian desert.[19] Even

King Abdullah of Trans-Jordan, though he acknowledges in his memoirs Lawrence's influence among the Arabs of the desert tribes, is at the same time resentful of it.[20] One young resident of Amman (not a Bedouin) told me after an interview I had had with a Bedouin shaykh: "Shaykh Muhammad [who had been too young at the time to take part in the campaigns] said to me after [your] talk [with him]: 'Why would I want any British foreigner like Lawrence leading me. I am an Arab. You are an Arab. You would not want a foreigner leading you.'" My young companion did not tell me how he had answered Shaykh Muhammad, but he told me his own view: "I would say yes, he helped me. I would never say he was the leader. I would say I was."[21]

One must assume that Lawrence understood this aspect of Arab psychology in choosing to work through Faisal and the other Arab leaders. The assumption was well substantiated in my interviews with the Bedouin shaykhs. One Howeitat shakyh said to me: "Lawrence was like a servant to our master Faisal. He used to teach us plans, but the war was carried on by the brave Bedouins." Another said: "He was not a leader but a guide (dalil)." From a third: "He was a servant of the Ashraf [the sharifs]."[22] Another Howeitat shaykh, who did take an active part in the Revolt, told me that he talks about the events of the Revolt and about Lawrence with his children, but he does not tell them to be courageous like Lawrence. Rather he says to them, "You should be like I was, strong and courageous before Lawrence."[23]

From the political standpoint, Arab writers who are or might otherwise be appreciative of Lawrence's service to the Arab peoples, deeply resent his singleminded espousal of the sharifian cause, whereby Hashemite governments were imposed on other Arabs, especially the Syrians. On three occasions the sons of King Husayn were installed as rulers of other Arab groups.

Anis Sayigh, a well-known Arab nationalist and journalist, is representative of these writers. He has described in his book on the Hashemite leadership in the Arab Revolt the problems for Arab political unity that have derived from Faisal's preponderance as a military leader during the Revolt and from Faisal's willingness to rely on Lawrence for political liaison among the Allies, while at the same time becoming the instrument of Lawrence's personal dreams for the Arab peoples.[24]

'Abd al-Rahman Shahbandar, a Syrian nationalist who was assassinated in 1940, wrote a series of articles in 1931, in which he attempted to evaluate Lawrence's role among the Arabs. Shahbandar met Lawrence in Cairo in 1916 and was one of the "Syrian Seven" who approached British authorities there in 1918. He warned against assessments of Lawrence that merely served political propaganda purposes. "If you ask a hundred of those who have struggled in the Arab Revolt and saw Lawrence on the battleground 99% will say that he is only loyal to his nation," Shahbandar wrote in his first article of his series. "But the information I will publish in my coming articles will cause most of my readers to think differently, because history is one thing and political propaganda which the newspapers compete in publishing is another thing."[25]

Most difficult to assess are the various Arab accounts of events that Lawrence has written of himself, especially in *Seven Pillars of Wisdom*. Suleiman Mousa, a Jordanian working in the Press and Information Department of Amman, published in 1966 the only full-length biography of Lawrence by an Arab writer. His book has been translated into English.[26] A strong supporter of Arab and other Muslim political positions, Mousa has set out to show that the Arab Revolt was predominantly an Arab affair and that Lawrence exaggerated his own part in it, which was a minor one, and gave insufficient credit to the Arab leaders and fighters. Mousa supports his theses by relating interviews with surviving participants of the Revolt who dispute Lawrence's statements regarding his services in planning the strategy, and even contest his claim to have been present in various journeys, battles and raids.

The most controversial of these journeys is the one into Syria of June 1917, which Lawrence reported in his letter to Clayton of July 10, 1917.[27] Mousa, on the basis of his investigations, has concluded that the story of the trip was entirely fabricated and that the journey never took place.[28] He has based much of his argument on the recollections forty years later of Nasib al-Bakri, a Syrian nationalist whom Lawrence described in his letter to Clayton as "volatile and shortsighted." Bakri claimed that Lawrence never left the base where they both were at the time the journey began. Arnold Lawrence has rebutted Mousa's account and has referred to independent confirmation by Antonius, who had details in his own account other than those of Lawrence's report. But Mousa asserts that Antonius must have relied on accounts by Lawrence, Robert Graves and Basil Liddell Hart.[29] Subhi al-'Umari, a young Syrian officer who joined the Arab armies in October 1917 (four months after the events in question), considers the trip impossible, that Lawrence could not have moved about so freely in the lands in question or reached the points he claimed he did because they were full of Ottoman forces. According to al-'Umari, only a foreigner with minimal knowledge of the country would believe Lawrence's story.[30] On the other hand, Anis Sayigh, a Palestinian, accepts the fact of the trip but turns its purposes against Lawrence. According to Sayigh, Lawrence traveled to Damascus and met its mayor, Ali Ridah al-Riqabi, in a suburb, but his purpose was to prevent an uprising of Syrian nationalists and thereby to delay an Arab victory.[31] His letter-report to Clayton indicates that the purpose of the journey was to determine the loyalties of various Syrians and tribal groups. After seeing it, Hogarth wrote Clayton: "The W.O. [War Office] is optimistic about Arabia and Syria, however, and much bucked by T.E.L.'s report and scheme"[32] — hardly what one would write about a plan of delay.

Lawrence's own war diaries, one of which contains a contemporary draft of the Clayton report, tend to support his account of the trip. The diaries are written in pencil, upside down, and are very difficult to decipher, but two colleagues of mine were able to make out the following words, using special lighting and magnification: "Clayton. I've decided to go off alone to Damascus, hoping to get killed on the way: for all sakes try and clear this show up before it goes further. We are calling them to fight for us on a lie, and I can't stand it."[33] Later in the account, according to Knightley and Simpson, Lawrence wrote, " '[I] learnt that Hachim was NE of Ragga [Rakka?] and Ibn Murshid in prison in Damascus and my plan thus failure. . . . I was able to get satisfactory assurances . . . in El Gabbu [Gaboun] . . . has been entrusted by the Turks with the defense of Damascus!' "[34] Lawrence has himself compounded the question of what ("if anything") occurred on this journey by his own incomplete treatment of it.

I find myself unable to reach any conclusion as to what actually happened, and am not sure that even with investigation by an impartial scholar familiar with the country and peoples in question could the matter be resolved. It should be noted, however, that for the accounts of the trip to have been fabricated, as Mousa and al-'Umari claim they were, Lawrence would have had to falsify not only detailed official reports but his penciled diaries as well, and have persuaded Clayton, Hogarth and Wingate of their truth (Wingate recommended Lawrence for the Victoria Cross on the basis of this journey). Furthermore, since the information in the report was evidently used by British intelligence afterwards in the campaigns, without disclosure of errors or misleading data in it, Lawrence certainly made the journey unless he was able to obtain a great deal of quite specific information from some other source.

My own Bedouin informants, who were active in the engagements along the Hijaz railroad and from Aqaba northward, attribute a major responsibility to Lawrence in planning, supplying and coordinating (not leading) the campaigns in contrast to the statements of al-'Umari and Mousa, which repeatedly disparage his role. Al-'Umari even dismisses Lawrence's function in teaching the use of explosives for demolition purposes. According to al-'Umari, demolition was an easy thing to do, readily mastered by the Arabs, which Lawrence purposely made sound difficult in his reports in order to claim credit for himself and make himself a hero. This contrasts sharply with what my Bedouin informants told me. One Howeitat tribesman, who fought in the campaigns along the railroad, told me spontaneously (I did not ask him about the demolitions): "He was the only one in charge of the explosions. He was the only one who knew the explosives and he used to go from one place to another and try to explode the trains and railways . . . he was an expert on trains, on mines. He used to plant the explosives, and then the Arabs used to shoot and kill the Turks."[35] Another tribesman told me, "He used to put in the dynamite himself because they were ignorant about this and did not know how to place it themselves."[36]

James D. Lunt, a British officer who served in the Jordanian desert, dined with a Howeitat shaykh at Bayir. This shaykh recalled, as had the Bedouin whom I had interviewed, that Lawrence was as tough as the toughest Bedouin, among the finest of camelmen, lived like a Bedouin, had an uncanny knowledge of the scandal of the desert which he used to good effect, and seemed to know all the wadis, wells and hills from Azraq to Aqaba.[37] At the conclusion of the evening Lunt's Bedouin host said to him of Lawrence, "Of all the men I have ever met he was the greatest Prince," and the Arab audience present signified their assent.[38] Ja'far al-'Askari, an Iraqi who commanded the Arab regular army and engaged in many activities during the campaign with Lawrence, spoke of him as the bravest man he had known.[39]

W. M. M. Hurley, an RAF officer with whom Lawrence later served, had had occasion in 1928 to travel in Trans-Jordan and meet Arabs there who had taken part in the campaigns. "I saw the places he had wrecked on the railway," Hurley wrote, "the areas where he had maintained his camps, and, above all, the people whom he had inspired to victory. On every side his name was still a legend: 'Aurens Bey' whom the older Sheikhs spoke about in awe and veneration, and whom the younger generation of the Bedouin accepted in their tradition as akin to deity."[40] Carl R. Raswan, who journeyed extensively among the Bedouin, wrote in 1935, "I have met many of his [Lawrence's] old companions and also enemies, and whether they loved or feared him, they all agree that 'Aurens' was the most sincere friend that ever came from Europe to take up the Arab cause, though most of them regretted that he did not have a chance to side with Ibn Saud."[41]

Sometimes the Arab accounts, even when more than one reporter was an eyewitness of the events being described, contradict one another. The events around Tafas in the last days before the capture of Damascus provide a case in point. Al-'Umari describes the atrocities at Tafas committed by the retreating Turks against the villagers and his own desire to take revenge against the Turkish prisoners, but he says that Nuri al-Sa'id and Ali Jawdat (who was in charge of the Arab forces) calmed him and no vengeance was taken.[42] Ali Jawdat, on the other hand, states in his own memoirs that he tried without success to control his soldiers and officers from avenging themselves for the massacre upon the Turkish prisoners.[43] Mousa cites a report from a former Ottoman officer denying that any killing of women and children took place at all.[44] For a Western writer such as myself to extract the truth from the self-serving distortions in all this is a difficult task indeed.

Nuri al Sa'id, one of the ablest of the Arab officers, an Iraqi who later served his country with distinction until his assassination in 1958, was

warm in his praise of Lawrence and generous in his estimate of
Lawrence's value to the Arab cause.[45] When Lawrence's abridged version
of *Revolt in the Desert* appeared in 1927, Nuri reviewed it for the
Baghdad *Times*. In his review he wrote: "It was possible for Lawrence
to understand the Arabs at the first instance better than any other
Britisher who worked for the Arab cause; and perhaps even now he
surpasses all others in this knowledge. Without exception I remember
Lawrence whenever we now encounter any difficulty, and ask myself
whether we shall be again so fortunate as to have another friend of
Lawrence's type." With regard to the accuracy of the book Nuri wrote,
"Lawrence is thoroughly candid in his book, which is throughout accurate.
If the book is lacking in any way, it is information to which the author
had no opportunity of access."[46]

George Antonius was not a participant in the campaigns, but in his
important history of the Revolt, looked at from an Arab perspective, he
consulted Faisal, other members of the ruling family, and officers who
took part in the war. He questions the accuracy of some of the statements
of fact and interpretation in *Seven Pillars of Wisdom*, citing barriers of
culture, language and temperament from which Lawrence suffered, but
he is unequivocal in his acknowledgment of Lawrence's value in the
service of the Arabs. "On more than one occasion in the years that followed the war," Antonius wrote, "have I heard the late King Faisal declare that, with the exception of Lawrence whose genius entitled him to
a place of his own, the claims of Colonel S. F. Newcombe or of Major
Joyce to Arab gratitude were not less strong than those of any other
Englishman."[47]

Shahbandar has also written of Lawrence's value to the cause of Arab
nationalism, and understood the limitations placed upon him, and the
ambiguity of his position that resulted from the secret Anglo-French
agreements. "Lawrence spent all possible energy to establish the strongest
foothold for the Arabs to have full independence under their own flag,"
Shahbandar concluded in the fourth and last article of his series, "but
what use was there when the British had understandings with their allies,
the French, which tore apart any possibility of full independence."[48]

In summary, there remains a need for an objective analysis by a scholar
familiar with both the Western and Arab cultures of Lawrence's part in
the Arab Revolt from both the military and political standpoint. My own
view — which I in no way claim to hold in freedom from the cultural
biases that have been described — is that Lawrence's role in the Arab
Revolt was an extraordinary one. Although there may have been distortions and exaggerations in Lawrence's accounts of the Revolt, especially
the romanticization in *Seven Pillars of Wisdom*, these are not so great as
some Western and Arab denigrators have claimed. His basic description
of the development, leadership and course of the Revolt, and of his own

participation in it, are much as he described. My assessment of the evidence largely bears up the prediction Lawrence made to Robert Graves in 1927: "All the documents of the Arab Revolt are in the archives of the Foreign Office, and will soon be available to students [not for almost forty years] who will be able to cross-check my yarns. I expect them to find small errors, and to agree generally with the main current of my narrative."[49]

Without in any way reducing the value of what other Allied officers, British and French, accomplished in the Revolt, or detracting from the heroic efforts of the Arabs in their own behalf, the evidence, taken all together, supports the view that Lawrence was predominant in organizing, coordinating and shaping the Revolt, in conceiving its possibilities, in obtaining effective British support for it, and in transforming the raw energies of Arab frustration and idealism into an effective guerrilla movement of national liberation.

Nor is the charge that he claimed credit for himself while denying the important role of his British and Arab colleagues accurate, although he could be biting in his criticism of those who disappointed or betrayed him. In the introductory paragraphs of *Seven Pillars of Wisdom* Lawrence tried to explain why the book takes on such a self-centered cast. With his characteristic false modesty (false not because it was not genuine but because it gave a false picture of reality) Lawrence downplayed his own role and elevated that of others: "Then there is the question of my British colleagues. This isolated picture throwing the main light upon myself, is unfair to them. Especially I am most sorry that I have not told what the non-commissioned with us did. They were inarticulate, but wonderful, although without the motive, the imaginative vision of the end, which sustained their officers. Unfortunately my concern was limited to this end, and the book just a designed procession of Arab freedom from Mecca to Damascus. It was intended to rationalize the campaign, that everyone might see how natural the success was, and how inevitable, how little dependent on direction or brain, how much less on the outside assistance of the few British. *It was an Arab war, waged and led by Arabs, for an Arab aim, in Arabia* [italics added].

"My proper share was a minor one, but because of a fluent pen, a free speech, and a certain adroitness of brain, I took upon myself, as I describe it, a mock primacy. By the accidental judgment of a publicist who visited us in the field, this mock primacy was published abroad as truth. In reality I held a subordinate official place. I never held any office among the Arabs; was never in charge of the British mission with them."[50]

As will be discussed later, the most serious limitation of Lawrence's effort grew out of his fantasy of the shape of the Arab world, a conception that derived as much from the need to fulfill a dream of his own as it did from the political and national actualities he found in Arabia and Syria.

This romantic fantasy of a pure race of Bedouin — God's original children living closer to Him than other human beings, closer surely than the overcivilized English — whom he would enable amirs of Mecca to lead to a new tomorrow began to take shape in the early years of the war.

The dream grew, as we shall see, out of deep personal roots. Because of the power of his drive and the scope of his talents, he was able to impose it for a time upon the Allies and the Arabs alike. From his standpoint it was shattered with deeply disturbing consequences by the events of the war. The results of his capacity to live it out still persist in the Middle East, but some of the most important constructive forces for change in that troubled region are linked to Lawrence's dream if, indeed, they do not grow out of it.

15

The Question of Motivation

A decade after the desert campaigns were over, Lawrence wrote Robert Graves: "During the Revolt I had a motive, within me, for activity, and therefore became capable of imposing my will on others. The very accident that normally I am empty of motive, helped make the rare motive, when it finally came, overpowering."[1] With this statement Lawrence draws our attention from the activity itself to the motive behind it.

A discussion of someone's motivation in relation to events in which he has taken some vital part implies the possibility of choice: that he was not simply performing actions required by a situation he had no part in creating, or to which he was drawn by circumstances beyond his control. The more effectively a person like Lawrence can impose his will upon events, shape their course or influence their outcome, the stronger our fascination with the psychology of his motivation becomes — even stronger if these events have a sufficiently sharp impact and continue to affect our own lives. For we recognize then among the determinants affecting the course of history — and ourselves with it — the internal drives and purposes of an unusual person. We wish to understand him, to learn why he chose the directions he did.

On the other hand, no person's life conforms to a grand design. It is a popular pastime for readers as well as biographers to discern in the childhood or adolescence of a great man the antecedents of his later choices and actions, especially since Freudian psychology has called so forcefully to our attention the early motivational roots of so much later behavior. A great man himself is no less guilty of this retrospective harmonizing of the past and the present than the rest of us, as he looks back upon his life and tries to make intelligible to his followers and to himself the turns he took and the choices he made.

But the reality is more complex. Personal drive and need are influenced throughout the course of one's life by the shifting actualities of the human and nonhuman environment, and their outlet and expression must conform with or be adapted to a great variety of what, for lack of a better expression, is called historical circumstances. In fact, the "historical figure" may be defined as one who is uniquely able to adapt his internal drives, capabilities and personal conflicts to historical situations and to the opportunities he discerns, or with which he is confronted. To the extent to which he uses these characteristics to fulfill the political or other purposes of a government or a people — as Lawrence did with Whitehall and the Arab leaders — the historical figure or leader is himself "chosen" by his times.

Finally, when one considers motivation one must recognize its multiple dimensions and levels. On the surface, motivation is usually highly practical and relates simply to influencing or conforming to an immediate set of circumstances or realities. Motivation of this kind, dictated as it is by the exigencies of day-to-day reality, is readily discerned by the observer, who does not require that the subject let him in on his purposes. Between this level and the deepest or "ultimate" levels of motive and need in the dark recesses of the soul are various strata of motivation deriving from different psychological levels of consciousness and periods of development, which find outward expression in the multiple confluences of private purpose and public opportunity.

Lawrence's importance as a historical figure derives from his ability to impose his will not only through actions and decisions of his own, but through his unusual capacity to influence his superiors — men like Allenby and later Churchill — to act in directions of his choice. "Allenby, Winston, Trenchard. I have a fine taste in chiefs," Lawrence wrote to another British officer many years later.[2]

But beyond his work through such men as these Lawrence gains importance as a historical figure by virtue of his introspective nature and gifts of psychological perceptiveness regarding the motivation of himself and others. He teaches us what "a person like Lawrence" is like, insofar as it is possible to generalize from his psychological characteristics to those of others who live out their inner fantasies and conflicts in the public domain. The extraordinary consciousness of self that is most evident in *Seven Pillars of Wisdom*, in letters to Charlotte Shaw, Lionel Curtis and others, and in *The Mint* (his book about his experiences in the RAF) was not so evident before the war.

Lawrence was particularly aware of the multiple levels of his motivation, and taught us to expect to find a number of motivational levels in any leader, rather than to conclude that he or anyone else is likely to be motivated by one purpose alone. I believe the efforts of Lawrence's biographers to find *the* definitive motive for important periods of his life, such as the years of his participation in the Arab Revolt, to be in error.

Lawrence retained, as is well known, the child's pleasure in teasing and in making riddles — for example, in the merry chase he has led his biographers regarding the identity of "S.A.," the object of his dedicatory poem in *Seven Pillars of Wisdom*. Like Rumpelstiltskin he provoked interest in his own identity and piqued his audience with clues, but at the same time he seemed to dread their really "finding" him. Yet his psychological torment and his need to live out private conflict in public action or, after abandoning action, in writings that would find their way to public scrutiny, have made it possible for us to learn about the internal sources of his actions.

There are two summary statements by Lawrence, both written during 1919, of his motivation in pursuing what he called "the Arab affair." The first is a letter to a British Foreign Office staff member, written probably in November 1919; the second appears in the epilogue to *Seven Pillars of Wisdom*. In both expositions Lawrence refers to motives of personal caring, patriotism, curiosity and ambition, ranged in that order. This ranking reflects more accurately, in my opinion, Lawrence's estimate of the worthiness of these motives, or their relative freedom from conflict, than it does their actual order of strength or depth. The Foreign Office letter (I) and the epilogue (II) are reproduced here for comparison:

I

Dear ——,

You asked me "Why" today, and I'm going to tell you exactly what my motives in the Arab affair were, in order of strength: —

(i). Personal. I liked a particular Arab very much, and I thought that freedom for the race would be an acceptable present.

(ii.) Patriotic. I wanted to help win the war, and Arab help reduced Allenby's losses by thousands.

(iii). Intellectual curiosity. I wanted to feel what it was like to be the mainspring of a national movement, and to have some millions of people expressing themselves through me: and being a half-poet, I don't value material things much. Sensation and mind seem to me much greater, and the ideal, such a thing as the impulse that took us into Damascus, the only thing worth doing.

(iv). Ambition. You know how Lionel Curtis has made his conception of the Empire — a Commonwealth of free peoples — generally accepted. I wanted to widen that idea beyond the Anglo-Saxon shape, and to form a new nation of thinking people, all acclaiming our freedom, and demanding admittance into our Empire. There is, to my eyes, no other road for Egypt and India in the end, and I would have made their path easier, by creating an Arab Dominion in the Empire.

I don't think there are any other reasons. You are sufficiently Scotch to understand my analysing my own mind so formally. The process intended was to take Damascus, and run it (as anyone fully knowing the East and West could run it), as an independent ally of G.-B. Then to turn on Hejaz and conquer it: then to project the semi-educated Syrians on Yemen, and build that up quickly (without Yemen there is no re-birth for the Arabs) and finally to receive Mesopotamia into the block so made: all this could be done in thirty years directed effort, and without impairing British holdings. It is only the substitution of a 999 years' lease for a complete sale.

Now look what happened when we took Damascus: —

Motive (i). I found had died some weeks before: so my gift was wasted, and my future doings indifferent on that account.

Motive (ii). This was achieved, for Turkey was broken, and the central powers were so united that to break one broke all.

Motive (iii). This was romantic mainly, and one never repeats a sensation. When I rode into Damascus the whole country-side was on fire with enthusiasm, and in the town a hundred thousand people shouted my name. Success always kills hope by surfeit.

Motive (iv). This remained, but it was not strong enough to make me stay. I asked Allenby for leave, and when he gave it me, came straight home. It's the dying remains of this weakest of all my reasons which made me put up a half-fight for Feisal in Paris and elsewhere, and which occasionally drives me into your room to jest about what might be done.

If you want to make me work again you would have to recreate motives ii and iii. As you are not God, Motive i is beyond your power.

I'm not conscious of having done a crooked thing to anyone since I began to push the Arab movement, though I prostituted myself in Arab Service. For an Englishman to put himself at the disposal of a red race is to sell himself to a brute, like Swift's Houhynyms. However my body and soul were my own, and no one can reproach me for what I do to them: and to all the rest of you I'm clean.

When you have got as far as this, please burn it all. I've never told anyone before, and may not again, because it isn't nice to open oneself out. I laugh at myself because my giving up has made me look so futile.[3]

II

Needless to say, when the Arab thrust northward from Hejaz began, Damascus was not my ultimate end: but by the time it was taken most of my springs of action were exhausted, and so I withdrew myself. Throughout my strongest motive had been a personal one, omitted from the body of the book, but not absent, I think, from